WRESTLING WITH THE WORD

CHRISTIAN PREACHING FROM THE HEBREW BIBLE

FOSTER R. McCURLEY

TRINITY PRESS INTERNATIONAL
Valley Forge, Pennsylvania

Trinity Press International, P.O. Box 851, Valley Forge, PA 19482-0851

Library of Congress Cataloging-in-Publication Data

McCurley, Foster R.
Wrestling with the Word : Christian preaching from the Hebrew Bible / Foster R. McCurley.
p. cm.
Includes bibliographical references and index.
ISBN 1-56338-142-7 (pbk. : alk. paper)
1. Bible. O.T.–Homiletical use. 2. Preaching. I. Title.
BS1191.5.M33 1996
251–dc20 96-23
CIP

Printed in the United States of America

96 97 98 99 10 9 8 7 6 5 4 3 2 1

WRESTLING WITH THE WORD

To Jannine,
my wife and best friend,
on the fifteenth anniversary
of her ordination into the ministry
of Word and Sacrament

List of Abbreviations

Translations of the Holy Bible

JB	Jerusalem Bible
NAB	New American Bible
NEB	New English Bible
NIV	New International Version
NRSV	New Revised Standard Version
RSV	Revised Standard Version
Torah	*The Torah: The Five Books of Moses*

Sources in the First Several Books of the Bible

D	The Deuteronomic editors
E	The Elohist
J	The Yahwist
P	The Priest

Contents

Part Three
SERMONS ON SELECTED PERICOPES

Preface

This book is intended for preachers. Primarily it is directed to those who stand in the pulpit to deliver sermons on Sunday mornings, but it seeks to provide guidance also for those who announce the good news in their teaching ministries and in their private conversations with one another.

In 1973 I published the core of this book under the title *Proclaiming the Promise: Christian Preaching from the Old Testament.* They were different times. As a nation we were beginning our recuperation from our involvement in Vietnam, and as a society we were exploring the ramifications of new freedoms, sexual and otherwise. The cold war between the two superpowers continued without thawing, and "white glove diplomacy" sent Henry Kissinger all over the world. They were opportune times for preaching.

Recently, at my wife's insistence, I cleaned my study. She and I had come to the realization that though God promised never to flood the earth again with water, nothing was said in that Noachic covenant about paper. We were becoming deluged with clippings from magazines ten years old, copies of lectures I never should have presented in the first place, and all those sermons from the 1960s and 1970s. Recalling the occasions and the situations and the people filled my mind with nostalgia. More important at this point in our lives, the sermons filled the filing cabinets and cardboard boxes all over the house, and so out they went with the packaging from frozen food and unwanted advertisements and obsolete issues of news magazines.

I tossed the sermons not because they were no good (Who can determine that but the listener?) but because they were written and delivered to a people who lived at a different time. Like the original version of this book, they were written when no one ever heard of AIDS, when no one could have imagined the splitting apart of the Soviet Union or the reunification of Germany, when no one dreamed of the possibility of Contragate or Whitewatergate.

Times and people change. If it were not so, we could do with a very concise Bible — a few pages of timeless truths about sin and salvation, about creation and new creation, and about what it means to be the people of God in the between-time. But the Bible covers almost two thousand years of history — from the days of Abraham and Sarah to crises in the second-century church — and includes literature from a span of time lasting almost a millennium and a half. It contains sixty-six books by at least as many authors, no one of whom wrote in order to contribute to the formation of a canonized book of faith.

In a sense all the biblical books were originally sermons for their days. Whether they took the form of proverbial instruction, history, prophetic oracle, Gospel, or epistle, they all attempted either to address the word of God to their contemporary audiences or to demonstrate how faith operated in response to God's word. Those audiences lived in many different situations, and with each surprising turn of events the dynamic God of scripture inspired spokespersons to speak or write words that would effect an encounter between God and the people. Such is the nature of dialogue — God speaking, people hearing or refusing to hear; people speaking, God answering or choosing not to answer or responding in unexpected ways.

Over the past couple of years professors of homiletics and pastors have asked me to reprint *Proclaiming the Promise*. But too much has changed, even many assumptions of biblical scholarship, and so have I. Honesty to the nature of biblical dialogue required that I not reprint but rewrite the book. It might not be any better in the present day than the original was in the middle of the 1970s. But like preaching itself, this book attempts to witness to God's word anew.

The title of the present book differs from the original in two ways. First, the present book is called *Wrestling with the Word* rather than *Proclaiming the Promise*. The new title originated in a project I began in 1989 and continue to the present day: a monthly audiotaped discussion on the pericopes and the possibilities in them for preaching. The title appeals to me because it reflects the ongoing struggle with interpreting the biblical passages in terms of their meaning today. The task never ceases to be a wrestling match — for me and for all engaged in the awesome task of preaching.

Second, the subtitle of the original book was *Christian Preaching from the Old Testament* while that of the present work is *Christian Preaching from the Hebrew Bible.* Throughout this book I refer to the first thirty-nine books of the Bible sometimes as "the Old Testament" and sometimes as "the Hebrew Bible." In part, the inconsistency is due to my own ambivalence about the terminology. On the one hand, in order to maintain the integrity of the scriptures composed in Hebrew and passed down to us in and through the Jewish community, "Hebrew Bible" seems to provide the appropriate description of the first thirty-nine books of the Christian Bible. On the other hand, the structure of those books has been altered by the church. While the sequence of the parts of the Hebrew Bible is Torah–Prophets–Writings, the order of the parts in the Christian Old Testament is Torah–Writings–Prophets. The change indicates the church's conviction that the prophetic books immediately precede the Gospels in order to demonstrate the explicit relationship of prophecy and fulfillment. Thus, the Hebrew Bible and the church's Old Testament are not identical, and so perhaps the term "Hebrew Bible" does not do justice to the structure of the Christian canon.

The terminological issue becomes even more confused when we deal with the intriguing use of passages from the Torah, the Prophets, and the Writings in the New Testament. In such quotations and allusions we are often examining quotations from the Greek translation of the Hebrew Bible (the Septuagint) rather than from the Hebrew texts themselves. Because of that reality, perhaps we should speak of the "Greek Old Testament" in contrast to the "Hebrew Bible," but it is not always entirely clear which version is quoted in the New Testament book. I ask the reader to forgive my ambiguity and my inconsistencies in regard to these terms as I struggle with appropriate nomenclature for the first portion of the Christian Bible.

While I have rewritten major portions of the original book here and have expanded considerably the number of pericopes and sermons, some readers will think I have not changed the book enough. Some will wonder, for example, why I have paid almost no attention to structuralism or to narrative criticism popular in recent years and have instead continued to expound the historical-critical method popular in previous decades. My reason for continuing the method in this book is that I intend the exegesis here to focus on the theological issues in the texts, and I am still convinced that the situations in which people lived their lives provided the arenas in which God's word was proclaimed, written down, edited, and expounded. At each new turn in the experiences of God's people, the stories themselves and the words that expressed them changed. Such redaction was done not lightly but homiletically, so that God's word would constantly address the people anew. For the theological task of continuing that kind of preaching today I find nothing that can take the place of the historical-critical method. It is my hope that the following pages will demonstrate that conviction.

As I think about what has changed in me since I wrote the original volume, I pause to give thanks. My gratitude, first of all, goes to my wife, Jannine, to whom this book is dedicated. Her patience and support, as well as her friendship, have enabled me to think and write more freely than I had before. I am indebted, too, to my children — Scott, Brett, and Dana — who have become for me exciting friends as well as sons and a daughter. Their enthusiasm about my writing pushes me onward even when I might otherwise avoid the task at hand. Certainly I owe a debt of gratitude to my former colleague at the Lutheran Seminary at Philadelphia, John Reumann. As my teacher and colleague he helped me discern the relationships between the two testaments and encouraged me to test my own wrestlings alongside his in joint publications. I thank Joan Piasecki for her painstaking work typing onto disk the pages of the original book. Her hours of tedious labor enabled me to concentrate on revising the original and developing the new. Finally, I thank Harold Rast, Director of Trinity Press International, for his enthusiastic support and for his allowance of the creative spirit to present this book anew.

Part One

REFLECTING ON SCRIPTURE

Chapter 1

The Bible as Word of God

Christian preaching from the Hebrew Bible or Old Testament assumes an understanding of the entire Christian canon as the word of God.[1] The biblical witness as a whole oversees every part of the testimony, and an interpreter's presuppositions about the Bible affects what is done with any excised piece, a pericope, of someone else's age-old sermon.

People within the church speak of the Bible and the word of God in the same breath, however they define the connection. For the purposes of preaching we who occupy the pulpits are compelled to take a position on how the two connect. The listening audience waits for clues on how scripture and the word — be they identical, antithetical, complementary, or separate — address their lives.

The "word of God" is one of those expressions that elicits various emotions and reactions. While some complain they "don't hear the word of God from the pulpit anymore," others tremble before the preaching of the word, especially when it is based on apocalyptic judgment. In some homes the word of God is nothing more than the large dusty book on the coffee table. For others the word is found in the confrontation with the suffering on the streets of urban blight and in the loneliness of homes for the elderly.

The many reactions to the hallowed phrase reflect confusion and even conflicts among Christians. Yet, on the positive side, this same multiplicity of interpretations is indicative of the dynamic nature of the word of God itself. Far from leading to division among Christian groups, this rich diversity of God's word can be the means by which the Body of Christ recognizes unity among its members and with its Head.

At the heart of understanding the word of God is the realization that the word is the means by which God confronts us in words and accompanying symbols. When this confrontation results in the awareness of our sinfulness and in the judgment of God, then we call that encounter with God the *law.* When God comes forgiving, comforting, and accepting us in spite of our sinfulness, we call that encounter the *gospel.*

Martin Luther taught that this effective word occurs in the preaching of sermons, in the administration of sacraments, and in the mutual consolation of sisters and brothers in the name of Christ. What is striking about all three expressions is the commonness, even the feebleness, of the means God uses to meet humans. That ordinary words and such meager elements as water, wine, and bread serve as the vehicles for God's powerful word is completely consistent with the vulnerability God demonstrated in the cross of Jesus Christ.

Definitions of the Word

Three classic definitions of the word of God have emerged in theological and ecclesiastical circles: (1) the message about Jesus Christ, (2) the person of Jesus Christ, and (3) the Bible itself. The sequence of this list of definitions puts the Bible in its place, but at the same time the Bible itself contributes to its position at the end of the list.

1. *The word of God is the message about Jesus Christ, particularly about what God accomplished in Jesus' death and resurrection.* Theologically and chronologically Paul's writings provide an appropriate starting point for defining the word for Christians. His letters addressed to congregations in Asia Minor, Greece, and Rome proclaimed the message of Christ's death and resurrection and related their meaning to particular issues raised in each community. These audiences consisted mostly of Gentile Christians, yet some, such as that in Rome, clearly included Jewish Christians as well.

Paul's profound understanding of the word was communicated both in terms of his own cherished scriptures (what we call the Old Testament) and in terms of new imagery derived from the Greek and Roman cultures of the day. For Paul the new time that was promised in the scriptures of old had already begun in the event of Christ. Indeed, for Jewish Christians the Christ-event meant confirmation of the promises of God to the ancestors. For Gentile

Christians the Christ-event meant that the eschatological miracle of their inclusion in the Kingdom was already being fulfilled (Rom. 15:8–9).

In this early collection of Christian literature, Paul's use of "the word" is instructive. He uses the actual expression "word of God" only six times (Rom. 9:6; 2 Cor. 2:17; 4:2; Phil. 1:14; Col. 1:25; 1 Thess. 4:15), the corresponding expression "the word of the Lord" only twice (1 Thess. 1:8; 2 Thess. 3:10), and "the word of Christ" only at Colossians 1:25. Yet other expressions such as "the word of truth" (Col. 1:5; Eph. 1:13), "the word of life" (Phil. 2:16), "the word of the cross" (1 Cor. 1:18), and "the word of reconciliation" (2 Cor. 5:19) all serve to highlight "the word" as the message Paul delivered to the churches. This message, Paul maintains emphatically, is not the result of his own invention but that which was delivered to him by the Lord (1 Cor. 11:23–26; 15:11–12).

This word of God was spoken by Paul on the basis of the Lord's commissioning (2 Cor. 2:17). It is, therefore, not something with which to tamper. Proclaiming the word is the task for which Paul became a minister (Col. 1:25), for the word itself is the power that accomplishes salvation and reconciliation. In particular, it is "the word of the cross" that is "the power to us who are being saved" (1 Cor. 1:18). This understanding of the word as power to save clearly derives from Paul's scriptures, where God's announcement of a salvation event for Israel was itself the means by which the deliverance will be accomplished (Isa. 55:10–11).

As the word of God accomplishing salvation, "the word of God" is interchangeable with "the gospel" in Paul's writings (see above all Rom. 1:16). In many instances Paul equates "word of God" and "gospel" in the same passage. Paul's "gospel" was proclaimed to the church at Thessalonica, they "received the word," and from them "the word of the Lord sounded forth" (1 Thess. 1:4–8). Paul's imprisonment, he himself argued, has "served to advance the gospel," for other Christians "are much more bold to speak the word of God without fear" (Phil. 1:12–14). The apostle reminds the saints at Colossae who had previously heard of the hope laid up in heaven about "the word of truth, the gospel which has come to you" (Col. 1:5–6a), and that same "word of truth, the gospel of your salvation," had been proclaimed in Ephesus (Eph. 1:13).

The content of this gospel-word preached by Paul is "the Son of God, Jesus Christ" (2 Cor. 1:18–19), whose death on a cross is the power and wisdom of God for salvation (1 Cor. 1:18; Rom. 1:16; Eph. 1:13). This message of universal significance, far from having occurred in a vacuum, was promised beforehand in Israel's sacred scripture (Rom. 1:2; 9:6) and continued in the words and deeds of the early church, which received it and proclaimed it anew (1 Thess. 1:4–8; see also 1 Cor. 15:1–8).

2. *The word of God is the Son of God who became truly human in order to effect reconciliation.* The relationship between the gospel-word about Jesus Christ and the person of Jesus is very close indeed. The author of Mark's Gospel draws the two together in a veritable equation by setting twice on Jesus' lips the expression "for my sake and the gospel's" (Mark 8:39; 10:29).

It is, however, in the Prologue to John's Gospel that the word of God is explicitly stated to have become incarnate in Jesus of Nazareth. Apparently employing a hymn that reflects the development in Hellenistic Judaism of word, wisdom, and *tôrâ,* the author proclaims that the divinity of the Son began not with his baptism (so the impression given in Mark), not even with his conception (so Matthew and Luke), but "in the beginning," before creation itself. The word that not only was with God but was God provided the source of life for the whole world, but neither the world nor the Jewish people welcomed that word. Finally, that "word became flesh and dwelt among us" in the form of Jesus of Nazareth (John 1:14).

This understanding of the word of God as incarnate is not again attested explicitly in John's Gospel. It appears elsewhere in the New Testament only at Revelation 19:13 and possibly also in a sacramental sense at Hebrews 6:5. Perhaps the closest one comes to such a notion apart from these instances is Paul's use of Christ crucified as "the wisdom of God" (1 Cor. 1:24). ("Word" and "wisdom" had become virtually identified with each other in late Judaism, especially in the apocryphal book called the Wisdom of Jesus ben Sirach.)

3. *The word of God is the Holy Bible.* No single verse in the Bible claims that the sixty-six book collection is the word of God. The mention of "scripture" in the New Testament (see 2 Tim. 3:16; 2 Pet. 1:20–21) and even of scripture as "the word of God" (Mark 7:13) refers primarily to the writings of the Hebrew tradition that became the Old Testament for the church. In one case the term "scriptures" seems to include Paul's letters (2 Pet. 3:15–16).

How then can we speak of the whole Bible as the word of God? One way to approach the question is to note that in Paul's letters, as we have seen, "word of God" and "gospel" are interchangeable terms for the message about Jesus Christ. We can indeed move beyond Paul to all other books of the New Testament to assert the same: the entire collection of twenty-seven books of the New Testament is witness literature to the gospel about Jesus Christ. In this sense the entire New Testament is the word of God. Yet, as we stated above, the message that is the good news fulfilled in Jesus Christ was already promised in Israel's scriptures (Gal. 3:8), and so we speak likewise of the Old Testament as the word of God.

Such an approach should not leave the impression that "the word of God" is simply a phrase imposed on the Old Testament from the New. On the contrary, those Hebrew scriptures of old abound in expressing the dynamism of the word as that encounter between God and people that results in the experience of law and gospel. From Genesis to Malachi the word of the Lord and the corresponding expressions "Thus says the Lord" or "The Lord spoke" result in God's creative, judging, and saving work. The word of God that addressed Israel over the span of biblical history provided a powerful experience of God in the past, in the present, and in the future. The Law, the Prophets, and the Writings (*TANAK: Tôrâ, Nebî'îm, Ketûbîm*) witness to the God who addressed Israel in the word. Therefore, proclaiming the word of God in Israel's scriptures is not simply a matter of paving the way for the New Testament but is itself a living and dynamic reality in Israel's own history.

The Dynamic Word in Changing Situations

The word of God is so intimately bound up with Israel's history that God's verbal expression only rarely takes the same form twice. Indeed, the phrase "the word of the Lord" or "the word of God" occurs 241 times in the Old Testament, only in a few cases repeating itself verbatim (cf., e.g., Isa. 2:2–4 and Mic. 4:1–3).

This dynamic diversity of God's expression of will and action for Israel and ultimately for all people demonstrates that the word is always directed to the changing situations that people experience. This characteristic of God's word cannot be overstated: in the word God meets people in ways that are relevant to the needs of the moment.

In his "Preface to the Prophets," Martin Luther stressed the necessity of understanding the word in its relationship to concrete situations:

> For if one would understand the prophecies, it is necessary that one know how things were in the land, how matters lay, what was in the mind of the people — what plans they had with respect to their neighbors, friends, and enemies — and especially what attitude they took in their country toward God and toward the prophet, whether they held to his word and worship or to idolatry.[2]

A few examples from the Bible will suffice to support this approach. At Hosea 1:2–3 the Lord commands the prophet to take "a wife of harlotry and have children of harlotry" (RSV). In contradictory fashion, the same Lord exhorts the prophet Jeremiah not to marry or have children (Jer. 16:1–2).

How are we to interpret these contradictory commands on the basis of "how matters lay in the land"? According to the superscription of the Book of Hosea, the prophet preached in the northern kingdom of Israel during the second half of the eighth century B.C. It is clear from the preaching of Hosea and other sources that the rich, lush territory later known as Galilee was the hotbed of Canaanite fertility religion. This seductive religion managed to lure into its devotion and practice many of the Israelites who had been called to worship the Lord exclusively. The mission of Hosea (and that of his predecessor Elijah) was to call the people back to the God who had delivered them from the bondage of Egypt. The means that God chose to express Hosea's message was the prophet's marriage to an Israelite girl who had participated in the fashionable Canaanite rites of initiation in order to ensure fertility for a would-be husband. Marriage to such a woman representing Israel's infidelity to the Lord would provide the means for Hosea's proclamation of God's unfailing love for Israel.

The prohibition to Jeremiah, however, occurred at the end of the seventh century B.C. in the city of Jerusalem, capital of Judah. Because of constant rebellion over the years, Judah was about to be devastated by the Lord by means of Nebuchadnezzar's Babylonian army. Jerusalem would not be a suitable place to raise a family, for destruction was its immediate future. Thus the word of God to Jeremiah in Jerusalem was different from that addressed to Hosea almost a century and a half earlier in Israel. "Matters in the land" had changed, and so also did the Lord's word to a prophet.

In the New Testament as well it is clear that different times, communities, and purposes provide the background for understanding diverse expressions of the word. The Synoptic Gospels offer ample illustrations of situations affecting the proclamation of the word. Christ's teaching of the Lord's Prayer has a quite different thrust in Matthew's Gospel when compared to the version in Luke's. Addressing an essentially Jewish Christian community, Matthew reports Jesus' instructions to his disciples in terms of *how* they should pray in contrast to the Gentiles: "Pray then like this: . . . " (Matt. 6:7–13). On the other hand, Luke's audience, consisting essentially of Gentile Christians apparently unfamiliar with the practice of prayer, can identify with the plea of one of the disciples, "Lord, teach us *to* pray, as John taught his disciples." And he said to them, "When you pray, say: . . . " (Luke 11:1–4).

Biblical Faith as Dialogue

God's word is so directly related to each situation that we should speak of the biblical faith as a constant dialogue between the Lord and the people rather than as a monologue delivered by some aloof deity. In fact, apart from the dialogue, we cannot really talk about the God of the Bible at all. The witnesses of scripture are not concerned about describing God apart from the dialogical relationship that exists between Israel and God, humanity and God, or the church and God. God is known only in relationships with those people who witness in faith to what God says and does. Likewise we cannot speak of the people of God — Israel or the church — apart from the God who called the people into being. This relationship is constant throughout the Bible, although its form changes, depending on various circumstances.

The dialogue exists in terms of God's word and human words. It is an interplay between initiation and reaction. God's word initiated the act of creation (Gen. 1–2) and the call and covenant with Abraham (Gen. 12; 15; 17). Between these two acts of God, humans took over the verbs and initiated a variety of acts. All of those described between Genesis 3–11 end in some negative result, for each act initiated by humans runs counter to the order of relationships established by God's word at creation. Thus God's initiating word to Abraham in Genesis 12 is simultaneously God's response to the actions taken by humans in the previous nine chapters. The human reaction to God's initiating promises to Abraham is a mixed bag. The patriarch's doubt is evident in his scheme to save his own neck (Gen. 12:10–20) and in his attempt to solve the progeny issue on his own terms (Gen. 15:2; 16:1–16; 17:18).

Ultimately his faith (Gen. 15:6) in God's promises leads him to risk the life of Sarah and his only beloved son (Gen. 22).

To continue the story of action and reaction, God called Moses to be the agent of deliverance of the Hebrew slaves in Egypt; God's act on this occasion was a response to the cries for help from the children of Israel (Exod. 3:8). Yet the people were not delighted at Moses' intervention into their lives (Exod. 5:20–21) and bitterly murmured over the inconvenience their salvation brought (Exod. 16–17; Num. 11–21). When they praised the god who brought them out of the land of Egypt, the deity — "lo and behold" — turned out to be the image of a calf, a representation common among Canaanite deities (Exod. 32).

The bestowal of divine sonship on Jesus — whether at baptism, at conception, or before the creation of the world — was strictly God's act, as was the promise of the Reign of God through the prophets. Yet that promising and fulfilling word of God was addressed over the centuries to an Israel who had become the world's punching bag.

Dialogue does not occur in a vacuum. The divine word and human words take specific form in light of the situations in which people live and on the basis of the relationships in which they are involved with one another and with God. The relationship God established with Israel is special indeed. God held Israel especially responsible among all peoples because "you only have I known of all families of the earth" (Amos 3:2). Certainly the Lord was cognitively aware of the existence of other nations, but only Israel, with whom God has been intimate (God "knew" her in the biblical sense!), can be sued for divorce by the aggrieved husband, the Lord (Hos. 1:1–13). The choice of imagery by these prophets, even the selection of words, is directly related to the husband-wife or parent-child relationship between the Lord and Israel, a relationship described by some authors as a covenant.

Words themselves are, of course, human inventions, and so words have meaning only within particular cultural contexts. When the Old Testament describes God as "Redeemer," for example, the Hebrew word behind the term (*gō'ēl*) reflects that ancient cultural phenomenon in which the next of kin settled matters on behalf of one's own clan member; the *gō'ēl* would pay damages so that a kinsman might go free, or he would take vengeance on another clan that had deprived his own of a member. In either case, the notion that the Lord served as Israel's "Redeemer" meant something in terms of their kinship with each other; it also promised what the people could expect of their nearest kin. The culture changed by the time the New Testament was written, and so the word that is translated "redemption" (*apolytrōsis*) reflects the Greek practice of emancipating a slave by a particular economic process.

The Hebrew traditions spoke of the Lord's "atonement" (*kippēr*) by which were removed sins that prevented fellowship between God and the people. This term, derived from Israel's cultic life, did not fit the need at a later time when the apostle Paul carried the message about Jesus Christ to the Gentile world. This different cultural setting demanded new words and images in order to communicate what God had accomplished in Jesus Christ. Thus "justification" and "reconciliation" were added to the biblical vocabulary. Beyond the mere use of vocabulary, moreover, different issues were raised in that cultural setting of the Gentiles, and so the gospel took on new forms while simultaneously remaining true to what God had accomplished in Christ.

Such a relationship between culturally laden human words and the word of God raises the question about the extent to which words and "the word" can be separated or even distinguished. Recognizing the limitation of human communication, some interpreters speak of the Bible as "containing" the word of God. The human words are accepted, but somehow God's word is in the midst of them all. The result of that understanding is a scavenger hunt in which believers attempt to separate the sacred and eternal from the profane and limited. Such a separation — perhaps even merely such a distinction — is theologically problematic, for God demonstrates throughout the Bible, especially in the incarnation, the will to use precisely the finite in order to proclaim the infinite. There is no word of God to humans apart from the words and other symbols by which humans communicate. Thus, rather than saying that the Bible contains the word of God, the Reformation tradition drives us to speak of the Bible *as* the word of God in written form.

If the word of God is so indissolubly bound up with the many human words that comprise the Bible, then we are at a loss to select only a few as those that adequately define the word. Even the popular John 3:16 cannot by itself limit the word to the extent that the rest of the Bible's syllables are superfluous. In that passage a particular set of human words proclaims God's word, but much more is to be said about the word's richness. In fact, the word takes so many diverse forms due to the changing circumstances of human life that finally it is necessary to say that God's word is nothing less than God's meeting people to judge and to save, to create and to destroy, to comfort and to afflict.

The Effectiveness of the Word

The dialogical character of the word makes it possible for the same word to have different effects on hearers. Luther explained in his discussion of the Introduction to the Ten Commandments that the words "I am the Lord your God" might be experienced by one person as law and by another as gospel. If the first hearer considers himself to be his own lord and master, then the declaration "I am the Lord" comes as judgment. To the second hearer, one overcome with loneliness and a loss of self-worth, the same words are comforting and affirming. Thus the word reverberates not only on the human eardrum but on the human heart as well.

Understanding this effectiveness of God's word is essential to comprehending the biblical faith. Because the word is God's, the message is not simply a presentation of information but the means by which the divine presence is communicated to the expectant listener. The word came to the exiled Jerusalemites in Babylon in the sixth century B.C. in order to announce salvation. The hearers could be assured the promise would have this effect because it is the nature of the word to fulfill the purpose it sets out to accomplish (Isa. 55:10–11). It is the same understanding of effect that defines the gospel as "the power of God for salvation to everyone who has faith" (Rom. 1:16).

Announcing and achieving the return of the exiles from Babylon to Jerusalem, the word was thus effective in moving history toward the divine goal. The entire historical corpus from Deuteronomy through Kings, the so-called Deuteronomistic history, is based upon this view that the word of God directs local and world events in terms of judgment and salvation. To cite just one example, a man of God prophesied to Jeroboam, king of Israel, that his altar in Bethel would one day be destroyed by a Davidic king named Josiah (1 Kings 13:1–2). More than three hundred years later, the prophecy was realized (2 Kings 23:15). More than twenty such cases of history-directing prophecy guide the story of the people of Israel in the Deuteronomistic work. Such fulfillment of prophecy not only confirmed God's credibility for the people but distinguished Israel's God from the idols of Babylon (see the discussion in part 2 on Isa. 44:6–8).

Along with the judging and saving effects of the word, the speaking of the Lord brought creation itself into being. The divine "Let there be" brought into existence the entire universe and ordered all things secure. The account in Genesis 1 and the solitary verse at Psalm 33:6 are the only passages in the Bible that explicitly expound a creation by the word, but by its very position at the beginning of the Bible the confession about the effectiveness of the creative word assumes particular significance.

Simultaneously the strategic position of Genesis 1 has established that creation account as a major source of debate and open conflict. Among the many issues raised by this chapter is one related to our query about the word: To whom was it spoken? Or to put it another way: Who was there to give the report? The question itself seems to throw into difficulty the assertion that the word never occurs as a monologue but always addresses people in dialogical form. If there was no human eardrum on which to vibrate, how can we speak of a dialogue? Obviously we cannot — if the account is considered to be a report of what actually happened during the first week of the world's existence. However, if we interpret the profound story from the perspective that the word is always addressed to people in particular circumstances and that the word takes the form of human words in a given cultural setting, then we must ask why Genesis 1 was written as it was. What did the writer have in mind by framing the creation account in this particular form? What problems and questions raised by the audience was the author addressing, or to use Luther's words, How did "matters lay in the land"?

Scholars usually assign the authorship of this account to a priestly writer or school who addressed the exiled Israelites in Babylon in the sixth century B.C. This creation story focuses in one sense on a polemic against Babylonian religion and in another sense on the proclamation of God's word to an insecure and despondent people. That situation and that cultural milieu caused the story to take its present shape, and in that setting the word of God that brought creation into being addressed the exiles with good news: against the chaos of the present time the God of their ancestors is the one who made and rules the universe with goodness and orderliness, and that very God will have the last word as well as the first.

In another sense the creation account is certainly more than a historically conditioned message. Genesis 1 proclaims to audiences of all times and places that God created the universe in such a way that all things fulfill their expected role and that they work together to provide a fit neighborhood in which to bring up the children of humanity. Furthermore, standing as it does at the beginning of the canon, it becomes the first of God's mighty acts in history that culminate in the New Testament confession that the word became flesh and dwelt among us, was crucified by the powers of the world, and was raised as the first act of the new creation God promised through prophecy.

Canon, Inerrancy, and Inspiration

The Greek New Testament proclaims the gospel-word about Jesus Christ, and the Hebrew Bible prepares the way for the Kingdom fulfilled in his ministry, death, and resurrection. This collection of diverse literature covering a span of more than a thousand years represents our canon. As part of such a collection each individual passage serves a purpose in addition to its original one: it interprets and is interpreted by other passages and books, even in the other testament. Thus while it is essential to seek the original meaning of a pericope for a particular audience, it is likewise imperative that each portion of scripture be recognized as part of the whole. This realization prevents an absolutizing of favorite passages over less popular ones and simultaneously paves the way for an interpreter to expand the pericope's scope by including insights from the whole. For example, Psalm 90:10 speaks of the limit of human life as seventy years, while Genesis 6:3 more generously sets the number at one hundred twenty. The seventy-year limit is exceeded by vast numbers of people in our day. Should we consider them rebellious for living so long? Should we chide modern medicine for adding years to life? Should we take steps to intervene at age sixty-nine so that the limit stays in tact? Such questions are, of course, ludicrous, but they illustrate what can happen if one makes absolute a particular verse at the expense of the larger biblical message. In light of Genesis 6:3 and a host of other passages we can conclude that the issue is really a matter of the mortality of human beings rather than a specific time frame for the limitation of human life. The realization of our mortality paves the way for the hope of resurrection that is realized in Jesus Christ. The canon thus becomes a means for interpretation by insisting on a holistic view rather than one based on individual texts at the expense of others.

In addition to its role as interpreter, the canon functions to provide the norm or framework by which teaching and preaching the word of God can be judged. Bound between covers, the sixty-six books do not close the time of God's dynamic encounters with people but rather open the way for the church's continuing task of proclaiming the word anew. The relationship between that canon of scripture and the church's proclamation is this: within all the diverse witnesses to God's effective word, the Bible provides the framework and norm by which all preaching and teaching in the church must be evaluated. In other words, while the Bible attests to a dynamic God who acts differently in this or that situation, there are some ideas and teachings that are simply not included in that variety, some that are simply contrary to the witnesses of scripture. While no formula can limit God's word, neither can that word be made to fit every social cause or ideological fad. The canon thus provides not a prescription for every contemporary illness but the norm by which are measured the church's teaching and preaching in regard to such illnesses.

In this discussion of the Bible as the written word of God, we have thus far omitted any reference to inerrancy or to infallibility. Certainly we can assert emphatically that the Bible is without error in its understanding of the gospel. Likewise the scriptures do not err in their message about God and in their portrayal of the human condition both without the gospel and through the gospel. Indeed, the early church fathers repeatedly asserted that the scriptures do not deceive: they are perfect and true.

Yet another use of the word "inerrancy" — particularly the way it is used more recently — insists that the Bible is without error in all matters, even those that are historical, scientific, and literary. Such a view, similar to Islam's view of the Koran, is based on the understanding that God dictated all the words to humans, and since God cannot err, the scriptures themselves are without error. Therefore, inconsistencies and contradictions are not recognized to be such, and so some ingenious methods are employed to harmonize problematic accounts or explain them away. Sometimes the solution to the problem is said to be present in the original text to which we no longer have access.

The advocates of literalistic approaches seem to deny that dialogical quality of the scriptures by which God and humans interact. We have argued above that it is precisely in this dialogue that the scriptures come into being, for the human being — full of prejudices, biases, wishful thinking, fears, and misconceptions — is the very vehicle upon and through whom the Spirit acts. The resultant witness is therefore divine and human, infinite and finite.

Moreover, citing errors of scientific data, historical record, or authorship of books is not a matter of accusing the authors of deception. Incongruities occur in the Bible because of the obvious limits to human comprehension as well as to the purposes for which the author was addressing the audience. Far from regarding these issues as unfortunate problems, we should rather rejoice that God so chooses the common and ordinary to communicate the gospel-word. Such awareness enables us today to identify with God's spokespersons of old in the task of witnessing. We share their struggles in putting God's word into human terms. We stand in their shoes (or sandals) when we realize the awesome task God places upon us. We appreciate their predicament when the words are not heard or heeded. We can only pray that our words are as faithful as theirs in communicating God's will in our own time and place.

The use of the word "inerrancy," understood in different ways, has led to contention and divisiveness among the members of Christ's Body, the church. Such an issue tends to divert our attention from the one exclusive object of our faith and worship, the triune God in whom alone our unity as sisters and brothers is accomplished. For this reason perhaps the church would do well to eliminate the word "inerrancy" from its discussion of the Bible.

While avoiding the term "inerrancy," however, we emphasize the role of inspiration. "No prophecy ever came by human will, but people moved by the Holy Spirit spoke from God" (2 Pet. 1:21). The inspiration of God's Spirit has moved people in all ages — in biblical times, in the history of the church, and now — to witness to the word of God both in written and in oral form. Without such inspiration people are incapable of proclaiming that effective word that both judges and justifies the ungodly. Thanks to the Spirit ordinary people are inspired to choose the words that communicate, select the analogies that illustrate, and demonstrate the creativity that attracts and holds the attention of the audience. These people receive their inspiration to witness not in isolation but through the preaching of the gospel in the Spirit-filled community. "So faith comes from what is heard, and what is heard comes from the preaching of Christ" (Rom. 10:17).

Ultimately the community of faith regarded even the sacred

writings of inspired people to be nothing less than "inspired by God and profitable for teaching, for reproof" (2 Tim. 3:16). What was originally said of the authors came to be said of the words as well. Such was the respect that developed in the early church for holy scripture.

The word of God, then, takes the form of a message proclaimed, of the Son of God Incarnate, and of a book written. The same word in all these forms creates the community of believers called the church and simultaneously provides the only source of the church's authority by which to preach and teach. Indeed, the word in its various forms lays upon the church in every generation the responsibility to proclaim it anew, whether from pulpits, through the administration of the sacraments, or in the mutual consolation of the sisters and brothers of the faith community. This word reaches out to the world in order to bring people to faith and is likewise shared among us in the church in order to drown daily the old Adam in us all.

These reflections lead me to state — as I did at the outset of this chapter — that "the word of God" is not simply a phrase that elicits various emotions. Rather the word is nothing less than God acting on people in profound ways. Whatever the action, the word of God is the means by which the Almighty God effects the divine will on humans in ordinary human terms.

The word has become incarnate in Jesus Christ. The word has been written in books and collected as the canon of the church. The challenge to the church today is to join the witnesses of the past in the awesome task of preaching that word anew.

Chapter 2

The Reality of a Two-Testament Bible

Some Christians see the division of the Bible into two testaments as a reason to neglect the "old" because we have the "new." Others pay little attention to the division and regard both parts on an equal basis, suggesting there is nothing in the New Testament that is not already in the Old. The approach developed in this book is to maintain the tension between those two extremes so that one might preach God's word from a pericope derived from the Hebrew Bible and simultaneously deliver that word in terms of God's new act and revelation in Jesus Christ.

In the following pages we will consider first the relationship between the testaments in terms of the use of the Hebrew Bible/Greek Old Testament by the writers of the New Testament. Second, we will look at explicit "promise"-"fulfillment" formulas that connect the testaments, particularly in regard to the identity and work of Jesus. Third, we will consider the theme of the Reign of God as the promise that unites the two testaments. Finally, we will examine the harmony and the tension between the two testaments that define the challenge for the Christian preacher.

The Old Testament in the New

The New Testament writers derived much of their imagery, expression, and theological concepts from their Hebrew scriptures. Just as Christian hymn writers of today employ biblical terms and themes, so the early church found its religious language in the Torah, the Prophets, and the Writings. The emphasis on the Reign of God, the understanding of God as Shepherd, the image of the

Servant of God, the relationship between God and the people in terms of covenant, and many more concepts are derived from the Hebrew Bible, though they are usually reinterpreted in light of Jesus Christ.

In addition to employing themes and categories of thinking from the Hebrew Bible, New Testament writers quote specific passages, usually accompanied by a statement such as "it is written," "according to the prophet," or something similar. At times, however, the quotation is incorporated so smoothly into the new writing (common in Luke) that the reader might miss its origin as the scriptures of Israel.

Some of the instances in which early Christian authors used the Hebrew Bible are rather casual. The author of 2 Peter was dealing with the problem of Christians falling back into their old pagan ways. It would have been better for a person not to have been a Christian at all than, having been one, to turn away again. Then the author illustrates the point by quoting Proverbs 26:11: "It has happened to them according to the true proverb, 'The dog turns back to his own vomit.' " This not-so-delectable little quote summons the reader to recall the remainder of the proverb: so "is a fool that repeats his folly." The specific content is not as important for us as the recognition that the writer assumed the audience could fill in the blanks once the first part of the proverb was cited. That assumption, of course, included the audience's knowledge of their scriptures.

Most of the New Testament's use of the Hebrew Bible is more theological, or better, christological. One of the primary reasons for citing the scriptures is to demonstrate who Jesus is. The author of Matthew's Gospel was particularly fond of using such quotations in order to establish the identity of Jesus and to show how his name — the same as Joshua — indicates what Jesus was to do: "save" his people. At Matthew 3:3, for instance, the author defines the task of John the Baptist by citing Isaiah 40:3:

> The voice of one crying in the wilderness:
> "Prepare the way of the Lord,
> make his paths straight."

The author, however, alters the punctuation so that the passage from ancient scripture connects with John the Baptist "crying in the wilderness" rather than maintaining the original sense in which the voice cried, "In the wilderness prepare the way of the Lord." His point was that John, the preparatory voice in the wilderness, was paving the way for the coming of the Lord in the person of Jesus Christ and for the salvation he was bringing.

At Matthew 2:6, when Herod was told where the Messiah/Christ was to be born, the scribes read Micah 5:2, a passage that says nothing at all about anyone's birthplace. The prophecy does, however, indicate that the ruler to come would descend from the lineage of Jesse, whose home was in Bethlehem. By applying this verse to Jesus, the author of Matthew reaffirms the Davidic descent of Jesus, which was established through the genealogy in chapter 1.

The apostle Paul, too, displayed a fondness for quoting the scriptures in order to expound his Christology. Perhaps his most prominent attempt in this regard appears at Romans 10:5–13, where he quotes the Hebrew Bible three times. (1) In verses 6–8 Paul uses Deuteronomy 30:11–14 to demonstrate Christ is the word on which righteousness is based and that word is near the people; in doing so, Paul reinterprets the Deuteronomy passage that speaks of the word as the law promulgated in that book. (2) At verse 11 Paul cites Isaiah 28:16 (Septuagint version), where the object of faith is either the precious cornerstone or God himself; for Paul the object of faith is clearly Christ. (3) At verse 13 the apostle quotes Joel 2:32, which announces salvation for all who worship Yahweh; for Paul, the title "Lord" has been transferred to Christ on the basis of the resurrection, and so in Christ there is salvation for everyone who "calls on the name of the Lord."

On occasion, the connection with the Hebrew Bible is made by the use of a mere word, particularly a word reserved in the scriptures for God. Making the connection between Yahweh of the Hebrew Bible and Jesus Christ of the New Testament provided profound christological insights. Mark 4:35–41 (parallels at Matt. 8:23–27; Luke 8:22–25) describes Jesus and his disciples crossing the sea in a boat when a great storm arose and threatened to sink their craft. In deadly fear the disciples turned to the sleeping Jesus. The master "awoke and rebuked the wind and said to the sea, 'Peace! Be still!' " The forces of nature obeyed, and the disciples were filled with awe, wondering among themselves, "Who then is this, that even wind and sea obey him?"

Perhaps we should not be too hard on the disciples. They did not have, as we have, the essential clue about who Jesus was. That clue appears in the words of the narrator: he "rebuked" the wind and the sea. The Greek verb *epitimaō* in the Greek Old Testament is owned by Yahweh. Yahweh "rebukes" the channels of the sea (Ps. 18:15), the primordial Deep (Ps. 104:5–9), the sea (Nah. 1:3b–5), rivers (Isa. 50:2), rider and horse (Ps. 76:6), Assyrian armies (Isa. 17:13), wicked nations (Ps. 9:5), and Satan (Zech. 3:1–2). Therefore, when the writers of the Gospels state in their narration that Jesus "rebukes" the sea (Mark 4:39 and parallels), unclean spirits (Mark 1:25), and Satan (in the form of Peter [Mark 8:33]), they are announcing the beginning of God's battle against chaos that was expected to occur "on that day" (Mark 4:35; see Isa. 27:1). That the battle is being fought for God by Jesus indicates the filial identity of Jesus with Yahweh.

In addition to direct quotes and specific words of narration, images, epithets, and metaphors often make the connection between Jesus and the Hebrew Bible. When Jesus identifies himself as the Good Shepherd at John 10:1–8, he (or the author) is employing the image from Ezekiel 34:15, a metaphor already transferred to the future Davidic king only eight verses later. Further, the image of Jesus as Servant of the Lord derives from the poetic preaching of Second Isaiah, even though the "suffering servant" of Isaiah 52:13–53:12 is hardly ever quoted (Luke 22:37; Acts 8:32–35; and 1 Pet. 2:22–24 are exceptional). And the image of the "mound" on which the angels of God ascend and descend, marking the place where the divine and earthly worlds connect (Gen. 28:12), is transferred to Jesus at John 1:51.

Promise and Fulfillment

A Christian approaches the Hebrew Bible with a committed set of presuppositions about who Jesus is and what God accomplished in his ministry, death, and resurrection. While these presuppositions should not distort the original meaning of a passage, they do indicate that we read the Bible backward. As believing New Testament people of God, we search the Hebrew Bible to discern what God had said and done "before faith came" (Gal. 3:23) to those original people of God.

In discussing the categories of promise and fulfillment, we will, therefore, begin with the fulfillment passages of the New Testament. Only from the perspective of the revelation of God in Jesus Christ can we move backward to the Hebrew Bible to determine what the promise is.

Fulfillment in the New Testament

New Testament writers employ two Greek roots to speak of something being "fulfilled." First, the terms *teleioō* and *teleō* are used to designate something that has been "accomplished" or "brought to fulfillment," often without mention of an existing prophecy. *Teleioō* appears in the following passages (my italics):

John 4:34:	Jesus said to them, "My food is to do the will of him who sent me and to *accomplish* his work."
John 5:36:	"The works that the Father has granted me to *accomplish,* these very works that I am doing, bear me witness that the Father has sent me."
John 17:4:	"I glorified thee on earth, having *accomplished* the work that thou gavest me to do."
John 19:28:	After this, Jesus . . . said (to *fulfill* the scripture), "I thirst."
1 John 2:5; 4:12, 17, 18:	"*perfected* in love"

Teleō appears likewise in the following passages (my italics):

Luke 12:50:	"I have a baptism to be baptized with; and how I am constrained until it is *accomplished!*"
Luke 18:31–32:	And taking the twelve, he said to them, "Behold, we are going up to Jerusalem, and everything that is written of the Son of Man by the prophets will be *accomplished.* For he will be delivered to the Gentiles and will be mocked and shamefully treated and spit upon; and they will scourge him and kill him, and on the third day he will rise."
Luke 22:37:	"For I tell you that this scripture must be *fulfilled* in me, 'And he was reckoned with transgressors'; for what is written about me has its fulfillment (*telos*)."

John 19:28:	After this, Jesus, knowing that all was now *finished,* said . . . , "I thirst."
John 19:30:	He said, "It is *finished*"; and he bowed his head and gave up his spirit.
Acts 13:29:	And when they had *fulfilled* all that was written of him, they took him down from the tree and laid him in a tomb.
Revelation 10:7:	In the days of the trumpet call to be sounded by the seventh angel, the mystery of God, as he announced to his servants the prophets, should be *fulfilled.*
Revelation 17:17:	For God has put it into their hearts to carry out his purpose by being of one mind and giving over their royal power to the beast, until the words of God shall be *fulfilled.*

These passages show a particular emphasis in Johannine and Lukan material on Christ's fulfilling or accomplishing God's work. The terms *teleioō* and *teleō* point to the accomplishment of God's will, even if they do not always cite a particular promise. Striking is the preponderance of cases in which the setting or the fulfillment itself is the crucifixion of Jesus (Luke 12:50; 18:31–32; 22:37; John 19:28–30; Acts 13:29). In only one case is a passage from the Hebrew Bible cited as a promise (Luke 22:37), and that passage is the final verse of the suffering servant song (Isa. 53:12). Apart from specific reference to the crucifixion, the formula points to the work of God that Jesus said he was sent to accomplish.

The second root used in the New Testament for the fulfillment of God's work is *pleroō.* The formula "in order that what was said through the prophet might be fulfilled" is phrased in a number of ways in the material peculiar to Matthew's Gospel: 1:22 (citing Isa. 7:14: Jesus' birth); 2:15 (citing Hos. 11:1: God calling his son out of Egypt); 13:35 (citing Ps. 78:2: Jesus speaking to the crowds in parables); 21:4 (citing a combination of Isa. 62:11 and Zech. 9:9: Jesus' need to enter Jerusalem on an ass). The formula specifically mentions the prophet Jeremiah at 2:17–18 (citing Jer. 31:15: the weeping of Rachel for her children) and at 27:9 (citing Jer. 18:2–3; 32:6–15: the thirty pieces of silver paid to Judas). Isaiah is mentioned as the prophetic source at 4:14 (citing Isa. 9:1–2: Jesus is the light to the people in Galilee), at 8:17 (citing Isa. 53:4: rooting Jesus' healing ministry in prophecy), and at 12:17–21 (citing Isa. 42:1–4, the first servant song: Jesus withdrew from the crowds because of the Pharisees' intention to destroy him).

Similar expressions using *pleroō* such as "that the scripture might be fulfilled," "the scripture had to be fulfilled," "the scriptures have been fulfilled," and so on, occur in such places as Matthew 26:54, 56, explaining the necessity of the crucifixion; Mark 14:49, regarding the arrest of Jesus in the garden; Luke 4:21, about the eschatological fulfillment of Jesus' mission to the poor and oppressed; 24:44, about his death and resurrection and forgiveness of sins to all nations; John 13:18; 17:12, both regarding Judas's betrayal; 19:24, 36, both in narrative details about the crucifixion. Particularly interesting is Acts 3:18: "But what God foretold by the mouth of all the prophets, that his Christ should suffer, he thus fulfilled." This is the only passage in which God is explicitly said to have been the speaker and in which God fulfilled the promised word by actuating it; in the other cases, the fulfillment is stated as a theological passive: that is, God is assumed to be the subject of the action.

The *pleroō* formulae are used by Matthew in the infancy stories (1:22; 2:15, 17), the story of the passion (26:54, 56; 27:9), the entry into Jerusalem (13:35), the demonstration that eschatological expectation is fulfilled in the healing ministry of Jesus (8:17), and in the move to Galilee, where Jesus' preaching is cited (4:14). In all these cases Matthew is attempting to show that God's promise is fulfilled in the person and work of Jesus.

In John the formulae relate the details of the passion, but the primary concern is the betrayal by Judas (13:18; 17:12) and the rejection of Jesus by the Jews (12:38; 15:25). In Luke *pleroō* indicates that the promise of good news to the afflicted is fulfilled in Jesus' ministry (4:21) and that the cross and resurrection are rooted in the entire Hebrew Bible. Thus the *pleroō* formulae are used exclusively in the Gospels and in Acts to refer to the whole event of Christ.

Both the *pleroō* and *teleioō/teleō* formulae point to the fulfillment of the New Testament as the accomplishment of God's will in the person and work of Jesus Christ. While Paul does not use these *pleroō* or *teleō* formulae, his understanding of the gospel as a combination of Christology and soteriology corresponds to the formulae usage, and we find that understanding of fulfillment throughout the whole New Testament.

Promise in the Hebrew Bible

If the New Testament describes fulfillment in terms of Christology and soteriology, then finding the promise of that fulfillment in the Hebrew Bible presents an interesting challenge. The "fulfill" passages we have just examined include several events regarding the person and work of Christ, and that variety may mean we must speak of a number of promises in the Hebrew Bible. Indeed, we have already seen that the assumed promises come from Isaiah (7:14: the Immanuel passage; 9:2: a messianic prophecy), from Second Isaiah (42:1–4 and 53:4: both servant passages), from Jeremiah (31:15: a judgment passage), from Hosea (11:1: not a promise or prophecy at all but a quasi-credal statement), and from Psalm 78:2 (a historical survey that is neither a promise nor a prophecy).

Perhaps if we ignore for a moment the Greek New Testament quotations and concentrate on promise in the Hebrew Bible itself, the picture will become clearer. The word "promise" occurs frequently in English translations of the Hebrew Bible, but there is no word in biblical Hebrew that means exclusively "promise." The Septuagint uses the common *epaggelia/epaggelein* only rarely and then usually in late texts (1 Esd. 1:7; Esther 4:7; Ps. 55[56]:8; Amos 9:6; 1 Macc. 10:15; 4 Macc. 12:9). When "promise" appears in English translation, it usually renders Hebrew *dbr* (to speak) or *'mr* (to say).

Hebrew *dbr* appears in the sense of promise more than thirty times, some of which are as follows (my italics):

1 Kings 8:20:	Now the Lord has fulfilled his *promise* (*d*ᵉ*bārô*) that he made; for I have risen in the place of David my father, and sit on the throne of Israel, as the Lord *promised* (*dibbēr*), and I have built the house for the name of the Lord, the God of Israel. [For the promise itself see 2 Samuel 7.]
1 Kings 8:56:	Blessed be the Lord who has given rest to his people Israel, according to all that he *promised* (*dibbēr*); not one word has failed of all his good *promise* (*d*ᵉ*bārô*), which he uttered by Moses his servant. [For the promise itself see Deut. 12:10.]

Exodus 12:25: And when you come to the land that the Lord will give you, as he has *promised* (*dibbēr*), you shall keep this service. [For the promise see Gen. 12:7; 15:12–21; Exod. 3:8, 17.]

Likewise, Hebrew *'mr* appears in the sense of promise a number of times (my italics):

Exodus 3:17: "And I *promise* (*wa'ōmār*) that I will bring you up out of the affliction of Egypt to the land of the Canaanites, the Hittites . . . "

Numbers 14:40: And they rose early in the morning and went up to the heights of the hill country, saying, "See, we are here, we will go up to the place that the Lord has *promised* (*'āmar*); for we have sinned." [For the promise see the passage cited immediately above.]

2 Kings 8:19: Yet the Lord would not destroy Judah, for the sake of David his servant, since he *promised* (*'āmar*) to give a lamp to him and his sons forever. [For the promise see 2 Samuel 7.]

The promises mentioned in these examples of *dbr* and *'mr* include the promise of land, the promise of deliverance, and the promise of rest to God's people. Some of them relate to the nature and the actions of the royal covenant: the promise of an enduring dynasty and the promise that a temple would be built.

There are many more promises in the Hebrew Bible in which the words *dbr* and *'mr* do not appear at all. To Abraham the Lord promises descendants, along with land and blessing for all the land/earth (Gen. 12:2; 18:18, both J; 15:1–5; 22:17–18, both E; 17:5–7, P); the same promises are repeated to Isaac (Gen. 26:3–4, J) and to Jacob (Gen. 28:13–14, J). The Lord promises protective presence and guidance to individuals (e.g., Moses at Exod. 3:13; 33:14) and to the people as a whole (the entire wilderness motif). The Lord promises a Messiah to rule over God's Kingdom (Isa. 9:2–7; 11:1–10; Jer. 23:5–6; Mic. 5:2–4; Zech. 9:9–10) but more frequently promises (without mentioning the Messiah) the Kingdom of peace and harmony for those who at the present time experience upheaval, turmoil, and rejection (Isa. 2:2–4; 35:1–10; Jer. 31:31–34; Amos 9:13–15; Joel 2:28–29; Mic. 4:6–7). A whole collection of promises of salvation (e.g., Isa. 43:1–7) and of judgment (e.g., Joel 2) adds to the more specific promises mentioned above. So overwhelming is the list of promises in the Hebrew Bible that the collection of thirty-nine books might well be called "Promises! Promises!"

Many of the promises in the Hebrew Bible were fulfilled in the time of biblical Israel. Abraham and Sarah had their son, and their progeny became a great nation. The people who were enslaved in Egypt came out, as the Lord promised. The Lord led the same people through the wilderness and eventually into the promised land. The people of Israel and later those of Judah were carried away as exiles to other lands, as the Lord promised, and the Lord, faithful to the prophetic word, brought the exiles home. In the books of Deuteronomy through Kings a close correspondence exists "between the words of Yahweh and history in the sense that Yahweh's word, once uttered, reaches its goal under all circumstances in history by virtue of the power inherent in it."[3]

There are also promises in the Hebrew Bible that were not fulfilled in the time of biblical Israel. They include the blessing for all the families of the earth, the reign of the Messiah, the universal Reign of God, the new creation of Isaiah 65, the new covenant of Jeremiah, and the ultimate Day of the Lord. In light of these unfulfilled promises the Hebrew Bible always points forward, beyond itself and its own experience.

We have, then, two categories of promises: those fulfilled and those unfulfilled in the period of biblical Israel. As Christians we might be tempted to ignore the first category and move exclusively to the second, where Jesus and the New Testament witnesses proclaim the Messiah has come, the Day of the Lord has dawned, the new covenant has been established, and the Reign of God is breaking into human history. All of that is essential for the New Testament faith, but to ignore the first category is to dismiss the Hebrew Bible as having no significance except that it promises what is said in the New Testament to be fulfilled.

Perhaps we come to a more comprehensive view of God if we take seriously the entire range of God's promises. Since we cannot isolate one or even a few as those that are fulfilled in the person and work of Christ, perhaps we should ask about the significance of the frequency with which God issues promises and of the variety of situations they cover.

Why would God offer so many promises? Why is God so oriented to the future — both somewhat immediate and completely ultimate? The entire biblical story would lead us to answer that God is not satisfied with the way things are. God points always to the future because the present does not meet the standards for the life and faith God desires. Curse is contrary to God's Reign, and so God sends Abraham and Sarah — and through them, the people of Israel — to be agents of blessing. Bondage is not God's will, and so God promises to free the slaves in Egypt. Negligence of the poor runs counter to everything God stands for, and so God threatens judgment on the people held most accountable for their welfare, the people of Israel and Judah. Though God sent the people into exile, God was satisfied eventually that they had had enough, and so God promised to take them home. Dissension, conflict, and war contrast with God's Reign of peace, and so God promises the greatest recycling program of all time, the transformation of instruments of war into tools of agriculture.

These few examples of the many promises in the Hebrew Bible still leave us asking: What is *the* promise?

In the earlier version of this book I defined the promise as God. More specifically, I argued, the content of the promise is not some event in the future but God coming to be with people: "*The* promise is not different from the promiser!"[4] By that I meant that the constant among the many and diverse promises is God's commitment to encounter people in the word, whether to judge or to save. This divine encountering over the centuries of biblical history points toward a future coming of God that ultimately will be decisive not only for the people of Israel but for the whole world.

While I still hold to that basic understanding of the promise, I wonder about the times when God is distinct from the promises made, for example, in the nature of the Messiah. Jesus Christ was not identical to the nature of the Messiah expected on the basis of prophecy. Jesus was not the royal figure who ruled over the Kingdom of God after God had established it. Jesus as Christ was God's big surprise to the Jews and to the world.

That kind of distinction between the stated promise and the fulfillment in Christ leads me to wonder if the promise that unites the two testaments does not have a content apart from the identity of God the Promiser. At the risk of settling on a theme that itself might be restrictive and exclusive of much scriptural testimony, I offer now the understanding of the promise as that of God's Reign.[5]

The Reign of God as the Promise

The synoptic records of Jesus' ministry highlight the centrality of the Reign of God. They report that the message Jesus preached was the nearness of the Day of the Lord and the ensuing Reign of God (Mark 1:15 and parallels). Jesus' rebuke of demons (Mark 1:25), of Satan (Mark 8:33), and of the sea (Mark 4:39) reflects the fulfillment of God's eschatological victory over the forces hostile to the Kingdom, a victory that would occur "on that day" (see Isa. 27:1). Jesus' healing ministry announces in deed the fulfillment of that hope for the new day in Isaiah 35. The calling of a new community, the twelve apostles, sounds like the new covenant promised in Jeremiah 31:31–34. Further, the commissioning of that new community in Matthew 10 involves the announcement about the imminence of the Reign of God and includes a healing ministry as well.

While John's Gospel emphasizes "life" rather than the Reign of God, the two seem to be identified in Jesus' conversation with Nicodemus (John 3:3, 5). Furthermore, when Pontius Pilate asks Jesus if he is the king of the Jews, Jesus responds by saying that "my kingship is not of this world" (19:35; see also 36). By implication, Jesus' kingship is of another realm, the heavens.

The apostle Paul focuses on the crucifixion and resurrection as the beginning of the new day that began in Christ. His letters are filled with pronouncements about the time (*kairos*) in which the church lives. He writes that "now is the acceptable time, . . . the day of salvation," and so we speak of those in Christ as a new creation (2 Cor. 5:16–6:2). He announces that "we are *now* justified" even while we wait to be saved from the wrath to come (Rom. 5:1–11). It is no wonder that in the Book of Acts, Paul's preaching is said to include the Kingdom of God, as well as the message about Jesus (see Acts 19:8; 20:25; 28:23, 31).

With such an emphasis on the Reign of God, already inaugurated in the ministry, death, and resurrection of Jesus, the New Testament attests to the fulfillment of what God promised of old. Certainly the prophets of ancient Israel looked forward to the Reign of God and announced its coming as bad news and as good. The Day of the Lord, Amos warns, will not be a bed of roses, even for Israel and Judah, because God will judge them for their infidelity and for their oppression of the poor. That day will be one of judgment on all the obstacles that stand in the way of God's Reign. It will also be a time of blessing, for in the Reign that begins "on that day," God will turn darkness to light, sickness to healing, curse to blessing, poverty to abundance.

Portrayals of the Reign of God promise the opposite of what life is like in the present for the people of God. In the new time God will provide food and homeland (Amos 9:13–15), healing (Isa. 35:1–10), and fruitful labor (Isa. 65:17–23). Animals that presently devour one another will feed beside one another, and children will play safely in the presence of poisonous snakes (Isa. 11:6–9; 65:25). God will pour out the same Spirit on all people, regardless of gender, social status, or age, and they will prophesy (Joel 2:28–29). God will gather people from all nations on Mount Zion, where they will learn the Lord's Torah and live accordingly, and then, reconciled to God, they will transform the instruments of war into the tools of agriculture (Isa. 2:2–4). On that day the Lord will make a new covenant by writing the content of the old on their hearts so they are no longer able to disobey, and all people—great and small—will know the Lord intimately (Jer. 31:31–34).

God's rule portrayed in Genesis 1–2 includes living space, food, community and companionship, fruitful labor, equality, and, above all, fidelity to God. That which God intended from the beginning, God will have at the end, thus the promises of God's Reign by the prophets. The correlations between beginning and end lead to the impression that even Genesis 1 and 2 are eschatological promises rather than merely descriptions of a bygone Golden Age. They assert God's claim on the universe, a claim that God will one day make unambiguously.

God's will for humanity in the first two chapters of the Bible contrasts sharply with the description of life as it is portrayed in Genesis 3 and beyond, indeed through chapter 11. In a sense, the pronouncements in 3:14–24 define life as it was/is known in the world: hostility between snakes and people, gender hierarchy (male rule), physical pain even during the blessed event of childbearing, junk food in terms of thorns and thistles, the frustration of working and working but reaping little benefit (toil), and the reality of our mortality.

The biblical story of Genesis 3 reports the reason for the present disharmony is the disobedience of the first couple in eating of the forbidden fruit: the tree of the knowledge of good and evil represents the insistence on experiencing everything, defining for oneself what is right and good, in effect, autonomy. Autonomy means self-rule rather than submission to God's rule, and the results are evident in the pronouncements that follow. Yet the entire record of the Hebrew Bible pays little attention to Genesis 3. (What stands out more sharply throughout Judaism is the autonomous rebellion of each and every generation.) Its importance for Christianity, however, especially for the theology of the apostle Paul (see especially Rom. 5:12–14), cannot be overemphasized, because Christ's reconciling death on the cross is for all humanity, all the children of Adam and Eve, because "all have sinned." Genesis 3 is not simply the story of one couple's past but the experience of all humanity.

The biblical witnesses announced that God will not simply allow humanity to wallow in its self-inflicted misery until the glorious end time when God reclaims the creation. Rather, in the meantime God sends agents of healing into the world's brokenness. God called Abraham and Sarah and their offspring to turn curse into blessing (Gen. 12:3; 18:18; 22:18; 26:4; 28:14). God commissioned Moses to deliver the people from servitude under pharaoh to the liberty of God's Reign (see Exod. 15:18). God sent judges to rid the land of oppressors and prophets both to call the people to accountability and to offer the hope of restoration. This constant sending of people by God is the mission work of God, never satisfied with the status quo of Genesis 3 but ever faithful to effect the promise of the divine Reign.

God is always acting directly and through the spoken word to accomplish the opposite of what is. The specific illustrations of what God will do in order to transform the status quo into what God wills for individuals, a people, the world—they are the promises that define the God of the Bible. That divine involvement in the nitty-gritty of human life distinguishes our God from other gods—gods of timeless myths, gods of divine providence, gods that sanction the depravity of the power of a few over the "huddled masses yearning to breathe free."

The Two Testaments in Harmony and in Tension

The New Testament announces Jesus' resurrection as the eschatological victory by which God ushered in the promised Reign. His resurrection is the firstfruits of those who have fallen asleep (1 Cor. 15:20, 23), the beginning of the general resurrection of the last days. Through that victory God sent the Holy Spirit to call into being the eschatological people of God. For the church, then, the expected future has already dawned, and so the church lives its life in the age of fulfillment.

The letters of the apostle Paul overflow with references to the new time that began in Christ. "Behold, now is the acceptable time, now is the day of salvation" (2 Cor. 6:2). A Christian leaves the old time zone and enters the new through the sacrament of baptism: "*Before* faith came,... *until* Christ came,... *now* that faith has come, we are *no longer* under a custodian" (Gal. 3:23–26). The new time calls the church to act accordingly: "The night is far gone, the day is at hand. Let us then cast off the works of darkness and put on the armor of light; let us conduct ourselves becomingly as in the day" (Rom. 13:12–13).

Even given all that, no one will be surprised to read that the old aeon is putting up a good fight to stay alive. The new has already begun, but it has not yet fully arrived. The front page of any newspaper or the first five minutes on "Action News Tonight" or the experiences in our own lives make that observation abundantly clear. In apocalyptic terms, the dragon thrown down by Michael (Rev. 12:7–12) is literally "raising hell" because he knows that his time is short. Therefore, the community of the future, the church, still looks toward the end when all things will be made new, when evil and pain and death and grief will cease, when all people will be raised with new bodies that will know none of the pain, the hunger, the weariness, and the discrimination that torment our present bodies.

The future is already here but not yet fully consummated — so the formula goes. The implication is that the church, while looking back to God's act of fulfillment in Jesus Christ, simultaneously lives under the promise that God will send Christ again to make all things new.

As the church looks forward to the unambiguous day of God's Reign, it can identify with the people of God, Israel, in receiving God's promise that life as we know it will be transformed into its opposite. It is the mark of the people of God in both testaments that faith in that promise of God enables believers to endure the present and, beyond endurance, to live life faithfully and thankfully.

In addition to the forward look common to both testaments, both celebrate a salvation event that occurred in the past. Israel looks back to the salvation event we call "the exodus," the freeing of the Hebrew slaves. At the Passover celebration, the head of the family announces, "It is because of what the Lord did for me when I came out of the land of Egypt..." (Exod. 13:8). In so doing, the Israelites or Jews of all following generations make themselves contemporary with that ancient event. Likewise, the members of the church of every generation look back to the death and resurrection of Jesus Christ and in a variety of ways recognize that the effect of that event is for them. The words said at the Sacrament of Holy Communion proclaim the contemporaneity of the two-thousand-year-old event: "The body of Christ given for you.... The blood of Christ shed for you."

Both church and synagogue look backward to a salvation event at the same time they look forward to the coming Reign of God. That similarity between the testaments is only one of many.

A second similarity is the emphasis in both testaments on forgiveness. Some Christians have distinguished between the two testaments by suggesting that while the Old Testament is based on God's judgment and on human righteousness through works, the New Testament announces God's grace and forgiveness. That distinction holds true only if an interpreter eliminates an enormous amount of material in both testaments. In the Hebrew Bible the understanding of Yahweh as forgiving and gracious is of utmost importance in identifying the nature of God. God's own announcement of forgiveness and loyalty, in spite of the people's sin, introduced the second Decalogue after Moses broke the first when he saw the golden calf (Exod. 34:6–7). Further, God provided the entire sacrificial system as the means by which the sins of the people might be wiped away so that fellowship between God and the people might continue (most of the Book of Leviticus). It was God's forgiveness that allowed the people of Israel to exist over the centuries, and it was God's reputation for forgiving that led Jonah to jump overboard so as to avoid announcing God's judgment on Nineveh. God's forgiveness of the people led to their homecoming hopes in Second Isaiah (Isa. 40:1–2), and that same nature enabled the individual Israelite to petition God for mercy and forgiveness (Ps. 51:1–2). On the other side, the New Testament includes an abundance of testimony to the judging nature of God and recognizes that what people do is an expression of their faith. Even a cursory reading of the Sermon on the Mount (Matt. 5–7) and of Jesus' announcements about the last days prevents us from eliminating from God's nature the role of judgment and the need for people to act accordingly.

Still one more similarity between the two testaments is the understanding of the people of God as that community gathered by God's grace in order to be God's witnesses in the world. The people of God, Israel, came into being as the result of God's promise to Abraham and Sarah: "I will make of you a great nation" (Gen. 12:2). Their election to be God's people was the result not of their own size and numbers but rather of the simple, inexplicable fact that God loved them (Deut. 7:6–8). Their identification as God's people in the world was not a matter of status but of responsibility to be "a kingdom of priests and a holy nation" (Exod. 19:6). Likewise, the New Testament people of God developed from that community of unlikely disciples that Jesus gathered around him during his ministry and from that miraculous act of the Holy Spirit on the Day of Pentecost. Nothing they did qualified them for inclusion in the new community, only God's grace. Their role as "a chosen race, a royal priesthood, a holy nation, God's own people" (1 Pet. 2:9), was not a status but a responsibility to proclaim the gospel of Jesus Christ.

We have seen, then, that the two testaments share the following basic understandings: looking forward to God's Reign while simultaneously looking back to God's act of salvation; emphasizing the nature of God as forgiving, even while exercising the role of judgment; becoming God's people on the basis of God's grace for the purpose of a larger role in the world.

With such harmony in view, where is the tension?

Ironically, the tension lies first and foremost in the same issues that comprise the harmony. More specifically, the *content* of salvation, expectation, forgiveness, and the people of God distinguishes the one testament from the other.

In our examination of "promise" and "fulfillment" terms above, we concluded that the content of "fulfillment" in the New Testament is the person and work of Jesus Christ. That same content—who Jesus was/is and what God accomplished in his life, death, and resurrection—sets the two testaments in tension and, in doing so, presents the challenge to preaching the gospel of Christ from texts from the Hebrew Bible.

Salvation in the Hebrew Bible is a matter of physical release from bondage. Derived from the root *y-š-ʿ*, meaning "wide," the Hebrew term for salvation portrays a spaciousness in which all that confines the people of God is obliterated, and the people are literally set free. The exodus from Egypt in the days of Moses qualifies as the salvation event par excellence, and the release from bondage in Babylon in the sixth century B.C. becomes for the people a new exodus as they return to their land. In the New Testament, salvation is variously understood as freedom also, but the release is not from bondage to another nation. It is freedom from the power of sin and of death and ultimately from the wrath of God on the day of judgment (Rom. 5:9–11). What accomplished the present benefits of salvation (justification, reconciliation) is the death of Jesus Christ on the cross, and what enables the believer to face the judgment day with hope is the person of Christ, waiting to serve as our advocate.

That new understanding of salvation indicates that the concepts of sin also differ from the one testament to the other. In the Hebrew Bible, sins were the acts that the people did or did not do, sins of commission and omission that could be avoided if the people had the mind to do so. The choice between good and evil, thus between life and death, was ever present for the people, and the expectation was that the people were capable of choosing good (see Deut. 30:15–20).

By contrast, the New Testament understands sin as that power that controls us so profoundly that it gives us a new identity: sinner. It captivates us and imprisons us so that we cannot possibly free ourselves from its grasp. It prevents us from doing good in the eyes of God, even from doing the things we ourselves know to be good (Rom. 7:19). Sin is a power from which we are unable to save ourselves, and its force is so powerful that only the death of God's Son is sufficient to defeat it. Moreover, while we might console ourselves with the news that in comparison to others we are not all that bad after all, when we recognize in the person of Jesus Christ what a sinless person is, we all stand convicted. Further, the justifying work of God gives us new identities: we are not only sinners; we are also forgiven children of God. The new creature we have become regards Jesus from a new point of view (2 Cor. 5:16). Jesus Christ, crucified and risen from the dead, is not only the one in whom God effected our salvation; he is also our Living Lord whom we worship and praise and for whom we wait to come again.

As for the nature of the people of God, even though the people of Israel and the people of the church both become God's people through God's gracious election, the makeup of each is different. In the Hebrew Bible, the people of Israel is the people of God; that is, the nation and the religious identity are one and the same. Strictly speaking there is no distinction between religious law and civil law, between the crimes of the people and their sins, because there is no line between the nation and God's people. For that reason, too, salvation is the release of the nation from physical bondage. In the New Testament, however, the people of God, the church, is without national affiliation. God's people consists of both Jews and Gentiles. The account of humanity's sinfulness in Romans 1 and 2 (Gentile and Jew) leads to the acknowledgment that "all have sinned" (3:23), and so the gift of justification is offered to all as well. The coming together of Jews and Gentiles to hear the gospel and to offer their praises to God is the eschatological miracle (see Rom. 15:7–13). The line between Israel and others is removed by the gospel of Christ.

Further, the gospel accounts of Jesus' ministry confirm that difference between the testaments. Jesus refuses to become involved in the nationalistic parties that would wage rebellion on Rome (see John 5:15). Jesus' battle was not with armies of an earthly empire but with the power of sin (Satan, the devil, the raging sea, the demons) that stood in the way of God's Reign over the universe. Victory over these cosmic enemies paved the way for the inauguration of the Kingdom of God.

Recognizing that the people of God of the New Testament and the people of any given nation, including our own United States, are not identical must alert the preacher to beware against making that assumption, even implicitly, in preaching from the Hebrew Bible. Throughout the history of our country and even in our own time, confusion over that issue has led to unwarranted ideologies and practices.[6]

Even the promise under which the Christian lives differs from that of the Hebrew Bible. Christians live under the promise that this Christ who died on a cross and was raised from the dead comes again — daily when he is proclaimed and ultimately to consummate the eschatological day Jesus has already inaugurated. While we are children of promise as were the people of biblical Israel, the promise is not identical for the church. The promise for us includes not only the expectation of the Reign of God to come but the presence and the power of Jesus Christ in our lives even now.

The Christian who knows that Christ is the content of the promise and the content of the fulfillment can look backward to the passages from the Hebrew Bible that proclaim God coming to forgive the people of their sins; to guide the people through the entangling demands of the times; to give them direction in bewildering and chaotic circumstances; to set them loose on a mission to the "families of the land" or even to "the nations of the earth"; to release them from the confining bonds of imprisonment, slavery, exile, persecution; to judge the people for failing to do justice and for whoring after other gods; to drive people to their knees and to raise them in new hopes.

From the perspective of the fulfilling work of God in Christ, Christians see in the promises and actions of God in the Old Testament a depth of love and power and purpose the writers of the Hebrew Bible could not have had. Like Monday morning quarterbacks we call the game differently, knowing how it all comes out and in what way and by whom, and so those stories and sermons that proclaim God's coming to judge and to save, to comfort and to challenge, are filled for the Christian with new meaning.

Struggling with, rather than avoiding, the tensions between the testaments, the Christian preacher comes to recognize the opportunities that exist in the Hebrew Bible for proclaiming the word of God in concrete situations today. The life dilemmas, the devastations of individuals and the nation, the protests and laments and confessions, the hopes and confidence, the dreams and the promises — all these are as real in our day as they were in the days of biblical Israel. In the searching of those ancient witnesses we can find parallels to our own searching, and in their faith we can seek hope. Above all, we can rejoice in their testimony to the faithfulness of God, especially as we see from this side of Good Friday and Easter how far God will go to be faithful to the promise.

Does that struggling mean the New Testament must always come to the rescue of a pericope from the Old? Can the passage from the Hebrew Bible stand on its own? Some scholars argue that we should set beside each passage from the Hebrew Bible one from the New Testament in order to validate it for Christian preaching.[7] In theory I have taken issue with that position, because I feel the word of God addressed to ancient Israel can itself become the vehicle through which the word is proclaimed from Christian pulpits today.

In practice, however, I always include in a sermon based on a passage from the Hebrew Bible something about the revelation of God in Jesus, or the effect of the crucifixion, or the victory of the resurrection. The structure of the lectionary in which the first lesson is chosen on the basis of how it relates to the Gospel for the day often leads to the pairing that some scholars recommend. However, the use of uniquely Christian beliefs is not limited to specific New Testament passages that might stand parallel to the prophecy or psalm or historical narrative. Rather it is the entire Christ-event that inspires and informs me in the development of my sermon, and that presupposition shows explicitly in what comes from the pulpit — whether I cite specific New Testament passages or not.

At the heart of biblical preaching is the good news that in Christ, God was reconciling the world and beginning the divine Reign that will come to completion in God's good time. In the meantime, until God makes that unambiguous claim on the world, God calls us to announce that good news in sermons, in teaching, and in private conversations. Through our speaking God's word of promise out of both testaments, God calls us to become the future community of God's people, even here and now.

Chapter 3

Wrestling with the Written Word

The biblical witnesses testify that God's word confronts us in history, that is, in that time- and space-bound arena where we live out our lives. In both testaments of the Bible, God participates in the nitty-gritty events that drive our lives as individuals, nations, and as peoples. This divine involvement prevents the word from dissolving into a timeless myth that regards earthly activity as only a reflection of the actions that occur in heaven.

This understanding of history as the arena in which God acts binds the two testaments together in a unique way, and no religion except Judaism could so intimately connect to the message about Jesus Christ. "History is the garbage that clutters the mind and prevents true meditation," an old Buddhist monk once told me. The attitude is common among a variety of religions throughout the world. "I am divine," a Taoist teacher announced to me proudly when I asked him about his understanding of God. Representatives of other religious systems would express similar views. But the witness in the Hebrew Bible and the New Testament to a God who operates outside of ourselves but in time and space and who brings history to a promised goal binds the two together in an intimate way. Both testaments attest to the same God, to the way that God acts in history, and to the nature of that God as one who comes to people to judge and to save.

Historicity and the Story of God's Word

The first implication of God's historical involvement is the importance of historicity, what actually happened. Any quest to determine precisely what occurred thousands of years ago is fraught with problems, of course, because often the resources at our disposal are limited and sometimes contradict themselves in reporting what happened. For example, the scarcity of material available to determine precisely "what happened" at the Reed Sea is frustrating to the historian: the event related in Exodus 14–15 and alluded to in historical summaries (Deut. 6:20–23; 26:5–9; Josh. 24:2–13; and Pss. 105; 106; 135; 136) has no extrabiblical support to confirm those reports. Some mention of the incident in Egyptian records would certainly help the historian pinpoint the date, place, and details (Did the chariots get stuck in the mud after having their wheels removed or did the sea actually split in two until the chariots got in the middle?). Perhaps it is too much to expect an ancient army and a proud pharaoh to report their losing a battle, but their candor would help us considerably in a quest for historicity. On the other hand, in the case of Sennacherib's siege of Jerusalem in the days of Hezekiah (Isa. 36–37; 2 Kings 18–19; 2 Chron. 32:1–21), we do have an extrabiblical account in the records of Sennacherib himself. However, the records are not entirely consistent. While the biblical records proclaim that Sennacherib's siege failed because of the plague brought by the Lord's angel (2 Kings 19:35–36; 2 Chron. 32:20–23; Isa. 38:36–38), Sennacherib claims that he brought the city to its knees and locked up Hezekiah "like a bird in a cage." When more evidence is available from contemporary sources, it is often contradictory, and so "what happened" becomes even more of a mystery.

In spite of the difficulties and the resulting educated guesses regarding historicity, the scholarly quest for what happened must continue nevertheless, for without this concern we cannot identify the situation to which the word is addressed; and without such identification there is no concreteness of the testimony and no indication of the involvement of God in our historical arena. That earthly involvement of God in time and space distinguishes the biblical testimony from all other religions.

As necessary as this concern for historicity is for biblical study, historicity does not proclaim anyone. What happened must be interpreted as the act of God. God confronted those ancient witnesses as well our ourselves not in the precision of historical accuracy but in the word that was and is proclaimed through the biblical witness. The word of God is the means by which God comes to be present — to judge and to save, to comfort and to challenge. Only the proclaimed action of God in an event provides the event with theological significance.

The proclamation of God becomes more significant for preaching than the event itself. To fail to find the historicity of a passage or to conclude that such a story was essentially based not on an event but rather on a legend or saga or even originally a mythological allusion from another culture does not invalidate the message of the text. Suppose scrutiny into the Reed Sea accounts reveals that the origin of the story was really the mythological encounter between the god of order and watery chaos (the Babylonian story of Marduk and Tiamat or the Canaanite conflict between Baal and Yamm). Even that conclusion would not diminish the significance of the story for history, a theological history in which Yahweh defeats the pharaoh of Egypt in order to deliver the people from bondage to another god.

The entire biblical message is that God constantly breaks into human earthly existence to move all of creation toward the divine rule. Whether or not every event happened the way it is described in the Bible, or whether this or that event happened at all, is secondary to the testimony that the transcendent God participates in our lives, eventually becoming flesh to share our pains and joys, our sorrows and our deaths, and providing us promise of new life through death. What is crucial in our evaluation of a biblical story is whether or not the proclamation is consistent with the God who confronts people in history by the word made flesh and who creates history anew by that confrontation.

The major criterion for determining the value for preaching a passage from the Hebrew Bible is not the historicity of the biblical event but the history of the word of God. What God was up to in this story or that, where God was leading the individual or the whole people, how God responded to the cries for help and to the audacity of the uncaring — they provide the history of God's word as it is witnessed through the faith of believing proclaimers. The testimony to God's breaking into the world through individuals and through the people of Israel and ultimately in the person of Jesus Christ provides for us the model for preaching the word in our own day.

Our challenge today is to cut through — not cut out — the details of each testimony in order to discern the role of God in the ancient witnesses. For the purpose of preaching the word we need to appreciate the words of the texts and their phrasing, the historical and cultural realities out of which they grew, the literary forms and their uses in ancient times. Working through all these details will enable us to get to the purpose for which the texts were written: what they are saying about God and the impact of God's word on the people to whom they were addressed.

In short, the goal of the interpretive work is to answer a theological question: *What is God doing here?*

This question, first suggested to me by the late Paul Scherer in his lectures on homiletics many years ago, requires a theological answer consistent with the arguments presented thus far in this book. (1) God must be the subject of the sentence, and so the emphasis is on the word of God rather than on what we ought to be doing, as though we were delivering a morality speech. (2) The verb must be an active one, for in the biblical testimony God reveals the divine nature by actions — saving and judging, comforting and challenging. The use of a linking verb, as in "God is love," will not adequately answer the question. (3) The response to "here" demands that the interpreter deal with the specificity of the given pericope. While it might be safe to say that "God is rescuing the covenant people," the sentence might apply to so many passages in the Hebrew Bible that a listener would not be able to identify the pericope in question. Perhaps "God is rescuing the covenant people from bondage in Egypt" at least indicates the pericope at hand is somewhere in the narrative about the exodus-event. As the interpreter concentrates on *how* God is pulling off the rescue, such as by slaughtering the firstborn of Egypt or drowning the Egyptian army in the sea, the source of the sentence will emerge as that of Exodus 12 or Exodus 14.

In order to ensure that the passage maintain its connection with time and space, that is, with our earthly lives and dilemmas, I have found it helpful to add a second question: *What is the situation in which God is doing it?* Concretizing the issue of the people's plight and stating that predicament precisely not only puts the interpreter in the sandals of the original hearers but helps to focus the pericope for preaching today. The situation to be described is basically theological: What is the issue between God and the people that needs fixing? The dilemma might arise from the historical fact of slavery in Egypt or from the sociological problems connected with forced labor gangs or from the economic concerns on the part of the workers, but the reason all that is a concern to the prospective preacher is the theological dimension of those realities. The proclaimer of God's word is not essentially a historian, a sociologist, or an economist but a theologian.

Therefore the problem must be defined theologically, just like the answer.

A one-sentence answer as a response to both questions (What is God doing here? and What is the situation in which God is doing it?) will focus the preacher on the theological testimony of the passage and direct the sermon to address a specific audience with a particular expression of God's word. Conducting the exegesis of the pericope to answer those questions will also limit — gratefully — the kind of research needed for the task.

Textual and Contextual Exegesis

I. What the Text Meant

To determine the significance of a given pericope or book in the scriptures, the exegete is compelled to use all the scientific tools and methods at his or her disposal. In one sense, the Bible is a historical document (or rather, a collection of documents) and must be examined like any other historical document. At the same time, the Bible is that collection of witness literature that provides the norm for our faith as Christians. And so, unlike other historical documents, we approach the study of the Bible with some commitments to the God to whom it bears witness and with some presumptions concerning its nature. Carrying such presuppositions and commitments, one's exegesis will not be completely objective. Even one's purpose for examining the scriptures is, of course, based on some presupposition that will undoubtedly influence what one finds.

The position previously set forth in this volume is that the word of God is the means by which God confronts people in time and space and by which God effects the divine will. Such a position, true of the Old Testament as well as the New, means that one cannot define in absolute terms precisely what the word of God says. For if God is understood as the one who faithfully comes to judge and to save and ultimately to establish the Reign of peace, then God's word always has a message for a particular situation, and the content and structure of that word are always determined by the situation that God addresses. When the word of the Lord comes to a prophet, there always follows a specific message to be spoken to a particular people at a certain point in time. This word is no theological, philosophical, or moral absolute but the dynamic confrontation of God with people. This understanding is a presupposition that will undoubtedly influence one's understanding of what the text meant.

Taking seriously such presuppositions and commitments, the interpreter approaches the texts of scripture with all the tools and methods at his or her disposal.[8] The steps for exegesis outlined here differ very little from other such lists, although my theological and hermeneutical position will cause certain aspects of the list to be emphasized more than others. In addition, since the concern here is with exegesis of texts from the Hebrew Bible in particular, the emphasis on some items in the list will be somewhat different from a list concerned with New Testament interpretation.

1. *Establish a working text.* The ideal method of establishing the text is, of course, to translate it from the Hebrew and to render it as literally as possible. (The literal translation will prevent the exegete from making an interpretive rendering before the hard work of exegesis has begun.) Fortunately or unfortunately, the exegete of a text from the Hebrew Bible does not need to expend as much time and energy in establishing the text as the New Testament exegete must do with the Greek. This difference is due simply to the fact that we do not possess a multitude of ancient Hebrew manuscripts, apart from the limited and often fragmented texts from the Dead Sea community at Qumran.[9]

For those unable to translate the text from Hebrew, another method of establishing a working text is available: comparing various English translations or paying attention to footnotes in most translations to see if any significant differences appear. The simple use of synonyms is unimportant, but the different rendering of an idiom, the use or lack of use of an article, the tense or mood of a verb — any of these might at least hint at a problem.

2. *Work through literary matters.* The literary aspects of a text are many and varied — in fact, almost infinite. The major concerns, however, are as follows.

a. The author, the date, and the purpose for writing or speaking. To determine the probable answers to these issues, the interpreter should use a sound and relatively recent Old Testament introduction or a commentary by a reputable scholar, if such is available on the book in which the passage occurs.[10]

b. Literary devices and laws of composition. Is the passage prose or poetry? If poetry, does it follow the rules and patterns for parallelism? If so, which kind of parallelism — synonymous, antithetic, climbing? If synonymous, then two lines of poetry — by the use of synonyms — mean the same thing. Such a discovery can prevent serious distortion of a text. For example, at Isaiah 55:7 appears the synonymous parallelism:

> Let the wicked forsake his way,
>   and the unrighteous his thoughts;
> let him return to the Lord, that he may have mercy on him,
>   and to our God, for he will abundantly pardon.

It might be tempting to separate the way of the wicked from the thoughts of the unrighteous and to distinguish between the Lord's mercy and God's pardon. Such divisions may indeed be tempting in a sermon outline, but the text intends no such differentiation between lines 1 and 2 and between lines 3 and 4.

If the passage under investigation is prose, are there any important and typically narrative-type expressions that stand out? The famous Immanuel passage at Isaiah 7:10–17 begins, "Again the Lord spoke to Ahaz. . . ." The simple adverb "again" obviously indicates that Yahweh had spoken earlier, and that prior conversation in 7:1–9 might be crucial in interpreting the present one.

c. Key words and idioms. Theological terms like "righteousness," "salvation," "transgression," "iniquity," and "redeem" deserve attention. One way to grasp what the biblical writers meant by these terms is to use a Bible dictionary like *The Interpreter's Dictionary of the Bible* or *Harper's Bible Dictionary* or *Theological Dictionary of the Old Testament.* Another way, open both to those who can read Hebrew and to those who cannot, is to do a word study through the use of a concordance. Using a Hebrew concordance or an English one, however, requires the interpreter to follow a responsible method. The purpose of such word studies is, of course, to make some conclusion about the meaning of the word to the people of biblical times on the basis of how and in what contexts the word is used. But since the meanings of words change and since different authors use words in somewhat different ways, it is important to establish a set of priorities in carrying out such a study. First, how is the word used elsewhere by the same author? Second, how is the word used by the author's contemporaries? Third, how is the word used generally in the Hebrew Bible? The further down in this list the interpreter must move in order to acquire enough evidence to make some conclusion about the use of a word, the less precise will that judgment be for the passage under investigation. If a certain author nowhere else used the term in question and if no contemporaries used the word, then the greatest caution must be exercised in determining precisely what the author meant on the basis of word usage at that moment in time. To illustrate this point, let us consider the word *subdue* at Genesis 1:28, a word that has such profound significance in modern discussions on ecology. A word study of Hebrew *kbs* or the English word *subdue* reveals precisely what we do not want it to mean: to enslave, to oppress, to bring into bondage. The contexts in which the word appears give an entirely negative sense to the word. However, there is no other instance in which the author of Genesis 1 — the Priestly writer — used the term, and so the interpreter must be extremely careful in concluding that the Priest meant "subdue" in a negative sense, especially since the author speaks so positively about the created world throughout the chapter.

Key words, of course, are sometimes the problematical ones in establishing the text, and so at this point of the process, the exegete should try to determine whether Isaiah 7:14 should read "A virgin shall conceive" or "A young woman is with child" or "The young woman is with child." Such a problem involves a word study of the term for the female (Hebrew *'almâ*) as well as the use of a good commentary, which should define the verb as a present participle or as a simple adjective.

The investigation of idioms is crucial at this stage, too. Sometimes idioms are difficult to recognize as such, but often they stand out prominently. In the Aaronic benediction, "The Lord make his face to shine upon you" (Num. 6:25) is obviously an idiom. A word study of "shine" in connection with one's face shows that the idiom stands in synonymous parallelism with "save" (Ps. 31:16), "be gracious" (Ps. 67:1), "restore" (Ps. 80:3, 7, 19), and "redeem" (Ps. 119:134–35). Since the benediction of Numbers 6 and the psalms obviously have a common cultic setting, the meaning of the idiom is rather clear.

3. *Determine the situation in life.* The so-called *Sitz im Leben* involves an inquiry into the situation in which a given proclamation was issued. This "setting in life" includes, first of all, the historical events at the time of the author or authors of a text, for how can the preaching of Isaiah be understood apart from the Assyrian and other threats against Judah in the second half of the eighth century B.C.? What meaning has the preaching of Second Isaiah apart from the long exile in Babylon? To repeat what was said earlier, the word of God in the Bible always addresses particular situations, and so those situations in history are crucial to the interpretation of a passage.

At the same time, the "situation in life" includes more than the sequence of events in Israel or in the ancient Near East. It involves as well social, psychological, cultural, and economic factors. The willingness of Lot to give his virgin daughters to the mob at his door rather than surrender his guests (Gen. 19:1–11) is incomprehensible apart from the ancient rules of hospitality. The Philistines' guilt offering of five golden tumors and five golden mice (1 Sam. 6:1–5) is simply humorous apart from the ancient belief that one could ward off the evil effects of a disaster by making replicas of them. Such elements of a life's situation are usually described in a good commentary or in a volume such as Theodore H. Gaster's *Myth, Legend, and Custom in the Old Testament.*[11]

The determination of the setting to and in which the word of God was proclaimed by the Yahwist, Isaiah, or the Priest leads immediately and directly to the question of the theological implications of that situation. When Ahaz stood in danger of losing his throne to Rezin of Damascus as a result of the Syro-Ephraimite alliance (Isa. 7:1–9), the theological problem at stake was the credibility of Yahweh's promise that a Davidic king would always sit on Jerusalem's throne (2 Sam. 7). When the people of Judah were carried off as exiles into Babylon, the theological difficulties that the Deuteronomists, the Priest, Ezekiel, and Second Isaiah had to address were: What happened to God's promise of the indestructibility of Zion? Has God called off the covenant relationship in which God promised to protect the people? If so, why? Is God alive now that the temple and the Ark have gone up in smoke? How can God, if God is indeed alive, be reached when exiles in Babylon have no means of traveling to the temple in Jerusalem? Struggling with such questions was the reason many biblical writings were preserved. If the historical situation is at all related to the preaching of the word, then the modern interpreter must try to determine the theological problem of the given situation to which a theological answer was preached.

4. *Employ the criticisms (form, source, redaction, and tradition).* While full descriptions of the nature and methods of these disciplines are readily accessible,[12] brief descriptions of each are presented here in order to emphasize their usefulness for preaching from the Hebrew Bible.

a. Form criticism involves the task of classifying a passage on the basis of its structure and content. Usually the concern is with the oral or preliterary stage of the unit, but form criticism also applies to written documents. As is the case with a business letter, a sonnet, or a limerick today, so ancient people used prescribed forms for oral and written communication. The desired form was determined, as today, by the use it was intended to serve. A cultic, a legal, a sermonic, or a storytelling function determined which set of forms was to be used. An infinite number of prose and a likewise staggering list of poetic forms have been described in the Old Testament — forms that contain common sets of characteristics that modern interpreters label as sagas, legends, announcements of salvation and of judgment, psalms of lament, and so on.[13]

The identification of forms enables the interpreter to compare and contrast other uses of the same form in order to see which aspects of a pericope are typical of the way something was said or written, and which elements stand out as being different — the latter often being crucial to distinguishing the pericope's meaning. For example, if one compares the reports of prophetic calls at Isaiah 6:1–13; Jeremiah 1:4–10; and Ezekiel 2:1–3:16, one discovers some common expressions as well as a basic structure. In addition, the intended purpose of each of these accounts is the same: to provide some validity or authenticity for these prophets' preaching as messengers of Yahweh. At the same time, some obvious differences are present in these reports that, precisely because they are different, may enable the interpreter to discern an emphasis intended by the original reporter or by the composer of the piece as we have it. In Isaiah's call the event takes place in the Jerusalem temple, and the report includes the forgiveness of Isaiah's sins. These features are not present in the reports concerning Jeremiah and Ezekiel. When the Lord asks for a volunteer, Isaiah responds immediately; when Jeremiah is confronted by the Lord with the designated task, this prophet-to-be offers some excuses (like Moses at Exod. 3:11; 4:10) in order to avoid the task; Ezekiel does not respond at all in words but obeys the instructions given to him. Thus, the common features and purpose of the three reports are balanced by the particular emphasis of each — all of which should be noted.

When using a psalm or part of a psalm as a text for preaching or as part of the liturgy, form criticism again plays an important role. A commentary of recent vintage will help determine the type of a given psalm and thus give a clue concerning its use in Israel's worship life. To conclude that a psalm is a community lament might be significant in its use in a contemporary setting; the same is true of a hymn or a thanksgiving or any number of possibilities. Likewise, to recognize that some psalms (such as 2 and 110) were used as part of the ceremony when a king was crowned on the Jerusalem throne might severely limit their use in our liturgies. However, even psalms of such specific purpose might proclaim a theology that is useful for Christian proclamation.

The original level or form of a story can usually be determined only by working backward. Only by identifying, for example, characteristics of the Elohistic source in Genesis 22 (the sacrifice of Isaac), and by isolating these characteristics, can the interpreter work back to a pre-Elohistic oral narrative that seems to be a polemic against child sacrifice. Such an example forces us to move immediately to source criticism.

b. Source criticism is the science of identifying and separating the various strands of narrative and legal material in the first several books of the Bible. Ever since 1753 when Jean Astruc discovered two strands of narrative in the Book of Genesis, scholars have been debating how many strands of material are present and in how many books. Some scholars have argued for five sources, some of which can be discerned from Genesis through Kings; others have maintained there are essentially three sources that are interwoven in the Tetrateuch, but traces of a fourth source are present as well; that is, running throughout the books of Genesis, Exodus, and Numbers (Leviticus is almost exclusively Priestly instruction) are the words of the Yahwist (known affectionately to scholars as J), the Elohist (E), and the Priest (P).

Over the last twenty years the assumptions behind source analysis have been disputed and challenged by a number of scholars. At the moment the discipline is in such a state of confusion that an interpreter must use source analysis with the admission that the scope of the sources, the dates of their work, and their purposes can only be educated conjectures. Whether or not the sources in the patriarchal stories of the Book of Genesis are the same as those in Exodus and beyond is one of the major issues. Whether or not they represent distinct theologies is another. In the examination of the pericopes in part 2 of this work, I will use the traditional approach — not because I am convinced of the reliability of the discipline but because it provides one means by which we today can struggle to understand the specificity of a story to an audience rooted in history.[14]

The J source seems to have originated in Judah in the tenth century B.C. — at the height of David's or Solomon's glory, although some scholars, especially J. van Seters, have argued that J is much later, even exilic or postexilic. The E source is considered northern (Israelite) in origin, although the only significant block of E material in the Book of Genesis (20–22) takes place in the south; it is somewhat more fragmented than J and is usually dated about 750 B.C. The Priestly material seems to have been composed in the late exilic or postexilic periods (sixth or fifth centuries B.C.) and is characterized by its use of historical narrative as the outline for the giving of cultic ordinances. The dates and settings assigned for "origin" or "composition" are in no way conclusive for all the material contained in these sources; the dates simply represent the approximate times in which the Yahwist, the Elohist, and the Priest did their work of collecting, editing, and organizing such material that had been handed down for centuries.

In addition to these three narrative sources, which are sometimes set side by side and at other times are intertwined delicately in the Tetrateuch, there are traces of another hand, known as the Deuteronomic editors (D). This school of editors/historians might indeed have begun the editorial process shortly after the fall of the northern kingdom in 721 B.C., perhaps even combining J and E at that time. Before and during the Babylonian exile of the sixth century, the D school remained active in collecting, editing, and adding to many Tetrateuchal pieces. They were active as well collecting materials, editing them for their own purposes, and eventually producing the extensive history that runs from Deuteronomy through Kings.

Each of these sources has its own typical expressions and concerns, its own ideological and theological emphases, and its own set of historical, political, and cultural situations it had to address. The editors who joined J and E together also had a particular set of characteristics that are often discernible. The final compiler (perhaps of the Priestly tradition), probably active prior to 450 B.C., who gave us what is essentially the Tetrateuch as we have it, had yet another set of concerns and emphases. Each of the editors whose hands are involved in a particular story addresses a new situation with a testimony to what God says to the audience of that day. These proclamations are in addition to the proclamations of the oral stories that preceded and that were used by J, E, and P.

By way of illustrating the method, consider the record(s) of the Reed Sea event at Exodus 14:10–31. Present here are two entirely coherent and complete reports of the incident. The Yahwist's proclamation seems to be, "The Lord will redeem Israel from the oppressor Egypt if they stand still in faith," while the Priest proclaims, "In the midst of Israel's conflicts, Yahweh comes to prove who is Lord by showing strength and getting glory over the enemy." When the final compiler intertwined them and included as well the murmuring motif at verses 11–12 (apparently E?), that proclamation can be summed up as, "Yahweh redeems Israel from a bondage from which they are unable and even unwilling to save themselves." Thus, the event at Exodus 14:10–31 contains complete reports from two stories, some isolated fragments from E, and the theological emphasis of the editor who ingeniously intertwined them. This editorial work now leads to discussion of redaction criticism.

c. Redaction criticism examines the editing of a passage or story that eventually resulted in the text that we have before us. In some cases, the redactor of a passage might be the Yahwist, the Elohist, the Priest, or those who combined sources J and E at some time between the work of the Elohist about 750 B.C. and the exilic period. In Tetrateuchal materials, however, the *final* redactor is the one who combined P with the already existing combination of JE (and D?). In this case the present structure of the material would have been accomplished in the postexilic community.

The task of redaction criticism, however, involves far more than the combining and intertwining of Tetrateuchal sources. It applies as well to virtually all the literature, especially to prophetic books in which introductions to the books or to sections of the books, as well as additions to the books, are the result of the work of an individual or school in the later community. For example, it has long been recognized that the Deuteronomistic editors of the exilic period and still later editors expanded the preaching of Jeremiah. This expansion probably accounts for some of the biographical data on the prophet and for some duplications such as that of the temple sermon at Jeremiah 7 and again in chapter 26.[15]

The work of the redactors is determined by the use of characteristic terminology, ideology, theology, and historical circumstances. These criteria enable the interpreter to see once again the continuing, dynamic witness to God, who addresses each generation anew. Old traditions are not cast aside; on the contrary, they are reinterpreted and reasserted by directing them to new audiences. Such redactional activity itself should guard us against regarding the final form of a passage or book as the only legitimate one for our preaching today.

d. Tradition criticism stands between and, in fact, includes form and redaction criticisms, for it concerns itself with the continuing use and reinterpretation of traditions and/or motifs. Such reinterpretation of traditions includes, of course, the various sources of the Tetrateuch, as well as the works of the editors who combined them or added to them. The event of deliverance from Egypt is a crucial theological tradition: we have already seen that event interpreted differently by J and P; to those interpretations we added that of the redactor. But the development of this tradition reaches back to an oral period, to a poetic version in Exodus 15:1–12, and on into the preaching of the prophets, especially Second Isaiah, who portrayed the return from Babylon as a new exodus (Isa. 43:2; 51:9–11). Likewise, the important Sinai tradition is constantly reinterpreted in the Hebrew Bible — probably originally and orally as a place of theophany (Exod. 19:16–19), then as a combination of theophany and covenant (Exod. 24:9–11), finally as a covenant tradition with no concern for theophany (Exod. 24:3–8; the Book of Deuteronomy). Thus, the mere mention of, or allusion to, a certain tradition in a biblical text does not enable the interpreter to conclude automatically that we have before us "the same old story." The "old story" may be so reinterpreted by the author, speaker, or editor of the passage that the tradition speaks quite differently to the new generation.

e. The *context* of the passage deserves particular attention by the interpreter because at whatever level separate pieces were brought together — as sources, by editors, by redactors — some sequence or arrangement gave structure to the compiler's work. When dealing with any portion of chapters 7 and 8 of the Book of Isaiah, it is important to observe that the former chapter is biographical and the latter, autobiographical. However, the two chapters stand together because they deal with the same historical period, the Syro-Ephraimite crisis. This context may indeed make a difference when examining any part in this section.

Likewise in the Ten Commandments at Exodus 20:1–17, the interpreter must recognize the obvious fact that the act of salvation (Exod. 14) precedes the giving of the law. Thus the laws of the Decalogue are given not in order for the people to be saved but rather because they already have been saved. These laws are, then, guides for the way redeemed Israel ought to live. Whether or not the present Christian interpreter accepts the "third use of the law" (the commandments as guidelines for redeemed Christians), the context nevertheless shows that God's imperative follows rather than precedes God's indicative. That this sequence is also a New Testament pattern, one need only compare the structure of Paul's Letter to the Romans where the announcement of God's justification of sinners (Rom. 3–11) is followed by implications for the lives of those who are justified (chaps. 12–16).

Discerning the context of a pericope challenges the interpreter to consider the relationship of a passage to nearby verses, paragraphs, and chapters, as well as the position of a unit in the outline of a book or collection of books (the Tetrateuch), or even the entire canon. Such insight sheds much light on its intended use and meaning at various levels in its history.[16]

5. Construct an interpretive summary of the passage. Now that individual tasks of exegeting the text have been accomplished, it is time to pull together some of the results of this work. One helpful method of getting it together is to paraphrase the passage by employing everything that has been learned in the preceding steps. For example, the "working text" at Isaiah 7:10 might have read "Again the Lord spoke to Ahaz. . . ." On the basis of the study of *literary matters* (the importance of the adverb "again"), *context* (the preceding speech in 7:1–9 and v. 13 that indicates that the Lord is again speaking through Isaiah), and the *historical situation* (the Syro-Ephraimite crisis of 735–734 B.C. with its threat of deposing the Davidic king), the interpreter might paraphrase the verse as, "In the midst of the Syro-Ephraimite threat against the Davidic throne in 735 B.C., the Lord spoke to Ahaz, the Davidic king of Judah, through this spokesman Isaiah, in much the same way as God did in verses 1–9 with the promise that the threat would not come to pass."

Finally, the exegete must summarize in concise sentences what the text meant at its various levels (oral stage, sources, redactions, contexts). In order to be consistent with an understanding of the Bible, which gives witness to a God who speaks and acts, the question "What is God doing here?" must then be asked at each level. Such a question, we have seen, should be answered in a single sentence that describes the situation or the problem as a theological dilemma to which God, as subject of the sentence, addresses the word of comfort and of challenge. The interpreter might now have two, three, or four such theological statements that were, in fact, different proclamations to God's people in various circumstances.

2. What the Text Means

Not all proclamations or interpretations of a text are valid or suitable for Christian proclamation at a given time. We have already argued that a Christian approaches the Old Testament with faith commitments and presuppositions and, in a sense, reads the Old

Testament through the New. On the basis of the faith presupposition, the Christian must determine which levels of a story are appropriate or inappropriate for Christian proclamation, which interpretations are legitimate or illegitimate for proclaiming the God who is known to us as the Father of Jesus Christ.

When there are several levels of interpretation that might be appropriate vehicles for proclaiming the word of God, how does the Christian proclaimer decide on which to use? The answer to that question can only be made on the basis of the situation of the audience that is to be addressed. Since the expression of the word of God is always directed to people in a particular *Sitz im Leben,* the interpreter has another task: to exegete the contemporary scene, the audience, the problem. It is only in knowing the present situation that the proclaimer can select the level of the text that should be employed as the vehicle for the word; it is only in making the word relevant to the situation that the message becomes proclamation.

What is valid or legitimate in the proclamation of the Yahwist, the Priest, Isaiah, or Ezekiel is dependent upon the theological stance of the Christian interpreter. What is appropriate in choosing which of the several legitimate theologies to use as the sermon text is determined by the situation in which the proclaimer finds the audience.

An obvious difficulty presents itself at this point: How does the interpreter move from the chosen level of proclamation (the selected "text sentence") to the sermon? By carefully analyzing the situation of the text and the situation to be addressed, the preacher may find it necessary to sharpen the text's problem, to narrow it, or to broaden it, so that, without doing injustice to theological problems of the text, the sermon can more directly speak to the contemporary situation. For example, suppose the preacher chooses as text sentence the proclamation of the final editor of Exodus 14:10–31: *God redeems Israel from a bondage from which they are unable and even unwilling to save themselves.* The bondage is the problem: in the text it is the physical enslavement of one people to another and the apparent destruction of the oppressor; the theological problem at stake is the apparent threat to God's promise of life and freedom in the Promised Land. To the Christian preacher that bondage from which we are unable and even unwilling to save ourselves is the power of sin. Whether or not the preacher decides to change the wording of the text sentence in order to begin composition of a sermon sentence, the movement from the one "bondage" to the other deserves careful consideration in the outline of the sermon. Likewise, the theological answer or response to the problem needs some careful attention, since the rescue of the people by God in the text is not identical to the Christian's understanding of redemption or justification that God accomplished on the cross. Thus, moving from the selected text sentence to the sermon sentence, the preacher might now be prepared to summarize the sermon and use as an outline the following sentence: *From that constraining and overwhelming force that entices us to wallow in our own destructive pessimism, God sets us free by giving us Jesus Christ to die on the cross.*

A simple outline for such a sermon might be something like the following:

I. Problem: An overwhelming Force Entices Us to Wallow in Pessimism.

  A. Today's pessimism is a result of a broken trust in God's promises.

    1. The realities of modern life in which evil and violence seem to prevail

    2. The credibility gap involved in comparing these realities to the church's proclamation that the age of salvation is here

  B. Israel's pessimism in Exodus 14:10–31 is a result of apparent discrepancies in God's promises through Moses.

    1. The reality of the onrushing Egyptian army

    2. The distrust in the proclamation of Moses that freedom and a new life awaited them

II. Response: God Sets Us Free.

  A. God conquered the enemy as well as the will of the people to fulfill the promise of life and freedom in the Promised Land.

    1. Moses' call to trust God in the face of overpowering odds

    2. God's accomplishment of the promised deliverance

B. In Christ's death on the cross God once and for all set us free to be at home in God's presence.

1. The church's call to hear what God *has done* in Christ

2. God's reconciliation and the ultimate consummation of that act

This outline has the advantage of starting and ending with the present situation and of keeping the biblical story intact for the sake of continuity. Many other possibilities are available, of course, but such an outline works easily and naturally out of the type of text and sermon sentences that have been described. The content and structure hopefully are consistent with the entire approach described in this work.

Part Two

INTERPRETING SELECTED PERICOPES

Genesis 22:1–19

Revised Common Lectionary, Year A, Proper 8 [13] (Sc)
Lutheran Book of Worship, Year B, Lent 1
Book of Common Prayer, Year B, Lent 2
Year C, Good Friday

I. Establishing a Working Text

A comparison of several English translations presents no major difficulties in accepting any one of them as a working text. However, while virtually all English translations read "the land of Moriah" at verse 2, such unanimity is not present in ancient translations of the phrase. Ancient renderings range from "the land of the Amorites" (Syriac) to "the land of the vision" (Vulgate and others) or to "the lofty land" (Septuagint). Some of these renderings are possible by slightly emending the Hebrew text. However, one of the basic principles in establishing the original text (textual criticism) is to accept the most difficult reading as most probably the original one. In this case, "the land of Moriah" is certainly the most difficult reading because no one knows where such a land is located. Therefore, "the land of Moriah" is the generally accepted reading.

The most important step in dealing with this text is determining its scope. The pericope listed in some lectionaries limits the passage to verses 1–14, but it is obvious that the story continues as far as verse 19. Whether or not the interpreter decides to limit the passage to the first fourteen verses can only be determined *after* the exegetical work is done. For the purpose of establishing a working text, then, the scope of the passage is Genesis 22:1–19.

Once the text includes verses 15–19, however, an interesting comparison is evident in verse 18: the RSV translates, ". . . shall all the nations of the earth bless themselves" (see also JB); the

NRSV renders, "...shall all the nations of the earth gain blessing for themselves"; similarly the NAB renders, "All the nations of the earth shall find blessing"; the NIV reads, "All the nations of the earth will be blessed"; and the NEB, "All nations on earth shall pray to be blessed as your descendants are blessed." The difficulty here is due to the Hebrew verb form that literally means "bless themselves" (RSV). But what does such an expression mean?

2. Literary Matters

The two problems raised above deserve attention first. "The land of Moriah" (v. 2) is not attested as such elsewhere in the Hebrew Bible. But "Mount Moriah" occurs at 2 Chronicles 3:1 as a substitute for Mount Zion, where Solomon built the temple. This only other occurrence can lead to two possible conclusions. (*a*) There really was a land of Moriah that became unknown to later generations in Israel. At the time of the writing of Chronicles, Moriah became the new name for what had been known as Mount Zion, perhaps to connect this story to the place of the temple, and the name has stuck to this very day. (Indeed, the tradition surrounding the rock over which Jerusalem's Dome of the Rock is built includes the Abraham-Isaac story.) (*b*) The writer of Chronicles was the first to use the name Moriah for the temple mount (for what reason is impossible to say), and a later editor of the Abraham-Isaac story inserted it into Genesis 22. In either case, a relationship between the hill on which the Abraham event took place and the mount on which Solomon built the temple seems to be intentional by someone. By whom or when this probable relationship took place is now impossible to determine, but the relationship certainly added an important tradition to the site on which the temple stood.

As for the problem in translating the blessing formula, the Hebrew verb here is clearly a reflexive one (*hithpa'el*), and that same verb form is used within the same formula at Genesis 26:4. Elsewhere, however, at Genesis 12:3; 18:18; 28:14, the blessing formula employs the *niph'al* form of the verb that can be either passive or reflexive, that is, "be blessed" or "bless themselves." Using a concordance will reveal that the word "bless" appears to be strictly reflexive (*hithpa'el*) at Deuteronomy 29:19; Isaiah 65:16; Jeremiah 4:2; and Psalm 72:17. The term seems to mean "to boast" at Deuteronomy 29 and in Jeremiah 4, the latter in a positive sense of boasting in Yahweh, the former in the negative sense of boasting in a false sense of security. At Psalm 72:17 people "bless themselves" by Jerusalem's king. And so it seems that the reflexive use of the word means "consider oneself fortunate" on the basis of something or someone. In this respect, Genesis 22:18 might best be rendered "and because of your descendants shall all the nations of the earth consider themselves fortunate." This expression would mean that the fame of Israel-to-be will be seen and in some sense shared by all people. In that sense the promise sounds like the worldwide effects of the return from Babylonian exile, especially as that message appears in Ezekiel and in the Priestly writings of the exilic period.

In addition to these two issues, several others deserve mention. At verse 8 the Hebrew verb *r'h* (to see) is used in the sense of "provide." The only other case in which this common verb seems to have the same meaning is at Deuteronomy 33:21, where "see" makes little sense: "He *furnished* for himself the best of the land"; thus, at least one parallel can be cited as evidence for the use of *r'h* as "provide" in Genesis 22:8. However, in verse 14, where the same word occurs twice in connection with the meaning of the place-name, it is not clear whether the translation should be "So Abraham called the name of the place Yahweh-yireh; as it is said until this day, 'On the mount of the Lord it will be provided' "; or "So Abraham . . . , 'On the mount of the Lord he appears (is to be seen).' " The *niph'al* form of the verb has already been used for theophanies at Genesis 12:7; 17:1; 18:1. We shall return to this problem in our study of form criticism.

Several times in the narrative God addresses Abraham by name (announced once in v. 1 and twice in v. 11), to which Abraham responds (as he does also to his son in v. 7), "Here I am." This address by God using a person's name (usually repeated twice), followed by the "Here I am" response, occurs also at Exodus 3:4; 1 Samuel 3:4–10; and, without mention of the person's name, the response appears at Isaiah 6–8. The repeated use of this expression indicates a formula of some kind when God singles out individuals for specific tasks.

3. The Setting in Life

The situation in the ancient world that immediately comes to mind in reading the narrative is the practice of child sacrifice. The Hebrew Bible testifies to the atrocious practice at 2 Kings 16:3;

Jeremiah 7:31; 19:5; 32:35; Ezekiel 16:20–24; 20:31, as a custom that some Israelites borrowed from their Canaanite neighbors. In addition, laws against such a practice are expressly stated at Deuteronomy 12:29–31; 18:9–12, with permission granted to use an animal as a substitute for a child at Exodus 13:11–16. There also exists evidence from Mesopotamia and from Canaan that seems to affirm that these biblical passages are not unfounded.[17]

4. The Criticisms

Source analysis deserves attention first. The story is almost exclusively E. The common characteristics of E that are present here include (*a*) the word "God" (Elohim) is used at verses 1, 3, 8, 9, and 12; (*b*) the notion that God tests people (v. 1) appears in the E passage at Exodus 20:20; (*c*) the purpose of such testing is to determine if one fears God (v. 12; again compare Exod. 20:20); (*d*) God is so transcendent for E (speaks "from heaven") that God always uses mediators to confront and address people; here, as often, it is an angel (vv. 11, 15); and (*e*) the description of the multitude of descendants at verse 17 is quite similar to the descriptions of E elsewhere (cf. Gen. 15:5).

At the same time, some non-Elohistic elements appear in the story: the use of the name Yahweh (the Lord) at verses 11, 14, 15, and 16; and the blessing formula for all nations at verse 18. Both these characteristics are typical of J, although the formula here uses different words and forms of words than the formula of J at 12:3. In addition, the Elohist's concern was for northern (Israelite) sanctuaries, but the "mount of the Lord" in verse 14 seems to be an allusion to Jerusalem's Mount Zion.

If one removes the characteristic elements of E from the narrative in order to work back to an original *oral form,* it seems that we have before us a story that served as a polemic against child sacrifice — like the legal prescriptions from Deuteronomy and Exodus mentioned above. The original form would then have had a polemical intention, and its proclamation would have been: *Appalled at the sacrifice of children, God provided an animal as a substitute.*

One could also argue that the narrative should be classified as etiological: it might have been told to explain the origin of the place-name Yahweh-yireh. Recent studies have demonstrated, however, that very few narratives in the Hebrew Bible were composed originally for this purpose; even the formula "as it is said until this day," which appears at verse 14, seems to have been added to an already existing story.

In all probability the story was originally a polemic against child sacrifice. When the Elohist took up the old story and edited it according to his interests, the story became something quite different. From the introduction in verse 1 to the announcement that Abraham was a God-fearer (v. 12) and on to the reward for his piety (vv. 16–17), the Elohist has made the story into a wisdom tale in which God tested Abraham in order to learn where his heart was and to reward him because it was in the right place. In wisdom literature such testing and discipline refine people and bring them closer to God. In this sense the proclamation of the Elohist might be summarized: *When God made an unreasonable demand on Abraham, God was testing his faith in order to refine him and reward his obedience.*

The presence of the name Yahweh (the Lord) in several places in the narrative and the use of the blessing formula at verse 18 do not seem to be sufficient evidence to argue that a J version of the story is intertwined with E. The story seems rather to be a unity; it cannot be divided into two separate strands. Thus, the use of the name and the blessing formula are probably the result of a *redactor* who supplied some J or D characteristics in order to provide continuity within the entire Abraham cycle.

This mention of continuity should lead directly to the question of context, but first let us consider how the *tradition* was used in the Bible. It is astonishing that, in spite of its popularity today, the story is mentioned nowhere else in the Hebrew Bible. The New Testament used the story as E intended: as an example of the way the person of faith acts (Heb. 6:13–14; 11:12, 17–19; James 2:12). But the New Testament writers are interested also in the promise of God (vv. 16–18) and not simply in Abraham's faith (see Luke 1:73; Acts 3:25; Gal. 3:16, where Paul allegorically relates Isaac and Christ). But this same promise appears in other Genesis stories, particularly 15:6, and so we cannot be certain that the New Testament writers refer specifically to Genesis 22.

5. Context

The continuity of the JE document and the continuing reference in the Genesis narratives to God's promise of descendants and blessing make the context of Genesis 22:1–19 particularly important.

The redactors wove the material together in such a way as to provide continuity, and at the same time they established the structure of the narratives that the final redactor followed.

In the structure of the Genesis narratives, the one thread that continues from Genesis 12 up to the Joseph story is the promise of God concerning land and descendants (J adds the blessing formula). This promise is repeated by God in spite of the patriarchs' weaknesses and all other obstacles. From Genesis 12 to 21 Abraham waited for God to start working out the promise of descendants. Finally, when Abraham was more than a hundred years old, God gave him a son, the first of many descendants to come. Genesis 21 reports the birth of Isaac, and only one chapter later God asks Abraham to sacrifice this only child, thereby jeopardizing the fulfillment of what had been promised for so long. This story, in other words, presents a contradiction of God to Abraham, but the patriarch nevertheless responds obediently, and God continues the way of the promise.

The inclusion of verses 15–19 emphasizes the continuing promise that began in Genesis 12:1–3; here, however, it is expanded from the earlier "families of the land" to "nations of the earth." These verses, furthermore, point toward the future, as the promise of God constantly does.

6. Interpretive Summary

In light of the previous work some paraphrases at certain points in the passage might help to pull together isolated bits of important information. The context might enable the interpreter to render verse 1 as, "After these things God seemed to contradict the promise of progeny by testing Abraham with the command that he sacrifice his only son, Isaac, on whom the promise of descendants depended." Furthermore, one could add here, "While God seemed to demand what the gods of the Canaanites and others demanded regularly, God addressed Abraham in a way that singles out the patriarch to cease the practice of child sacrifice." (This interpretation combines both the setting in life and the literary matter concerning the meaning of God's address to an individual, followed by "Here I am.") In verses 11 and 15 the significance of the use of the angel and the phrase "from heaven" might be paraphrased as, "The transcendent God spoke through a mediator." And in light of the word study on "bless themselves," the promise at verse 18 might be stated as follows: "And because of your descendants shall all the nations of the earth consider themselves fortunate at seeing and sharing in the fame of Israel."

7. Theologies of the Passage

Work on the text has indicated at least three levels of proclamation in the narrative. First, there was the proclamation of the oral stage that declared that God accepted and desired the sacrifice of animals rather than children. Second, there was the theology of the Elohist, who used the piece like a wisdom storyteller in order to show that God's testing refines people and ultimately leads to reward for obedience (fear of God). Third, when the entire story is seen in its context of the promise and when the problem of child sacrifice is combined with that promise, then the theology of the whole passage seems to be: *Even through an apparent contradiction God brought Abraham to commit himself in faith, refining the relationship between them and setting him apart from the world in which he lived.*

How useful for preaching the first of these proclamations might be is questionable. In our society where child sacrifice is not practiced (at least, publicly or legally), the message might be irrelevant. However, in certain circumstances this interpretation might be the most useful one for a missionary working in the midst of a tribe that still sacrifices children or for a preacher in American society faced with the presence of satanic cults in the neighborhood. The proclamation of the Elohist sounds much like the theology of old optimistic wisdom: the righteous are rewarded and the wicked are punished. The third interpretation of the whole passage with emphasis on the present context provides the basis for a sermon that proclaims the action of God through the means of Christ's death on the cross. The startling news is that God's own child was not spared death as God spared Abraham's. The death of the Christ/Messiah, in fact, is the Bible's greatest contradiction, but through this scandal God brings humanity into a new relationship and thereby sets apart those who believe in the scandal to be instruments of blessing in the world.

Genesis 28:10–17 (22)

Revised Common Lectionary, Year A, Proper 11 [16] (Sc)

Lutheran Book of Worship, Year A, Pentecost 17
Year B, Lent 2

Book of Common Prayer, St. Michael and All Angels

I. Establishing a Working Text

Any one of the seven translations used in this comparison might be used as a working text. However, the substantive differences that should be borne in mind are as follows:

Verse 12:

RSV/NRSV:	"There was a ladder set up on the earth."
NEB:	"He saw a ladder, which rested on the ground."
JB:	"A ladder was there, standing on the ground."
Torah:	"A stairway was set on the ground."
NIV:	"a stairway resting on the earth . . . "
NAB:	"A stairway rested on the ground."

Torah adds in a footnote that an alternate translation is "ramp," and the NRSV follows by including in a footnote "stairway" or "ramp." The alternative "ramp" most clearly approximates the Hebrew, where *sullam* seems to mean a "mound."

In verse 13 the translations are divided over where the Lord was standing. The RSV and NIV render "above it" (the stairway, ladder, or whatever); the NRSV, NEB, *Torah,* and NAB read "beside him"; the JB translates "over him." In footnotes the RSV and NIV allow the possibility of reading "beside him"; the NRSV, "stood above it"; the NEB recognizes as possible "on it" or "by it." The difficulty here is due to the ambiguity of the Hebrew preposition *'al,* which can be translated according to all these possibilities and even more. Such a variation in a preposition, while at first glance insignificant, is crucial to observe and then examine because the question of God's standing *above* or *on* the mound or *beside* Jacob betrays a certain view of God: transcendent or immanent. Such a distinction, among other things, is related to the analysis of sources.

In verse 14 occurs an expression repeated often in the Genesis narratives, one indeed we encountered in our study of Genesis 22:18. Here, the expression is identical to that at 12:3: "the families of the land." The difficulty lies in understanding how others benefit from Jacob and his offspring. Here the differences among the translations appear as follows: they shall "bless themselves" (RSV, JB, *Torah*); "be blessed" (NRSV); "pray to be blessed" (NEB); "find blessing" (NAB). The problem here has again to do with the ambiguity of the Hebrew verb form that can be translated as a passive or as a reflexive.

2. Literary Matters

Verse 12: "stairway," "ladder," or "ramp." Unfortunately, the noun *sullam* occurs nowhere else in the Hebrew Bible. It does seem, though, that the word derives from a verb meaning "lift up, cast up." The verb is used for casting up a highway (Isa. 62:10), siege works (Job 19:12), and heaps (Jer. 50:26). *Sōl^{e}lâ,* a related noun derived from the same verb, means a mound used in besieging a city (2 Kings 19:32, which is identical to Isa. 37:33; Jer. 6:6; Ezek. 4:2; 26:8). On the basis of the meaning of the verb and of the uses of the related noun, *sullam* seems to mean a "heap" or "mound" rather than a ladder.

The translation of the term *sullam* as "mound" brings to mind a pyramidal tower that was popular as a temple tower among the Babylonians and known as a *ziggurat.* These temple towers (see Gen. 11:1–9) were constructed in order to reach up to heaven, and in this way they served as the places of communication between the heavenly and earthly worlds. By climbing up to the highest levels of these towers, the priests could approach the gods for worship and with petitions on behalf of the people. Among the Canaanites, such places of intercourse between gods and humans were not such ornate towers but nevertheless mounds known as "high places," which served as sanctuaries and upon which altars and cultic symbols were constructed.

Many biblical scholars agree that Jacob's vision of a "mound" is related to such cultic places. However, when we recognize this mound that reaches up to heaven as a Near Eastern worship site, we must at the same time ruin the old familiar song, for we are not "climbing Jacob's ladder." At Genesis 11:1–9, the story of the Tower of Babel, God stops the construction and disperses the people so that they will not climb up to him; the emphasis in that story is that God comes down to humankind. Likewise in our story, it is not humans but God's messengers (angels) who go up and down on the mound. In this way the Bible has reinterpreted the old mound concept in such a way as to announce that the biblical God is one who comes to people and not one whom people approach through our own ways and means.

Verse 13: "above it" or "beside him." As indicated above, the translation of the preposition *'al* betrays a certain view of God: if God stands *above* the mound or *on it,* then God is aloof from Jacob (transcendent); if the divine one stands *beside* Jacob, then, of course, God is immanent. Since the Hebrew preposition *'al* is itself ambiguous, the exegete must seek to determine by studying the combination "stand beside/upon" which of the alternatives is most probable. Even this method, however, leads to ambiguous results. While *niṣṣab 'al* usually refers to people standing *beside* things (Gen. 24:13, 43; Exod. 7:15; 18:14; Num. 23:6, 17; Prov. 8:2; Isa. 21:8) or *beside* persons (Gen. 45:1; 1 Sam. 4:20; 22:6, 7, 9, 17), the expression also seems to be used for persons standing *upon* things (Exod. 17:9; 33:21[?]; 34:2). In only two of the cases where the combination of words occurs is Yahweh the subject: Amos 7:7 portrays Yahweh standing *beside* a wall, and Amos 9:1, *beside* an altar. Now herein lies the ambiguity of the results of our word study: whenever the combination *niṣṣab 'al* is used with Yahweh as the subject (as in Gen. 28:13), the preposition means "beside" rather than "upon." However, in those two cases in the Book of Amos, Yahweh is standing beside objects rather than human beings. Nowhere in the Hebrew Bible is Yahweh portrayed as standing beside a person; but nowhere either is the Lord described as standing above an object.

Therefore, the decision must be based on grounds other than comparable word usage; before getting to that decision, however, we must first say a word about *source analysis.* We have seen in our examination of Genesis 22 that one of the major characteristics of the E source, apart from its use of the name Elohim, is its understanding of the transcendence of God. Contrariwise, our study of Genesis 32:22–32 below includes a description of the J source that designates the deity by the name Yahweh and often portrays the Lord in rather anthropomorphic terms. For J, Yahweh is an immanent deity who is forever getting involved in human affairs. If we could determine the source of verse 13, then the translation of the preposition would take care of itself: E would never describe God as standing beside a person; J would probably not describe the Lord as standing above a mound. Since the subject of our questionable expression is Yahweh and not Elohim, and since the speech of introduction uses Yahweh ("I am the Lord"), the verse seems to be J. Thus the prepositional phrase should be translated "beside him" rather than "above it." Such an immanent portrayal of Yahweh, without the same terminology, is used by J to describe God's presence with people at Genesis 18:1–33 and 32:22–32.

Verse 14: The blessing formula has been discussed above in connection with Genesis 22:18. See the examination of that passage for details.

Verse 17: "house of God" and "gate of heaven." Jacob's vision enabled him to awake from his sleep with the realization that he was in a holy place. His exclamation that this place was "a house of God" (the translation "*the* house of God" is debatable) certainly is leading up to the naming of that place as Bethel ("house of God") in verse 19. Jacob's further description of the place as "the gate of heaven" is quite understandable in light of what we said above concerning the mound. Since the mound (a *ziggurat,* a high place) is the point of contact between the heavenly and earthly worlds, then that site can appropriately be named "the gate of heaven." Indeed, the ancient Babylonians erected a tower called E.TEMEN.AN.KI (the house of the bond of heaven and earth), and they built that tower in the city of Babylon (in their own language *bab-ilāni* means "the gate of the gods").

The passage, however, includes both a theophany and a set of promises — enough indeed to construct a sermon or two. To stop the passage at this point would be to place undue emphasis on Jacob's exclamation of surprise. The report of the incident goes on to include further activity and a speech by Jacob in verses 18–22, and so the scope of the passage exceeds verse 17. In the additional five verses Jacob sets up and anoints a pillar (a Canaanite symbol) in order to designate the spot as a holy place, changes the name of the place to Bethel, and then proceeds to make a vow that if God will bring him back safely to his father's house, he will worship Yahweh and tithe all of his possessions.

3. Setting in Life

Because of the nature of this passage, the setting in life will be discussed under source and redaction criticism. It is sufficient to repeat here that the common ancient Near Eastern cultic concept of a mountain sanctuary as a place of contact with the divine world is attested (but reinterpreted) in this text.[18]

4. The Criticisms

Source analysis of the passage reveals some interesting data for interpretation. Many scholars assign verses 11–12 and 17–22 to E, and verses 13–16 to J. Verse 10 is variously assigned to J, E, or a later editor who used it as a transition piece from the previous passage to the present one. Such an assignment of sources, however, seems to me to be oversimplified, and as a result, the importance of the passage in terms of tradition history is diminished.

The E source indeed comprises verses 11–12 and 17–19a. To read these verses together provides a complete story that bears the marks of E throughout. The name for the deity in verse 12 is Elohim (God); since God is transcendent, God uses mediators to relate to human beings; frequently God comes to people in visions and dreams. All these characteristics distinguish verse 12 as E, and since verse 11 has no meaning apart from the following verse, it too must be E. Verse 17 continues the marks of E: fear before God, the awesomeness of a vision, and again the use of the name Elohim. Verse 18 picks up the action and elements of verse 12 and must likewise be E. The first half of verse 19 provides what seems to be the climax of E's narrative by recording the origin of the name Bethel, one of the favorite sanctuaries of the northern storyteller.

J's story probably includes verses 10, 13–14, and perhaps a portion of 16. The record of the journey from Beer-sheba toward Haran (v. 10) is directly related to the preceding narrative of J at 27:41–45 (27:46–28:9 is clearly P). After Jacob had thoroughly aroused the anger of his brother, their mother, Rebekah, sent the "cheater" off to Haran to stay with her brother Laban. Our story begins with that journey and is thus J. As for verse 13, the Yahwist is identifiable here, first, by the twofold use of the name Yahweh (the Lord); the Elohist does not use the name Yahweh in a self-introduction or in a narrative until that name is revealed to Moses at Exodus 3:14. Second, the promise of land to the patriarchs is of particular interest to J; E is concerned, it seems, only about the promise of descendants.

Verse 14 continues the promise to include descendants; because that promise is then tied up with the blessing formula, the verse must be J. Verse 16 seems to belong to J, at least in part, because of the name Yahweh in Jacob's exclamation and because it forms a needless repetition with Verse 17. (Such repetitions or parallels are one major indicator of multiple sources.) The problem with the assignment of the whole verse to J is that the reference to Jacob's waking from sleep occurs without reference to his going to sleep (v. 11 was E). Moreover, it is not one of the marks of J to describe Yahweh as coming to people in dreams. Thus it seems that "Then Jacob awoke from his sleep" belongs with verse 17, which records his fear (E), and that Jacob's speech in verse 16 (probably J) is simply his verbal response to the promise he had just heard. The redactor who combined J and E moved some of the material around in order to make one story out of two separate ones.

Thus far we have not assigned verses 15, 19a–22, to any source. None of the characteristics of J or E is present here. On the contrary, all the key phrases and expressions seem to be D (more specifically, the Deuteronomistic school of the exilic period). Verse 15 contains God's promise to be present with Jacob: "I am with you" occurs more than twenty times in the Hebrew Bible, more than half of which appear in the Deuteronomistic history. More important than that expression by itself, however, is the combination of that promise with "in all the way that you go" (cf. Josh. 1:9) and with "I will not forsake you" (Deut. 31:6, 8; Josh. 1:5). That these combinations occur only in the Deuteronomistic corpus and in our text indicates that the contributor of Genesis 28:15 is D. Furthermore, while no exact equivalent to "until I have accomplished that which I promised you," the content sounds very much like the Deuteronomistic concept of the word of the Lord as effecting the fulfillment of divine promises.[19] Finally, the promise "I will bring you back" is a favorite expression of the Deuteronomists in the prose section of the Book of Jeremiah, where it is addressed to the exiles in Babylon (see Jer. 12:15; 16:15; 23:3; 24:6; 27:22; 29:14; 30:3; 32:37; 33:7).[20]

While the first half of verse 19 has already been assigned to E, the parenthetical expression "but the name of the city was . . . at the first" is paralleled only in the Deuteronomistic passage at Judges 18:29. From this point on, the rest of the passage — Jacob's vow — is D. To begin with, the Hebrew reads literally, "Then Jacob vowed a vow." This seemingly redundant expression appears in exactly the same form in a number of passages that belong to the Deuteronomists (Deut. 12:17; 23:22, 23, 24; Judg. 11:30, 39; 1 Sam. 1:11; 2 Sam. 15:7, 8; Jer. 44:25). Other passages where the same expression occurs are unidentifiable as regards source or are generally recognized as late (Num. 6:2, 21; 21:2; 30:3, 4; Isa. 19:21). Even more interesting are some of the elements in several of D's "vow a vow" sayings. The expression at 1 Samuel 1:11 introduces a deal that Hannah makes with the Lord, as Jacob does in our text. Judges 11:30, 39 describe Jephthah's bargain with the Lord, also introduced by "vow a vow."

Most interesting, however, is 2 Samuel 15:7–8: "Absalom said to the king, 'Let me go and pay my vow which I have vowed to the Lord in Hebron. For while I lived at Geshur in Aram, your servant vowed a vow, "If the Lord will indeed bring me back to Jerusalem, then I will offer worship to the Lord in this place." '" This last example is strikingly similar to Jacob's vow at Genesis 28:20–22: (1) the expression "vow a vow"; (2) the condition of returning at the will and action of the Lord; and (3) the promise to worship Yahweh upon return.

Finally, but also significant among the "vow a vow" sayings, there is Deuteronomy 12:17, where the vow is combined with the regulation concerning the tithe. Nowhere else in the Hebrew Bible does this combination occur except for Jacob's vow in our passage.

Furthermore, within this vow occurs a favorite expression of D: "Yahweh will be to me as God" (see Deut. 26:17; 29:12; Judg. 8:33; 2 Sam. 7:24; Jer. 7:23; 11:4; 24:7; 30:22; 31:33; 32:38). Apart from D the expression occurs almost exclusively in exilic or postexilic texts (mostly P and Ezekiel, neither of which have anything to do with our pericope).

The preceding source analysis now leads us to deal with *form, redaction,* and *tradition* criticism — each of which contributes something of significance to the interpretation of our passage.

The Elohist's version of the story is a theophany narrative or cult legend that is used as an etiology; it explains the origin and the name of the sanctuary at Bethel. Since most scholars agree that Bethel was probably a Canaanite sanctuary before it was used for the worship of Yahweh, it is not unlikely that this cultic etiology existed among the Canaanites with one of their heroes of antiquity as the recipient of the "mound" vision. The significance of the mound can best be understood from this environment. If the story was indeed connected to the cultic site of the Canaanites originally, then E redacted that story in such a way that the hero became Jacob and God's angels traveled up and down the ramp. In this way the old cult site would have been legitimized for the worship of Yahweh by the Israelites. Since Bethel was one of the two sites selected by Jeroboam when the northern kingdom separated itself from Judah (see 1 Kings 12), such a story would have authenticated the site as kosher for Israelite worship. In the midst of this concern to legitimize a particular cultic site, however, E tells us something about God: *Precisely because God is transcendent and cannot be reached, God came to Jacob to establish a place of worship and to call Jacob and others to service.*

The Yahwistic version of the story appears to have nothing to do with Bethel. Neither does J record a theophany of any sort. Rather his narrative is a saga in which God intervened in the life of Jacob as the patriarch fled from Beer-sheba to Haran. It was J who had just recorded that Jacob fled due to the patriarch's cheating of his brother (Gen. 27:41–45). Now, as was so typical of J, he records that to Jacob, the cunning refugee, God continued to reiterate the promise made to Abraham and to Isaac years before. Thus J's proclamation about God is: *Even to Jacob, the rebellious cheater, God announces faithfulness to the promise of blessing and descendants made earlier to Abraham and Isaac.*

The JE redactor put the two proclamations together in such a way that J's promise to Jacob occurred *within* E's story of the theophany at Bethel. The combined account seems to proclaim: *When the transcendent God appeared to Jacob, God communicated by speaking the promise of blessing and descendants even to the "cheater."*

For the Deuteronomists the passage had other possibilities. After all, D had to address the exiles in Babylon with the message about a God who was not tied down to unreachable holy places or to destroyed holy architecture. God was present even apart from the territory of Judah and Israel because God came to the people through the spoken word, wherever they were living. The situation of Jacob in Genesis 28:10–22 suited those needs perfectly. Jacob, like the nation later, was exiled from his homeland because of his wicked deeds; furthermore, he was on his way to Mesopotamia (Haran) where he, like the exiles later, would sojourn for some time. But the Lord appeared to him as he was leaving his homeland and promised to give him the land where he lay. To this promise of land (which itself was important for D) D added the promise of verse 15, which declared that Yahweh would go with Jacob wherever he went, that the Lord would not forsake him, that the Lord would bring him back to accomplish the promise. Jacob, in other words, was Israel in exile, to whom God promised both divine presence in a foreign land and the return of the exiles to their own land.

Furthermore, D supplemented the vow at verses 20–22 in order to demonstrate to the exiles that when God made this promise to Jacob, the patriarch promised that, upon return to the land, Yahweh and none other would be his God, and that he would worship and thank the Lord by giving a tenth of all that he had. This vow is not really the conniving deal it might appear to be! God had already promised to care for the patriarch and bring him home (v. 15). Thus Jacob's vow really means: "*Since* God will be with me, . . . my response will be one of worship and praise and tithe." According to D's understanding of the effectiveness of the spoken word of God, once the promise is made by the Lord in verse 15, there can be no "if's." This vow serves to show the exiles that, like Jacob, they should respond to God's promise by exclusive worship of Yahweh and by tithing their possessions.

Thus D took the old tradition of "Jacob's ladder" and reinterpreted it in such a way that it spoke not of a sacred place but of God's presence in a foreign land and of the promise of the exiles' return to receive the land as their own. Further, as recipients of this gracious word, the people are to worship God and God alone. Thus D's proclamation to the exiles was: *The transcendent God whom Jacob worshiped at certain places is present for the exiled people in the word wherever they are, to protect them and lead them home, in response to which they will worship the Lord as God.*

5. Interpretive Summary

On the basis of the preceding investigation, the old familiar "ladder" of verse 12 should be rendered as "mound." The prepositional problem in verse 13 should read "the Lord stood beside him," and the blessing formula (on the basis of our study of Gen. 22:18) can be paraphrased "and because of your descendants shall all the nations of the earth consider themselves fortunate." Beyond these literary problems noted in the work of establishing the text, we have seen that the "if" of Jacob's vow at verse 20 should be changed to "since" on the basis of D's understanding of the effectiveness of the spoken word of God. Apart from these few comments, the working text can stand as it is for the interpretive summary.

6. Theologies of the Passage

The text, as interpreted above, obviously meant many things to many people as it was passed on from generation to generation in the traditions of Israel. The cult legend or etiology, as redacted by E, proclaims that *the God of the Hebrews, unlike the gods of the surrounding religions, reached out to Jacob to establish for him and for the people a place of worship*. Such a proclamation is consistent with the New Testament witness to God who reaches out to us so dramatically that the word-made-flesh actually lived among us and provided a new means by which God could be worshiped. The one problem I have with E's theology at this point is that E has God *appear* rather than *speak;* E does not emphasize the spoken word, as do J, D, and the New Testament witnesses.

The proclamation of J — *even to Jacob, the rebellious cheater, God announces faithfulness to the promise of blessing and descendants made earlier to Abraham and Isaac* — is quite meaningful for Christian proclamation. The New Testament makes abundantly clear that God sent Jesus Christ to die for sinners, that God accepts us not because of what we do but in spite of ourselves. Furthermore, this act of God comes about by the proclamation of the word that is effective in our lives.

The testimony of the JE redactor — *when the transcendent God appeared to Jacob, God communicated by speaking the promise of blessing and descendants even to the "cheater"* — relieves the problem with E's method of describing the coming of God in visions and, at the same time, preserves both E's concern for transcendence and J's understanding of God's faithful promise even to sinners.

Finally, the use of the tradition by D provides a powerful message for the church today as it struggles with demonstrating God's presence among us when the nightly reports on television newscasts seem to indicate the absence of God in the world. To an apparently God-forsaken situation D proclaims that *the transcendent God whom Jacob worshiped at certain places is present for the exiled people in the word wherever they are, to protect them and lead them home, in response to which they will worship the Lord as God.* In the Word Incarnate, God is present whenever sermons are preached, sacraments administered, or Christians console one another with the good news. God brings home the prodigal children and summons us to lives of praise for God's faithfulness to the promises fulfilled in Jesus Christ and still to be experienced in the Kingdom to come.

Genesis 32:22–32

Revised Common Lectionary, Year A, Proper 13 [18] (Sc)
Year C, Proper 24 [29] (Pd)

Lutheran Book of Worship, Year C, Pentecost 22

Book of Common Prayer, Year C, Proper 24

1. Establishing a Working Text

A comparison of the English translations reveals only a few differences. At verse 28, the RSV and NEB are similar in translating "for you have striven (strove) [NIV: 'struggled'] with God and with men [NRSV: 'humans'], and have prevailed." *Torah* at this point reads the same in a footnote but in the text translates "for you have striven with beings divine and human and have prevailed" (similarly NAB). The JB renders "because you have been strong against God, you shall prevail against men."

At verse 30 where most translations read, "I have seen God face to face," *Torah* translates, "I have seen a divine being face to face." In both cases the offensive thought of Jacob wrestling with God is softened in *Torah* by the rendition of *ʾᵉlōhîm* as "divine being."

The only other noteworthy difference in the translations appears at verse 29. Most render, "And there he blessed him" (or similarly NEB, "But he gave him his blessing there"), while *Torah* translates simply, "And he took leave of him there."

2. Literary Matters

The passage belongs to the collection of stories known as the Jacob cycle. Like most other such stories in the Tetrateuch, the question of the identity and date of the original author is not relevant. Most of these stories come from an oral tradition, and so no known writer can claim credit for the creativity behind them.

The "man" (Hebrew *'iš* means only "a certain one") who came to wrestle with Jacob (vv. 24, 25) remains quite anonymous and unidentifiable until verse 30 when Jacob announces that it was God. Apparently this realization came to him when the "one" said, "You have striven with God" (see the previous verse). Given this identification of the "one" with "God," it is at first tantalizing to consider a word study on "wrestle" in order to discover other cases of God wrestling with individuals. Unfortunately, the word (Hebrew *'ābaq*) occurs only in this passage.

Perhaps the greatest literary problem in the passage lies in the explanation of the name Israel. The one offered here, namely, "You have striven with God and with humans and have prevailed," is impossible. But then almost every such explanation in the Hebrew Bible is wrong from a grammatical or etymological standpoint. If the name Israel is at all related to the Hebrew word *sārâ,* "to persist" or "to persevere" (and that is indeed debatable), then the explanation would have to be translated "God perseveres" or "May God persevere." The explanation "You have striven with God" is based on a word play due to similarity in sound rather than an accuracy in grammar.

3. Setting in Life

The tone of the whole story sounds quite unhistorical, and so the setting is to be understood culturally rather than as an incident that actually occurred. The attack by a river demon before a traveler crosses the raging current is obviously a relic from an animistic world of thought. The taboo against eating the thigh muscle on the hip socket is clearly a cultic or even superstitious proscription. The change of Jacob's name to Israel reflects the ancient understanding of the name. These elements, we shall see, belong to different levels of the story's development, and so at no level are we dealing with a historical event.

At this point we shall comment about the meaning of a person's name in the ancient world and reserve remarks about the other features for our discussion of form and redaction criticism.

For us a name is simply a matter of *identification;* it is something we have by which others can recognize us and address us. For the ancient Semites, however, the name was far more important; for them it was a matter of *identity.* A person or a god did not simply *have* a name; he or she *was* that name. The person and the name were so inseparably bound together that to know the name was to know the person intimately. This knowledge of a name meant that one could influence and exercise control over the other, precisely because the knowledge and use of the name were so intimately related to the knowledge and use of the person. In this way we can understand that when Adam named the animals in Genesis 2:19–20, he was given the same dominion and control as that accorded to him in the Priestly account of creation at Genesis 1:28.

In our story the significance of a name appears in two ways. First, we shall consider the change of Jacob's name to Israel. While Jacob is usually the name of the patriarch, the name is used also, especially in poetic literature, for the nation. Likewise, while Israel is usually the name of the nation, that name is sometimes employed to speak of the patriarch. With that flexibility of terminology in mind, the interpreter cannot always be certain that a given text is speaking of the individual or the nation or both. A narrative or a poetic reference to the patriarch Jacob might, in fact, be an allusion to or a description of the experience of the nation.

The use of the name Jacob/Israel for the nation means that the naming belonged to a story that originated not in the patriarchal period but rather at some time after the establishment of the nation. Such a dating of this piece of the story would fit, of course, the time of J, who wrote during the Davidic-Solomonic reigns. The same could be said, however, of a number of later redactors, among whom is P, for that composer/editor did indeed record the name change of Jacob to Israel at Genesis 35:10.

The change of Jacob's name to Israel could indicate that the man himself was thereby changed. If person and name are virtually identical, then the change of one should imply the change of the other. The meaning of Jacob's name has been variously explained, as can be seen in the earlier chapters about this patriarch. When he was born, he came out of his mother's womb hanging on to his brother's heel (*ʿāqēb;* therefore, he was named *Yaʿaqōb* [Gen. 25:24–26]). When the twins had grown up, however, Esau exclaimed that his twin was rightly named *Yaʿaqōb* "because he has cheated (*ʿāqab*) me twice" (Gen. 27:36). If this second explanation was remembered by the narrator of the story at the Jabbok or by one of its later redactors, then the intention of the name change might have been to announce that Jacob would now be different. Bearing the name "may God persevere," the patriarch is quite different from his prior life when he was called "he cheats."

Second, the significance of the name occurs in the attempt by Jacob to learn the identity of his attacker. The request by a human being to learn the name of a god or divine being is an obvious attempt to gain control of the deity, to use the divine one for one's own purposes, in effect, to acquire a genie, even if not in a lamp. In the Hebrew Bible such a request appears also at Judges 13:17 when Manoah, though not yet convinced that the herald of the birth of a son was a divine being, asked the visitor for his name. The response of "the angel of the Lord" (v. 22 indicates it was God) was, "Why do you ask my name . . . ?" In neither case does the petitioner receive the name.

In the biblical narrative about the burning bush on Mount Horeb, Moses asks for God's name when God commissions him to return from Midian to lead the people out of Egypt (Exod. 3:13). In that case God does provide a name, according to E, but the name "I am who I am" is such that God maintains freedom while nevertheless giving a name to be used in the cult.

In Genesis 32, Jacob ends up without a name but with a blessing, and the Nocturnal Wrestler vanishes before the sun appears on the horizon.

4. The Criticisms

There seems to be little evidence to indicate a conflation of several sources. To be sure, the story does not run smoothly, and indeed there are many diverse elements in the story. But the unevenness and the diversity cannot be explained by a division into sources.

Most scholars argue that the story belongs to the J *source.*[21] This assignment is based not only on terminology but on the nature of the activity and on a process of elimination. In the first place, none of the characteristic expressions of E or P is evident in the story. Second, neither E, with an insistence on God's transcendence, nor P, with such a lofty view of God and God's glory, could be responsible for writing a story in which a divine being wrestles with a human and barely comes out the winner. Those who propose the J source argue that J displays a fondness for dramatic flair, but clearly J did not invent the story. How much of the story belongs to J and how much was added by later editors is difficult to determine.

Form-critically, the original story J used appears to have been a narrative report about the attack on a man by a nocturnal river demon.[22] The "one" must return to his abode before daylight, and his function is to wrestle with trespassers before the intruder crosses the river. While a precise parallel story cannot be cited, there are numerous parallels from the ancient world for river gods and for nocturnal demons.[23] The closest parallel in the Bible itself is the nocturnal attack on Moses by a demon at Exodus 4:24–26. There the demon is identified as Yahweh in the final stage of the transmission, but the creature acts contrary to the nature of Yahweh: he seems to have as his goal to prevent Moses from making the journey to pharaoh, a trip commissioned by Yahweh. In both cases, that of Jacob in our pericope and that of Moses in Exodus 24, the identification of the creature with Yahweh appears to be a later theologization, perhaps to remove the impact of other supernatural beings on God's chosen people. Such an old tale is what J received. The first *redactor* of the old animistic tale was, then, J. The primary task was to fit the story into the context of the cycle about Jacob.

Like the story about the demon attack on Moses in Exodus 4:24–26, this one also occurs "on the way" to an encounter with a significant person: there, the pharaoh of Egypt; here, brother Esau, whom Jacob cheated several years earlier. In order to provide the traveling music, J first of all introduced the story by the addition of verses 22–23, which report that Jacob sent his family and all his possessions across the river.

Without such an addition the story of Jacob at the Jabbok stands out as an oddity in the movement of the surrounding material. The transition from verse 21 to the incident with the river demon is not at all smooth, and the further movement from verse 32 into the following chapter is worse. The roughness at the end of the story is due to the addition of the dietary taboo. Eliminating verse 32 from J's redacted piece enables us to see that J concluded the story with more traveling music, this time to the tune of verse 31: "The sun rose upon him as he passed Penuel, limping because of his hip."

The pericope, in other words, seems to have been an independent piece that was inserted into the present context by J. Without it the reader's eye could move easily and smoothly from 32:21 to 33:1. Why, then, did J insert this intrusion about the wrestling match into the total narrative? Perhaps the purpose was to prepare the patriarch for his encounter.

When the patriarch left his home and fled from his brother Esau

(Gen. 27:41–45), God encountered Jacob at Bethel and promised him, among other things, a safe return (Gen. 28:10–20). Jacob's stay in Haran with Uncle Laban is, for the most part, recorded without reference to God-appearances (although God remains active in his life [see 31:10–13]). The compiler tells us that when Jacob was returning home to meet Esau after all this time, Jacob experienced two confrontations: the first with the angels of God at Mahanaim (32:1–2), the second with a demon. Having survived the demonic attack, Jacob was strengthened (perhaps by God's angels) to meet his brother and endowed with a blessing from a supernatural being. In this way God's earlier promise of a safe return was fulfilled.

Added to J's story are three etiologies: explained are the origins of the name Israel, the name Peniel, and a cultic dietary taboo. All three etiologies seem to be attached to the narrative by someone other than J and do not seem to be significantly related to the story.

Just why Peniel ("Face of God") is included here is difficult to determine with any degree of certainty. If any place-name stands out in the narrative, it is Jabbok because of the play on that name with the Hebrew word *'ābaq* (wrestle) in verses 25 and 26. Penuel is mentioned as part of the itinerary at the end of J's story, and so perhaps a later redactor inserted Peniel in order to change the identity of the Nocturnal Wrestler to Yahweh: "I have seen God face to face." The result is that the reader of the *final* story regards the episode as one in which God wrestled with Jacob.

The etiology concerning the dietary law at verse 32 is even more difficult to comprehend because such a law is attested nowhere else in the Hebrew Bible. At some time in Israel's history the taboo meant something to someone, but more than that profound statement cannot be made!

As for the name change from Jacob to Israel (or rather the identification of Jacob and Israel), we have seen above that while it is possible that J was responsible, it is more likely that someone later supplied verses 27–28. The reader's eye can move easily from Jacob's demand for a blessing in verse 26 to Jacob's request for the demon's name in verse 29.

The *tradition* of God's encounter with Jacob at the Jabbok appears elsewhere in the Hebrew Bible at Hosea 12:3–4. There it is part of a Jacob tradition in which events in his life are used negatively. In order to establish the nation's guilt, Hosea points in a pejorative sense to the career of their ancestor whose shady dealings began while he was still in the womb and continued into adulthood when he brazenly strove with God. The details of Hosea's account show that the prophet uses the episode loosely and, in fact, in a way no longer evident in the Genesis story. However, Hosea's use of the word "strove" (*sārâ*) in verses 3 and 4 demonstrates that the term was related to the Jabbok incident as early as the middle of the eighth century B.C. Did Hosea's use of the term cause a later editor to insert the explanation of the name change into the story of Genesis 32? Or did Hosea know the story with the verb *sārâ* already included as an explanation of the name "Israel"? In any case, Hosea uses the incident as one more example of the negative behavior of Jacob as patriarch and as people that leads to the lawsuit Yahweh is bringing against them.

Hosea goes on in verses 4–6 to proclaim that just as Israel's proud and brazen ancestor was brought to tears and supplication, so the Israel of the eighth century must repent and entreat the favor of God in order to avoid utter disaster.[24]

5. Theologies of the Passage

The passage presents one of the most bizarre portrayals of God in the whole Bible. Yet, in spite of the mythical and animistic backgrounds, in spite of etiologies that have little meaning for today, the passage can speak to Christians in several ways.

According to the understanding of J's use of the old attack story, J's proclamation seems to be: *Faithful to the promise made to Jacob of safe homecoming, God equips the patriarch against hostile forces and even enables him to be gifted with a blessing for the confrontation that lies ahead.* This level of the story allows for the development of a sermon about the faithfulness of God to the promise of bringing us home, eschatologically understood. In the face of all obstacles, including confrontation with evil and violence and the threat of death itself, God continues to lead us "on the way" toward the fulfillment of God's plans for us all.

The etiological additions to this apparent Yahwistic piece differ in terms of their value for proclamation. The cultic taboo against eating the thigh muscle on the hip socket does not affect our lives in the least. However, the addition in verse 30 of the name Peniel and of Jacob's explanation "I have seen God face to face, and yet my life is preserved" identifies the demon with Yahweh, just as a redactor did at the attack on Moses in Exodus 4:24–26. This redaction indicates that the Nocturnal Wrestler was really

God, and it changes the proclamation to something like the following: *Just as Yahweh appeared to Jacob to promise him safe return when he fled from his brother Esau to his Uncle Laban, so now God wrestles with the patriarch on the way home from Laban to Esau, strengthening him for the encounter.* The three lectionaries pair this pericope with Luke 18:1–8a, the parable of Jesus about the widow's seeking justice from God by hounding God day in and day out. Jesus' instruction about constant wrestling with God over one's need for justice is probably the reason for the selection of this pericope about wrestling with God. In some ways the Gospel lesson recalls the psalms of lament that permit people in troubled times to wrestle verbally with God for response, presence, deliverance, and ultimately for praise.

Furthermore, in still another redactional addition, namely, the change of Jacob's name to Israel and the sense of nationhood that accompanies that name, the passage might be summarized like this: *As a result of one person's struggle with the divine, God brings Israel into existence and blesses them.* Such a proclamation is a testimony that the Christian can use to speak of God's creation of the church, the new people of God, through an encounter with us in and through the Risen Christ. One can become a "new person" only when God comes to wrestle down the "old one."

Redacted and positioned as it now is, immediately before the long-feared meeting with Esau, the encounter with God at the Jabbok seems to prepare the way for Jacob to face this crisis. If we recall the significance of the name in ancient thinking, we can look for the results of that change in the following episode. When Jacob meets his brother whom he cheated and from whom he fled years earlier, the patriarch approaches Esau as a new man — humble, generous, grateful, affectionate. Thus, in its present form and context the story announces: *In the midst of the worst crisis in Jacob's life, God wrestles with him to change his identity and to enable him to face the coming encounter as a new person.* In the day to day crises that beset people, God comes to be present in the word whenever one Christian proclaims it to another. God's coming, if it means anything at all, has a profound effect on us — sometimes accusing, sometimes comforting, but nevertheless an effect that makes a difference in our lives. That difference might be the way we handle fears, anxieties, or troubles of all sorts. Life cannot be the same when the gospel of Jesus Christ confronts us in the midst of our crises, especially over the way we relate to one another.

Genesis 50:15–21

Revised Common Lectionary, Year A, Proper 19 [24]

Lutheran Book of Worship, Year A, Pentecost 17

I. Establishing a Working Text

Setting side by side some of the major English translations discloses the following points of difference. In verse 15 virtually all except the NEB make the point that after Jacob was dead, the brothers comprehended the reality of his death: the NEB reads simply, "When their father was dead . . . " In the same verse the NEB interprets the brothers' reaction by reading they "were afraid and said," while the others read simply, "They said." Further, the speech that follows is rendered in various ways:

RSV:	"It may be that Joseph will hate us."
NRSV:	"What if Joseph still bears a grudge against us . . . ?"
JB:	"What if Joseph intends to treat us as enemies . . . ?"
NIV:	"What if Joseph holds a grudge against us . . . ?"
NEB:	"What if Joseph should bear a grudge against us . . . ?"

The difference lies not only in the severity of the RSV's "hate us" in relation to "bear a grudge" but also in whether or not he "still" (NRSV) holds such a grudge, implying that he had earlier given evidence of such contempt against his brothers.

Verse 16 indicates some ambiguity over the tactic chosen by the brothers on the basis of their concern:

RSV: "So they sent a messenger to Joseph, saying..."

NRSV: "So they approached Joseph, saying..."

JB: "So they sent this message to Joseph:..."

NIV: "So they sent word to Joseph, saying..."

NEB: "They therefore approached Joseph with these words:..."

The difficulty here lies in the Hebrew *wayeṣawwû 'el-yōseph* (and they commanded to Joseph). The differences in translations leave us wondering whether the brothers came to Joseph themselves or sent a messenger to speak in their stead.

The brothers' opening speech regarding their father's last words in verse 16 is represented by some translators strongly and by others less so.

RSV: "Your father gave this command before he died..."

NRSV: "Your father gave this instruction before he died..."

NEB: "In his last words to us before he died, your father gave this message for you..."

JB: "Before your father died he gave us this order..."

NIV: "Your father left these instructions before he died..."

Their own plea is usually translated literally as, "Forgive the crime of the servants of the God of your father"; however, the NEB states explicitly the motive for their forgiveness as their worship of God: "So now, forgive our crime, we beg; for we are servants of your father's God."

The conclusion of verse 17 is translated according to whether the brothers approached Joseph themselves or sent a messenger with their plea (v. 16). The rendering is either "Joseph wept when they spoke to him" (RSV, NRSV, NEB) or "Joseph wept at the message they sent to him" (JB, NIV).

The same assumption regarding their direct approach or their use of a messenger affects the reading of verse 18:

RSV: "His brothers also came and fell down before him."

NRSV: "Then his brothers also wept, fell down before him."

NEB: "His brothers also wept and prostrated themselves before him."

JB: "His brothers came themselves and fell down before him."

NIV: "His brothers then came and threw themselves down before him."

In footnotes the NRSV and NEB indicate that the Hebrew reads "came."

The translations offer subtle differences in rendering the key to the entire Joseph story in verse 20:

RSV: "As for you, you meant evil against me; but God meant it for good, to bring it about that many people should be kept alive, as they are today."

NRSV: "Even though you intended to do harm to me, God intended it for good, in order to preserve a numerous people, as he is doing today."

NEB: "You meant to do me harm; but God meant to bring good out of it by preserving the lives of many people, as we see today."

JB: "The evil you planned to do to me has by God's design been turned to good, that he might bring about, as indeed he has, the deliverance of a numerous people."

NIV: "You intended to do me harm, but God intended it for good to accomplish what is now being done, the saving of many lives."

The question we are left with is: Was God behind the harm done by the brothers to Joseph, or did God alter their devious plan in order to work good? The JB seems to lean toward the latter, while the other translations could lead to either understanding.

2. Setting in Life

This conclusion to the story of Joseph and his brothers demands that we consider the story as a whole, for without the previous material this pericope serves no purpose. The story begins in Genesis 37, skips over 38, and then continues from 39 until this final chapter of the Book of Genesis.

The story as a whole focuses on the tradition of seven years of plenty followed by seven years of want, for it is the provision of food during a time of famine that brings the brothers to Egypt, where they meet their long-lost brother. Joseph, having worked his way to a position second only to the pharaoh of Egypt, was the one responsible for the rationing of food during the good times.

The Nile River was considered by the ancient Egyptians to be the river of life. All life depended on its flooding on a regular basis so that the crops would grow, the livestock would be watered, and people would be refreshed. The river's flooding was somewhat unpredictable, and even the height of the water was measured carefully and records kept. At times the Nile was low, and so life was endangered. From the second century B.C. comes a text that speaks of "a space of seven years" in which the Nile was dangerously low. The text purports to be a contract dating from the reign of Djoser in the twenty-eighth century B.C., but that longevity is difficult to establish. In any case, a number of texts, some dating back to the third millennium B.C., tell of lean years in which the people struggled to keep alive, and one dating from late in the third millennium reports in the first person that some royal person "kept alive" a number of communities during the times of want.[25] Furthermore, a "report of a frontier official" describes the migration of Bedouin tribes from Edom into Egypt during a time of famine "to keep them alive and to keep their cattle alive."[26]

In the Bible itself, of course, there are several stories about migrations from Canaan into Egypt during a famine. The first of those is Abraham's movement there when he told the pharaoh that Sarah was his sister (Gen. 12:10–20).

This evidence does not prove that the story of Joseph is historically true. It does indicate, however, that the storyteller(s) placed the drama of Joseph and his brothers into a quite realistic setting for their day.

Under our discussion of form criticism below we shall note that Gerhard von Rad argued that the story, as we have it, belongs to a genre known as a wisdom tale. By that understanding the entire story belongs to the popular movement called "wisdom," which tried to explain the wonders of life and to set various phenomena into categories that lead to instruction and understanding.

3. Literary Matters

In our comparison of translations above we indicated some of the major differences and the possible implications for interpretation. One of the issues cited was the question of whether the brothers of Joseph came to him initially or sent word through a messenger. Part of the problem lies in the impossible "and they commanded Joseph" (v. 16), and the other part appears in the rendering of verse 18 concerning whether the brothers "also came" (i.e., in addition to the messenger) or whether they were present all the time, rendering the word "came" unnecessary.

As for verse 16, the Hebrew *way^{e}ṣawwû 'el-yōseph* (and they commanded Joseph) is clearly problematic, even corrupt. Obviously something is wrong because (1) the verb *ṣiwwâ* (to command) does not take the preposition *'el* to introduce the direct object of the verb, and (2) such an action would have been completely out of character for the brothers at this point in the story. Since the word for "command" occurs only four verses later ("Your father commanded before his death"), it is likely that a scribe duplicated the word and in the process eliminated the word that should have begun the verse. The LXX *paregononto* implies they "came to" or "presented themselves to" Joseph, but that translation does not solve our problem with the Hebrew text.

What, then, is the force of v. 18, which begins (as all the translations admit), "And his brothers then came" (NIV)? The Hebrew reads *wayyēl^{e}kû gam-'eḥāw wayyipp^{e}lû l^{e}pānāw.* It is important to note that the word is not *bô'* (to come) but *hālak,* which means basically "to go." Perhaps too much importance is given to the verb by the translators, for on several occasions the verb *hālak* appears in a weakened, almost auxiliary, sense, as though it is merely introducing the following verb. At 1 Samuel 19:12, after Michal lowered David through the window, David "fled away and escaped." The Hebrew at this point reads *wayyēlek wayyibraḥ wayyimmālēt.* Out of the six translations considered for this pericope, only the JB finds it necessary to translate *wayyēlek* (imperfect of *hālak*): "He made off and took to flight and so escaped." The others simply drop the word, considering it an auxiliary. If the same weakened use of *hālak* occurs in verse 18 of our pericope, then the meaning is simply, "And even his brothers fell down before him." The inclusion of "and also came" might, therefore, be irrelevant to the question about a messenger followed by a visit from the brothers. There is no compelling evidence to suggest that the brothers first sent a messenger to Joseph before appearing before him themselves.

At verse 15 we have observed that the RSV renders "Joseph will hate us," while the others indicate their fear of his bearing "a grudge." Other instances of the Hebrew verb *sāṭam* at Genesis 27:41; 49:23; Job 16:9; 30:21; Psalm 55:4 (Eng. v. 3) suggest the meaning "bear a grudge against" rather than the more powerful emotion "hate."

As for the force of Jacob's words in verse 16 about Joseph forgiving his brothers of their transgression against him, the RSV and JB correctly translate the Hebrew verb *ṣiwwâ* (he commanded; he ordered). The softer rendering of "instructing" offered by the other translations is not adequate. Clearly, the brothers want Joseph to understand the last words of "your father" as unambiguously as possible — whether Jacob ever said them or not.

In v. 20 we reach the meaning of the entire story. First, let us consider the Hebrew word *l^{e}haḥ^{a}yōt* (to keep alive). We have seen above that the expression occurs in several Egyptian texts in reference to preserving life in the midst of a famine. The clue to its significance here, however, probably lies in the context of the Joseph story itself. Early in the tale we are told that out of jealousy over their father's favoritism of Joseph, the brothers "conspired against him to kill him" (37:18). Against their plot to commit fratricide, God worked "to keep alive" a numerous people, including the brothers and their families. That people set out with one thing in mind and God changed it to something else is the teaching of numerous proverbs (Prov. 16:1, 9; 19:21; 20:24; 21:31).

As for the work of God in relation to the plots of the brothers, the first words of verse 20 are crucial. Literally, the Hebrew words mean, "And as for you, you devised against me harm; God devised it for good." What is the meaning of "it" in the passage? The Hebrew clearly indicates by use of a third person feminine pronominal suffix that "it" refers to the "harm" intended by the brothers. The brothers conspired to kill, but God took their evil and turned it to good. God did not initiate the whole event or cause the harm to come upon Joseph. What God did was transform the intended evil into something good. The point is important because in the parallel passage at 45:1–8 the brothers are excused from their sinful actions because "it was not you who sent me here but God." There Joseph explains twice, "God sent me before you to preserve life." Our pericope differs from 45:1–8 in its understanding that God did not initiate the action but transformed it for the purpose of life.

4. The Criticisms

Source criticism of the Joseph story has changed considerably over the decades. Martin Noth's division of sources in the Joseph story (*A History of Pentateuchal Traditions*) remains basically the opinion of recent publications on the subject. Noth assigns our pericope to the Elohist and is followed in that judgment by the *Anchor Bible, The Interpreter's One Volume Commentary,* and *Jerome Biblical Commentary.* Among the interesting questions about the division of sources is that about the relationship of a Reuben version (essentially E) and a Judah version (essentially J). Other studies of the Joseph story have concluded it is basically a unity and is divided into sources only at the cost of destroying the power of the story.

The divergence of scholarly opinion is true of *form criticism* as well. In 1953 Gerhard von Rad published an article in which he suggested that the Joseph story has numerous affinities with old Egyptian wisdom literature, particularly in wisdom's wide-ranging interest in human possibilities, limitations, and complexities.[27] The setting of "old wisdom" in court circles and the education of a young official who is taught to give advice to a king on matters of state parallels the role Joseph played in Egypt (see Prov. 22:29; Sir. 8:8). Moreover, the portrayal of the ideal wise one in terms of breeding, education, modesty, discretion, knowledge, friendliness, and self-control coincides with the character of Joseph throughout the story. The basis of Israelite wisdom as "fear the Lord/God" (Prov. 1:7; cf. 14:27) occurs in Genesis 42:18 as a chief quality of the hero of the story. Further, the theological reflection of 50:15–20 seems to interpret the entire story as a narrative that tells the same message as some single proverbs (Prov. 16:1, 9; 19:21): the human mind plans the way, but the Lord directs the steps. At the beginning of the Joseph story, the brothers "conspire against him (Joseph) to kill him," but at the end Joseph acknowledges that God used their evil intentions for good: to keep many people alive. Strikingly, God is mentioned only rarely throughout the entire story (39:23; 41:16, 25, 28, 32, 38–39; 42:18; 43:14, 29; 44:16; 45:5, 7, 8, 9; 50:17, 19, 20). Since God is actively involved in only a few of those passages, the reader is left with the understanding that divine providence is behind the story, even if God is not evident during its course. This feature of wisdom, along with the traits of Joseph, led von Rad to classify the story as "a didactic wisdom-story."[28]

Among the challenges to von Rad's classification are the works of Arndt Meinhold, D. B. Redford, George W. Coats, and Claus Westermann.[29] Meinhold designates the Joseph story as a *diasporanovelle:* a novella is an artistic form in which an individual comes to terms with his or her society, and since the story of Joseph, like that of Esther, tells of the human society as one in which Israelites are struggling in a foreign land, it is a novella of diaspora. Redford considers the story to be the Hebrew version of the general motif of a young man who dreams great things; he regards the purpose of the story as primarily entertainment. Coats questions the criteria used by von Rad in assigning the story to wisdom and suggests it is a "political legend," the real intention of which is to entertain. Westermann also objects to von Rad's original thesis, suggesting that the theological reflection at the end (our pericope) is an oracle of salvation addressed to the fear of the brothers over their guilt.

While no consensus has been reached in regard to the form of the Joseph story, it seems to me the influence of wisdom thinking in the theological reflection in our pericope cannot be discounted entirely. While the original story might have been told to entertain or even to provide the necessary literary transition from the patriarchal traditions of Genesis to the Moses traditions of Exodus,[30] the theological summary proclaims the unfathomable work of God in taking the evil that human beings do to one another and redirecting it for life and goodness. While that theme might or might not belong to Egyptian wisdom teachings, it does bear affinities with some proverbs in the Hebrew version of wisdom. At the same time, such a view of God is not limited to wisdom literature, and so perhaps the primary concern ought to be the action of God in the story rather than an obsession over naming the form.

As for *tradition criticism,* the Joseph story is not a common theme in the Hebrew Bible. While the name Joseph appears frequently, it is usually the name of the tribe or the land that the tribe occupied. Certainly the character Joseph provides the transition to Moses and the exodus at Exodus 1:5, 6, 8 and again at 13:19. But the story of Joseph is cited only at Psalm 105:16–22. In its recital of Israel's history, the psalm describes God's sending Joseph to Egypt as a slave, the man's imprisonment and his interpretation of dreams, his release from bondage and his position as overseer of the king's possessions. The summary concludes with a bicolon that would seem to support von Rad's analysis:

> . . . to instruct his princes at his pleasure,
> and to teach his elders wisdom.

In the New Testament the Joseph story is summarized in some detail in the sermon of Stephen (Acts 7:9–18). Its function in the sermon is simply to serve as the necessary link from Abraham, Isaac, and Jacob to the salvation act of God through Moses. It is, therefore, part of the salvation history that Stephen cites prior to his martyrdom.

In still another recital of God's history with Israel, the author of the Epistle to the Hebrews includes Joseph—along with Abraham, Isaac, Jacob, Moses, and the people of Israel—as an example of faith, mentioning at the end of his life the exodus of the Israelites from Egypt and his giving instructions about his own burial (Heb. 11:21–22).

5. Theologies of the Passage

In the light of the whole story and in terms of this pericope in particular, the proclamation might be summarized as follows: *God can and often does work good, even out of the evil intended by human beings*. God is not stymied by the evil we humans do to ourselves and to one another. Rather, even when God seems to be absent, God is at work and will ultimately have the last word. That word is for life.

Not to be lost in the entirety of the story and its theological reflection is the forgiveness the brothers seek and receive at the hands of their long-lost brother. In providing assurance and comfort Joseph lives up to the expectations of the teaching of the proverb:

> Whoever forgives an offense seeks love,
> but whoever repeats a matter alienates a friend. (Prov. 17:9)

This emphasis on forgiveness explains the selection of the pericope as the background for the Gospel lesson from Matthew 18:21–35. Peter asks Jesus how many times he should forgive one who sins against him: Should it be as many as seven times? Jesus responds with "seventy times seven" and proceeds to tell the parable about the king who forgave the debt of a servant and expected, therefore, that the servant forgive someone who owed him. The parable indicates not simply that we ought to forgive one another but more specifically that since God forgives us, God calls on us to forgive others (see also Matt. 6:12, 14–15). In light of this emphasis in the Joseph story's conclusion and in connection with the Matthew pericope, the proclamation of the passage might be summarized as follows: *Since the God we worship is revealed as forgiving and saving, that same God calls on us to forgive others, assuring and comforting even those who have offended us.*

Numbers 21:4–9

Revised Common Lectionary, Year B, Lent 4
Lutheran Book of Worship, Year B, Lent 4

I. Establishing a Working Text

A Literal Rendering of the Hebrew Text

The following is a literal translation of the Hebrew text of Numbers 21:4–9:

> And they journeyed from Mount Hor in the direction of the Reed Sea to go around the land of Edom, and the breath of the people became short on the journey. And the people spoke against Elohim and against Moses, "Have you brought us up from Egypt to die in the wilderness? For there is no food and no water, and our throat has felt a sickening dread at the contemptible food." And Yahweh set forth against the people the *sārāph* serpents, and they bit the people, and a multitude of the people died. And the people came to Moses and said, "We have sinned, for we spoke against Yahweh and against you. Pray to Yahweh that he might turn the serpent(s) from us." And Moses did pray on behalf of the people. And Yahweh said to Moses, "Make yourself a *sārāph* and place it upon a standard, so that anyone who is bitten might look at it and live." And Moses made a bronze serpent and placed it on the standard; and if the serpent(s) bit any one, the victim would look at the bronze serpent and live.

A Comparison of Some English Translations

In setting side by side the translations, one quickly notices that the only substantial differences occur in connection with the name of the serpents (vv. 6 and 8) and with an expression in verses 8 and 9 that is variously rendered as "mount it," "put it," or "set it on a pole" (RSV, NRSV, NAB, NIV), "mount it on a standard" (*Torah;* JB), or "erect it as a standard" (NEB). These slight differences present no major difficulty in accepting any one of the translations as a working text. The major difference between the translations cited and the literal translation from the Hebrew occurs at verse 4 where "the breath of the people became short on the journey" is obviously an idiom that needs some attention under literary matters.

2. Setting in Life

The possibility of a serpent attack on the ancestors of Israel is very real, and so the historicity of the event cannot be dismissed outright. However, in light of the fact that the nomads often encountered serpents in the wilderness, the emphasis on the situation in this passage seems to fall on the cultural or sociological rather than the historical background. The nomad's fear of the wilderness as the abode of deadly serpents is attested both here and at Isaiah 30:6.

But the situation here is difficult to determine precisely because there are several mythological and folkloristic elements intertwined in this story. One can see in the *sārāph* of Moses an allusion to the serpent as a symbol of healing in the ancient world. More generally, making a serpent image as a cure for snake bite reflects the magical notion, also common in the ancient world, that a plague or a demon can be avoided by making a replica of it, that is, homeopathic magic (cf. 1 Sam. 6:1–5).

3. Literary Matters

The author of the original story is impossible to identify, if indeed one can speak of an author at all. The story seems to be similar to many Tetrateuchal stories in which we are dealing more with a series of storytellers than with a literary author. Likewise it is impossible to date the original version of the story, although, as we will show below, it seems to have originated in a nomadic situation.

A study of the problems connected with the terminology bears little fruit. As is evident from the work on establishing the text, the words for the "serpent(s)" are problematic. The Hebrew word *srp* may or may not be related to the verb *sārāph,* meaning "to burn," and so *srp* serpents may or may not be "fiery" or "venomous" or "poisonous." The problem is further complicated by the fact that the word *srp* is used both as a qualifying word for "serpent" (*nāchāš*) in verse 6 and as a substitute for that noun in verse 8. Unfortunately, no amount of work in lexicons or concordances will lead to a satisfactory conclusion.

Especially interesting, however, in verse 4 is the idiom "the breath of the people became short on the journey." The use of the Hebrew verb *hiqṣîr* (became short) with the words for "breath" has a special meaning. When used with *nepeš* (as here) and with *rûaḥ,* both of which mean "breath" or "wind," *hiqṣîr* points to "reaching one's limit of endurance" (cf. Judg. 10:16; 16:16; Job 21:4; Mic. 2:7; Zech. 11:8). The last two of these references show that the object of utter discouragement is introduced, as in our verse 4, by the preposition *b,* which can mean "in," "on," "by," "with," "near," "at," and so on. The meaning of the idiom at Numbers 21:4, then, seems to be "the people reached their limit of endurance with the journey." In other words, it is not simply that "*on* the way" they became discouraged at something or someone. Rather they became discouraged with the journey itself.

4. The Criticisms

Form-critically the piece is a narrative. Furthermore, on the setting in life, the story seems to reach back to an oral period of transmission when Israel's ancestors lived in a nomadic or seminomadic state. Having moved from that early stage to a later development, the story might have become an etiology, that is, a story used to explain the origin of a name, place, or cultic practice. The story might have been used to explain the origin of the symbol called "Nehushtan," a bronze serpent in the Jerusalem temple, and to provide it with a needed sense of authenticity. The author of 2 Kings 18:4 makes precisely that connection, but the relationship is not so clearly indicated in our story. Thus, the classification of the account as an etiological narrative can only remain a possibility.

A quick glance at the story could also lead to its classification as a fairy tale, particularly because, as the narrative stands, there seems to be an emphasis on the magical aspect of the bronze serpent. Further, the notion of the people complaining against God and Moses points to a common motif in the wilderness narratives in Exodus and Numbers, namely, the so-called murmuring motif.

Finally, the interpreter must consider the whole story in its present context and conclude that in some way it has become a historical saga; that is, it deals with the migrations of tribes through the wilderness ("historical"), and it speaks of a direct intervention of God in the affairs of people ("saga").

In terms of *source* analysis, the passage seems to be a unity rather than an intermingling of sources. It is not possible to discern two narratives that can be set side by side; neither is there evident one basic narrative with loosely attached fragments from another. The only piece of evidence that appears to lead to source differentiation is the use of the divine names Elohim and Yahweh: Elohim (God) appears at verse 5, but elsewhere in the story the name Yahweh (the Lord) is repeated. This terminology could account for a distinction between the Yahwistic (J) and Elohistic (E) or Priestly (P) sources. But without evidence of two strands of material, the name change can better be explained as the work of the JE redactor, who regularly used both names in order to give cohesiveness to the account. Furthermore, E himself could have used the name Yahweh in this story, because according to E, the name Yahweh had already been revealed to Moses (Exod. 3:14–15). Because of this possibility and because the murmuring motif elsewhere seems usually to be E,[31] we conclude that the narrative was probably compiled by E.

The editor or compiler (E), then, took over an old fairy tale about the magical snake-bite cure and edited it in such a way as to establish a motive for the serpent attack (the murmuring motif) and to proclaim that God was the one who provided (or at least initiated) the means for the deliverance. E's proclamation seems to be: *When Israel scorned and rejected God's act of deliverance and the divine way to fulfillment, God judged them in the wilderness but nevertheless acted to save even the rebels.* By emphasizing the common murmuring motif in the wilderness stories, the proclamation of E might be stated: *God directed the people in spite of themselves and even against their wills toward the accomplishment and fulfillment of the divine promise.*

The *tradition* of this event is reinterpreted at Deuteronomy 8:15, where it is part of a sermon (vv. 11–20) proclaiming the gracious acts of Yahweh from the exodus through the wilderness to the giving of the Promised Land. In this reinterpretation there is no mention of the murmuring motif, no complaining by the people. Rather, the use of the tradition in Deuteronomy 8 is to stress that God brought the people through difficult situations in order "that he might humble you and test you, to do you good in the end." This wisdomlike proclamation of the story is: *God, far from granting the redeemed people immunity from danger, preserved them through such trouble in order to refine them in the knowledge that whatever they have and are is due to God's grace and faithfulness.*

Numbers 21:4–9 is paired in the lectionaries with John 3:14–21 as the pericopes for the Fourth Sunday in Lent (Year B). In fact, the allusion to Numbers 21 occurs in the very first verse of the prescribed Gospel lesson: "And just as Moses lifted up the serpent in the wilderness, so must the Son of Man be lifted up, that whoever believes in him may have eternal life" (John 3:14–15). The reference assumes knowledge of the wilderness story because the meaning of the typological allusion rests on the means by which Moses lifted up the serpent and the result of that action for the people: he raised it "on a pole," and whoever looked at the uplifted serpent, even after a venomous assault, would live. Although the author of John's Gospel uses "lifted up" also for Jesus' resurrection and ascension, this first use of the word points to the crucifixion. In that light the proclamation of the story through the eyes of the Fourth Evangelist might be summarized as follows: *Just as Moses' uplifted serpent served as God's means of drawing people to himself to preserve their lives, so the crucified Son of Man is God's act of drawing people forward to receive the gift of eternal life.* That this gift of life is not based on some magical quality about two crossed pieces of timber is evident in the following verse, which announces that "whoever believes in him might not perish but have eternal life."

The apostle Paul alludes to the pericope at 1 Corinthians 10:9 as an example of instruction for Christians. Included in a list of rebellious deeds from Israel's wilderness period, the destruction by the serpents came upon them because they "put Christ to the test" (some manuscripts read "the Lord," apparently to make clear the rebellion in the wilderness was not against Jesus but against Yahweh).

5. Context

The context of a passage can be as narrow as the preceding and following paragraphs or as broad as the Bible itself. Perhaps the most significant context for this passage is the recognition that it belongs to the wilderness traditions that lie between the salvation event of Exodus 14 and the Sinai traditions of Exodus 19–24, on one side, and the settlement of the land, on the other. In other words, the event takes place *after* the act of deliverance but *before* the fulfillment of the promise of land for which the people were delivered. At Exodus 3, in the revelation to Moses, God promised to deliver the people from Egypt in order to take them to the Promised Land. In our passage the redemption from slavery has occurred, but the final outcome of that promise is yet to be realized. Thus the people are "on the way," and it is this journey, the time of waiting, the frustration of not yet experiencing the land, that irritates the people and causes them to murmur against God and Moses.

6. Interpretive Summary

The only refinements to be made in this passage on the basis of our investigation occur at the beginning and at the end. Verse 4 can be paraphrased, "And the people, already delivered from bondage but not yet in the Promised Land, murmured against God." Verse 9 might be made clearer by the rendering, "And so Moses made a bronze serpent and set it on a standard, and if the serpent(s) bit people, they would look at the raised bronze serpent by which God drew them to himself in order to preserve their lives."

7. Theologies of the Passage

When the proclamations of the event are set down, the various possibilities seem to be as follows:

a. Some nomads, attacked by serpents, managed to survive by making a symbol of the serpent that healed those who looked at it (the original oral stage: a fairy tale).

b. When the people scorned and rejected God's act of deliverance and the way to fulfillment, God judged their rebellion but acted to save the rebels (E's redaction).

c. *God directed the people in spite of themselves and even against their wills toward the accomplishment and fulfillment of God's promise* (the murmuring motif; again probably E).

d. *God brought the people of Israel through the wilderness and preserved them through trouble in order to refine them in the knowledge that whatever they have and are is due to God's gracious faithfulness* (Deut. 8:15–16).

e. *God confronted the people on the frustrating road between redemption and fulfillment — judging them when they rejected their deliverance and preserving them when they looked to the Lord in faith* (the E account with particular emphasis on the present context of the passage).

When these theologies come into contact with that of the Christian proclaimer, the first possibility can be promptly eliminated. The other proclamations will be refined in the sense that the redemption of God with which we are involved is the decisive act in Christ, and the fulfillment to which we look forward is the consummation of God's Kingdom that has already been ushered in by that Christ-event. But like the people of ancient Israel, we too are *on the way;* we too become discouraged with waiting, with the journey; we too, though delivered, rebel against God in our frustration. As with Israel, God comes to meet us on the way, both judging us and rescuing us in the midst of our rebellion.

Whether the Christian preacher chooses to base the sermon on Numbers 21:4–9 by using the second, third, or fifth interpretations depends on the situation in which he or she finds the audience. If the fourth interpretation is more appropriate to that situation, then the preacher should use as the text Deuteronomy 8:11–20 and address the message from that pericope.

Certainly most appropriate to the Christian theology is the use of the story as it is reflected in John 3:14–15. While the serpent on a pole provides a graphic illustration of God's will to save lives from death, even deserved death, the crucifixion of Jesus Christ is the means by which God accomplishes eternal life for all who believe.

I Kings 19:9–18

Revised Common Lectionary, Year A, Proper 14 [19]

Lutheran Book of Worship, Year A, Pentecost 12
Year ABC, St. James Elder

Book of Common Prayer, Year B, Last Sunday after Epiphany
Year C, Proper 8

I. Establishing a Working Text

In setting side by side our six translations as well as John Gray's translation[32] it is clear that only one major difference occurs in the passage. That difference occurs in verse 12 at the description of the "voice":

RSV:	"and after the fire a still small voice . . . "
NRSV:	"and after the fire a sound of sheer silence . . . "
NEB:	"and after the fire a low murmuring sound . . . "
NAB:	"After the fire there was a tiny whispering sound."
JB:	"And after the fire there came the sound of a gentle breeze."
NIV:	"And after the fire came a gentle whisper."
Gray:	"and after the fire a sound of thin silence . . . "

Gray's translation is a quite literal one, which I would change only slightly to "and after the fire the sound of crushed silence." The obvious difference in meaning between the RSV and most of the others is that the former describes an audible and apparently communicable voice while the others range from a slight noise of some sort (NEB) to a poetic way of describing absolute silence (NRSV and Gray). Only the JB interprets the sound as a breeze.

No other significant differences occur in the comparison of these English translations. A relatively minor matter is that the Hebrew has a definite article in verse 9: "the cave"; the JB renders it as such while the other English translations use "a cave."

Keeping in mind these two matters, the interpreter can use any of the above translations as a working text.

2. Literary Matters

The books of Kings make up the last portion of the so-called Deuteronomistic history, which includes as well Deuteronomy, Joshua, Judges, and Samuel. While there is some debate as to the time of the work of this Deuteronomistic school, these writers apparently ceased their history about 560 B.C. (the date of the last detail recorded at 2 Kings 25:27–30). Furthermore, it seems that these historians/editors did their massive work in Babylon and addressed it to the exiles there. The Deuteronomists inherited and used large blocks of already existing material: stories about the judges, the court history of David, the succession narrative of Solomon, chronicles of the kings of Israel and of Judah, and legends about prophets. In some cases the Deuteronomists changed little in the works they had inherited; in other cases they edited material freely. Our passage belongs to the legends of Elijah that were handed down to the exilic historians; the present form of the story may or may not contain some of their editorial comments.

Verse 9: "there." The previous verse makes clear that the adverb refers to Horeb, the mount of God. It is clear from the Book of Deuteronomy and elsewhere that Horeb is another name for Sinai. One need only read Deuteronomy 4:1–11:32 to see that everything that happened at Sinai in Exodus 19–34 is said to have occurred at Horeb.

Verse 9: "the cave." Since a cave has not been mentioned in the preceding paragraph, the definite article here cannot mean "the aforementioned cave." Moreover, since the teller of the story does not seem to be standing in the vicinity of the cave, the article does not mean "that cave yonder." The article can only mean "*the* cave" or "the well-known cave." Since the word refers to a particular cave on Mount Sinai/Horeb, "the cave" must be the one familiar to the people from the story about God's appearance to Moses who was stationed in "a cleft of the rock" (Exod. 33:17–23).

Verse 11: "Stand on the mount before the Lord" and "the Lord passed by." In light of the mountain's identity as Sinai and on the basis of mentioning the old familiar cave, both of these expressions are reminiscent of the story at Exodus 33:17–23 where Moses was told to "stand" on (or by) the rock as the Lord "passes by."

Verse 12: "a sound of crushed silence." Unfortunately, no comparable expression occurs elsewhere in the Hebrew Bible, and so a word study is impossible. While the translation "sound of... silence" seems contradictory, it probably is a rather poetic way of describing absolute silence, a vacuum of sound, which is crushing in its impact on Elijah. This silence stands in sharp contrast to the preceding scene.

Verse 14 (and the end of 13): the repetition of the Lord's question, "What are you doing here, Elijah?" and the prophet's self-righteous response (first occurring at vv. 9–10) is often regarded as an error, an unnecessary repetition due to a scribe's mistake (dittography). However, the repetition may indeed be intentional by the author in order to emphasize something or to make a special point.

Verse 14: "your covenant." The word *covenant* (Hebrew *b^e^rît*) is one of the most important terms in the Hebrew Bible. Its use and development can be traced through an article in a Bible dictionary.[33] While "covenant" refers to a relationship in which God obligates himself (to Abraham at Gen. 15:12–21; 17:1–21; to David at 2 Sam. 7), it is also used of a relationship in which God puts the obligation on the redeemed people (Exod. 19:3–8; 20–23; 24:3–8). The use of the word *covenant* in verses 10 and 14 of our text refers to that Sinai covenant in which God set the rules for the people to live—rules that they broke in throwing down Yahweh's altars in order to worship Baal.

Verses 15–16: "anoint." The term is worth a sentence or so here simply because the word *mašaḥ* is that which provides the basis for Messiah, "the anointed one." That the term is used here for anointing kings and prophets signifies that the act of anointing designates someone or something for a particular task. A Bible dictionary is helpful for a summary of the uses of the word.

3. Setting in Life

Elijah was active as a prophet in the northern kingdom of Israel during the second quarter of the ninth century B.C. The dynasty of Omri was still in power in the person of Ahab, who, in order to establish some political ties, was married to Jezebel, a Phoenician and the daughter of the king of Tyre. Jezebel's presence in Israel's royal city of Samaria brought to a head the failure of the people of Israel to distinguish between Baal and Yahweh. Jezebel had her prophets of Baal and of Asherah who sat at the queen's table (1 Kings 18:19). The people, some offended by pagan worship in Israel and some impressed by it, were caught in a syncretistic situation in which they could no longer decide which god to worship (see 1 Kings 18:21). This struggle provided Elijah's reason for being: his very name "Yahu (Yahweh) is my God" describes his function in the life of Israel. His contest with the prophets of Baal on Mount Carmel (1 Kings 18:20–40) was his triumph in demonstrating the power of Yahweh over that of Baal. But for slaughtering Jezebel's prophets after that triumph, Elijah was in serious trouble, and so he fled to save his life.

4. The Criticisms

The story before us is, of course, a narrative about an incident in the life of a prophet. Since it deals with a holy man at a holy place, the narrative might be classified as a *legend*. However, unlike the story of Elijah with the widow of Zarephath (1 Kings 17) or the story of the many feats attributed to the prophet Elisha, this story has nothing about it which is complimentary for Elijah. It does not seem to portray him as a legendary figure. As for the holy place as a means for classifying the narrative as a legend, we shall postpone judgment on that issue until further investigation is made.

On the basis of the mention of wind, earthquake, and fire, some might classify the account as a *theophany.* These elements, typical of theophanic descriptions at Exodus 19:16–19; 20:18; Job 37; Isaiah 6:1–4, and elsewhere, play an important role in our story. However, just as the negative is more than a curiosity in the prohibitions of the Ten Commandments, so the word "not" here is essential to the understanding of the passage. Since the Lord was *not* in the wind, *not* in the earthquake, and *not* in the fire, the passage is precisely *not* a theophany. In fact, the narrator is so explicit about God's absence in these phenomena that we might call the story a polemic against theophany theology. In this way, the situation of Elijah is highlighted: unlike Baal of Canaan, who is identified with the phenomena of powerful natural forces, Yahweh is in no way identical to or identifiable with such phenomena, though he is indeed Lord over nature. Here is clearly an attempt to distinguish Yahwistic theology from that of the Canaanite worship of Baal. That distinction, we have already seen, was Elijah's mission in ninth-century Israel. However we classify the story in regard to form, the basic intention or proclamation of the story seems to be: *Unlike the gods of Canaan, Yahweh is not found in the natural phenomena usually associated with theophanies.* Such a proclamation is, of course, purely negative, and one must immediately ask: Where then is God to be found? The text seems to announce: *God is not to be found at all; rather God came to Elijah in the speaking of the word to send the prophet on a mission* (vv. 9, 15–18). That mission was to anoint kings and a prophetic successor. Yahweh is thus portrayed primarily as a God of history rather than a God of nature.

We have already begun a discussion of *tradition criticism.* In the narratives at Exodus 19:16–19; 20:18; 24:9–11, and above all at 33:17–23, Sinai is indeed a place of theophany. People see God (24:10–11) or God's back (33:23) or at least the signs of God's presence (19:16–19; 20:18) on Sinai. The story told about Sinai, alias Horeb, at 1 Kings 19:9–18, however, completely rejects the idea that Sinai is a place of theophany. In fact, as we saw above, our story is told in such a way as to call attention deliberately to the theophany to Moses at Exodus 33:17–23, which took place on the mount, at a (the) cave, where the Lord passed by. Moses saw God (at least, God's back), says the old tradition, but the new tradition tells us that God was *not* seen by Elijah. Rather the audiovisual demonstration showed Elijah that God was *not* to be found or seen, even on the famous holy mountain. The old Sinai tradition has been radically reinterpreted, and this reinterpretation explains the repeated use of the Lord's question to Elijah: "What are you doing *here?*" Elijah, not understanding the question, explained to God that he sought refuge on the holy mountain where Yahweh was known to be present. The divine response to that speech was the demonstration that God was *not* there on the mountain any more or any less than God was present in the cities and countryside below. But when God asked the question again, Elijah gave the same speech. He did not understand the point of the nonverbal demonstration, and so God clearly communicated to the prophet by articulate words, directing Elijah to leave the mountain and to do God's work "down there where the action is."

The sacred mountain is thereby desacralized by drawing intentional parallels to the earlier Sinai theophanies. How much of this reinterpretation belongs to the basis or original story directed against Baal worship is difficult to say. But it is quite possible, perhaps even probable, that the story is the result of some editorial work by the Deuteronomists. Simply by supplying the name Horeb and by wording verses 9–11 in such a way as to call attention the story of Moses on Sinai/Horeb, the Deuteronomists seem to have desacralized the mountain in order to proclaim their message: *Far from confining himself in holy places to which people must make pilgrimages, God confronts people in the word, sending them out into the world to accomplish God's will.*

Such a proclamation is typical of the Deuteronomists and crucial for the situation they were addressing. It would have been theological suicide to maintain the sacredness of places and objects to exiles in Babylon whose temple back in Jerusalem had been demolished years earlier. Indeed, if God were confined to mountains, temples, and thrones, then God was dead, or at least unreachable from Babylon. And so for the Deuteronomists, God chooses the temple for the divine name to dwell (Deut. 12:5, 11, and often), but God himself lives in heaven (Deut. 26:15). In this way the Deuteronomists reinterpreted the name of God: the view that the name *is* the person (see the discussion of Gen. 32:22–32) is changed to the notion that the name is God's means of relating to the people. In addition, by changing the concept of the name, the Deuteronomists also reinterpreted the significance of the temple. As for the Ark, in the old tradition it was the throne on which Yahweh sat enthroned (1 Sam. 4:4; Num. 10:35–36); this cultic object becomes for the Deuteronomists nothing more than a box that contained the tablets of the law (Deut. 10:1–5). Thus, the Deuteronomists reinterpreted several old sacral traditions in order to emphasize the presence of God in the word. Only in this way could the exiles experience God's presence in far-off Babylon after the destruction of the temple. Here indeed is a dynamic witness to the word of God that addresses people in a variety of situations in new and different ways.

5. Context

Set after the incident at Mount Carmel where Elijah had the prophets of Baal killed, the scene before us indicates that Horeb represents for the prophet security in a holy place. God sent Elijah back into the midst of the turmoil with some specific functions to perform. The context serves to confirm some of the interpretation described above. But the combination of this context with the announcement that God will leave a remnant in Israel (v. 18) gives a slightly different meaning to the story: *In the midst of Elijah's anxieties over doing the Lord's work alone, God announced that because there are many who are faithful, the presence and the future are secure in God's hands.*

6. Interpretive Summary

The following is an interpretive summary of our text:

> 9And there, on the mountain of God, Horeb (also known as Sinai), Elijah entered the old familiar cave that we all know from the story about Moses, and there he spent the night. And lo, the word of the Lord came to him saying, "What are you doing up *here,* Elijah?" 12 . . . and after the fire, absolute silence. 13And when Elijah heard this vacuum of sound, he protected his face and carefully stood at the entrance of the cave to see what was happening. Then out of the sheer silence God addressed him again, "What are you doing up *here,* Elijah?" . . . 15-17And the Lord told him that it was not on the mountain but down in the midst of turmoil that God's work was to be done and where God is active. Kings are to be replaced. A prophet must be commissioned. Judgment will come. 18But in spite of Elijah's claim that he alone is left in the land as Yahweh's faithful servant, God says the multitude that has remained faithful will be spared from judgment.

7. Theologies of the Passage

Several of the theologies summarized above, especially that which seems to be the original purpose of the passage and that of the Deuteronomistic editors, proclaim that the God of the Bible is not to be found in or as natural phenomena or in sacred places. Rather God is present in the word that is active in history. Nothing can make that proclamation clearer than the message that the word became flesh to dwell among us. The presence of God in the Incarnate Word makes sacred places, sacred objects, and theophanic signs idolatrous. This is not to say that church buildings are useless or unimportant; rather, God is present to confront people in such structures and anywhere else when the word is proclaimed and the divine will carried out. While several other sermons are possible on the basis of other interpretations of the passage, this concern about the presence of God and the divine work in the world seems most important from the standpoint of the pericope and from a variety of situations that a Christian preacher must address.

The *Revised Common Lectionary* pairs this pericope with Matthew 14:22–33. The Gospel lesson reports the activity of Jesus after the miracle of the feeding of the five thousand. Jesus dismissed the disciples from that scene by making them get into the boat and head for the other side of the sea, while Jesus himself dispersed the crowd. When they had gone, Jesus climbed "the mountain" so that he could pray in solitude. By evening the boat still had not crossed to the other side because of a storm, and so in the early morning Jesus came to them, walking on the sea, eventually calming the storm. The sequence feeding–praying–walking on the sea–calming occurs in all four Gospels and thus seems to make up a block of tradition that the early church cherished. Like Elijah, Jesus sought solitude "on the mountain," but also like Elijah, Jesus descended from the mountain to engage the powers of the world (in this case, the raging sea, representative of chaos;[34] in the Elijah story, two kings and a prophetic successor). Together the pericopes indicate that *while we seek and require solitude with God, God takes that opportunity to enable us to confront the world.* The christological significance of the Gospel story must not get lost here, for the punch line is the realization of the disciples: "Truly you are the Son of God."

2 Samuel 7:1–11, 16

Revised Common Lectionary, Year B, Advent 4

Lutheran Book of Worship, Year B, Advent 4

Book of Common Prayer, Year B, Advent 4 (2 Samuel 7:4, 8–16)

I. Establishing a Working Text

David's observation in verse 2 about the contrast in living quarters between himself and the Lord is rendered "house of cedar . . . tent" in all the major translations except the NEB: "house of cedar . . . curtains." Whether the NEB translators dislike camping or are suggesting a substantive difference or are merely using a synonym, we will consider below.

Translations are divided on the question that God asks David through Nathan (v. 5). The RSV and NAB read similarly, "Would you build me a house to dwell in?" while the others put the issue differently. The JB, NIV, NEB, and NRSV agree on "Are you the one/man to build me a house to dwell in?" The former places emphasis on the appropriateness of building the house, while the latter focuses on the identity of the builder: David or someone else.

Yahweh's recitation of past residence(s) (v. 6) indicates life "in a tent for/as my dwelling" (RSV, NIV), "in a tent" (JB), "in a tent under cloth" (NAB), or "in a tent and a tabernacle" (NRSV, NEB). The issue raised in these divergences is whether Yahweh had been living in one residence or two.

When in the future David's successor commits iniquity (v. 14), Yahweh promises to "chasten him with the rod of men, with the stripes of the sons of men" (RSV), "with a rod such as mortals use, with blows inflicted by human beings" (NRSV), "with the rod of men and with human chastisement" (NAB), "with the rod of men, with floggings inflicted by men" (NIV), "with the rod such as men use, with strokes such as mankind gives" (JB). Only the NEB renders this punishment in terms of family discipline: "as any father might, and not spare the rod." The issue is whether the Davidic king will be subject to the laws of state or to parental correction.

No matter what the guilt of the Davidic ruler to come, Yahweh promises in verse 15 not to take away from him "my steadfast love" (RSV, NRSV), "love" (*NEV, NIV*), "my favor" (JB, NAB). While at first glance these terms might be regarded as mere synonyms, the interpreter needs to ask if something is lost or gained in these various renderings.

2. Setting in Life

The story of the promise to David of an enduring dynasty plays an especially significant role throughout the entire Bible. Its importance in its own historical setting, however, cannot be overestimated. According to the sequence of narratives immediately prior to our pericope, David had recently become king of a united Israel. He had ruled Judah for seven years from his capital city, Hebron. When people from the northern kingdom, however, approached him with the invitation to become their king as well, David accepted — not reluctantly, we can be sure.

The combining of the two kingdoms, Israel and Judah, under one king raised questions, particularly two. First, where would David find a suitable city for his capital? Remaining in Judah would jeopardize his new alliance, but selecting a northern site would alienate those who had been his loyal servants. David's selection of Jerusalem was the perfect choice because until now that city was not affiliated with either north or south; it still belonged to the Jebusites. The second question was: How could David ensure that this new kingdom would remain intact after his death? That is, How could he structure the kingship for the sake of continuity? This pericope presents the answer — the establishing of a dynasty — and does so at the initiative of Yahweh.

In another setting, too, the passage plays a significant role, for during the exile of the sixth century B.C. the Davidic king, Jehoiachin, was himself carried off and enslaved in Nebuchadnezzar's land. The enduring promise to David needed to be told in those precarious times, and one can only imagine how this story was discussed, debated, affirmed, and even expanded among the exiles.

3. Literary Matters

The introduction to the passage relates the act of God to establish David's rule: "And the Lord gave him rest from all his enemies round about" (v. 1). The expression appears in precisely the same form at Deuteronomy 12:10; 25:19; Joshua 23:1. The view that Yahweh promised rest in the form of the land as inheritance appears also at Deuteronomy 3:20 and 12:9, as well as Joshua 1:15. During the period prior to the monarchy, "the land was at rest" thanks to Yahweh's raising up the judges to settle matters of conflict (Judg. 3:11, 30; 5:31; 8:28). The fulfillment of the promised rest is part of the reason for Solomon's gratitude at 1 Kings 8:56. The interpreter will note the frequent use of the concept of "rest" in the writings of the Deuteronomistic history and the exclusive use of our expression "rest from enemies round about" in that body of material.

The rendering of Yahweh's residence either as a "tent" or "curtains" (NEB) in verse 2 can raise questions about the nature of the edifice. Unquestionably, the NEB translates the word correctly, for the Hebrew here is not *'ōhel* (tent) but *y^e^rî'â,* a word that in Priestly writings is used for the curtains in the tabernacle. The difficulty with the correct translation of the word, however, lies in the impact—or lack thereof—that the term has on the readers. When we read "tent," we think of the "tent of meeting" that Moses was commanded to develop for the people all the way back at Mount Sinai. At that tent the Lord met with Moses and with others as they journeyed through the wilderness, and that edifice is most likely the one in mind in our pericope. The translation "curtains" tends to lose that impact. But how can the other translations be justified with their "tent"? Happily, *'ōhel* and *y^e^rî'â* occur frequently in synonymous parallelism, indicating they can mean the same thing (Jer. 4:20; 10:20; 49:29; Hab. 3:7; Song of Sol. 1:5). Thus, while the translations appear to differ, in substance they do not.

As for the question in verse 4 ("Would you build me a house to dwell in?" or "Are you the one to build me a house?"), either is possible on the basis of the Hebrew text. The use of the second person pronoun at the beginning gives the force "As for you, will you build . . . ?" The emphasis could lead to either interpretation. Whether the identification of the builder or the construction of "the house" itself is the issue can be determined only by the context. The solution occurs in verse 13. Referring to the descendant of David, that verse begins likewise with the emphatic use of the pronoun:

"As for him, he will build a house for my name." The issue is not, therefore, to build or not to build, but who will do the building.

As to the matter of whether Yahweh's dwelling had been a "tent" or "a tent and a tabernacle" (v. 6), the Hebrew words favor the latter. While it is possible that the two terms are pulled together as a hendiadys on the basis of their synonymous use at Exodus 40:34–35 (P), it is likely that two residences are intended. Yahweh traveled through the wilderness as a tent camper, but when the tribes settled the Ark of the Covenant in Shiloh, they housed it in a "tabernacle" (*miškān;* see Ps. 78:60).

In verse 9 Yahweh promises to David, "I will make for you a great name." While the words are not identical, the interpreter cannot help but recognize the similarity with the promise to Abraham at Genesis 12:2: "I will make great your name." The connection of the Abrahamic traditions with David's Jerusalem has long been recognized, and the use of such an expression for both men contributes to the likelihood of that relationship. The play on the word "house" throughout the pericope, especially in verses 4, 6, 11, and 13, provides the dramatic twist. Contrary to David's well-intentioned proposal to build for Yahweh a house, that is, a temple, Yahweh promises to build for David a house, that is, a dynasty. The theological significance of this promise throughout the Bible will be discussed below.

While none of the compared translations indicates any problem with the rendering of verses 10 and 11, the interpretation might not be as clear as it seems. All our translations link the beginning of verse 11 to the conclusion of verse 10, giving the impression that the violence inflicted on the people of Israel "formerly" occurred during the time of the judges. In order to make this transition from "formerly" to "from the time that," the translations need to omit the conjunction "and" at the beginning of verse 11. It is possible to conclude verse 10 with a period and thus regard the violence that oppressed Israel in verse 10 as the bondage in Egypt. Verse 11 would then mean something like, "And more than the day when I appointed judges over my people Israel, I will give you rest from all your enemies." We have seen above in our discussion of "rest from your enemies round about" that such rest was indeed given during the period of the judges. What Yahweh promises here is a rest that supersedes that of the preceding historical period.

The various translations of what God promises in verse 15 raise some question about what God will not take away from David. Is it "love," "favor," or "steadfast love"? The Hebrew word behind these renderings is *ḥesed.* Studies on the word indicate *ḥesed* is not simply "love," like Romeo loves Juliet, or "favor," which any one can receive from the Lord. Other terms exist for those important concepts, like *'ahᵃbâ* for "love" and *ḥēn* for "favor." Hebrew *ḥesed,* however, is more specific; it means essentially loyalty within a covenant relationship and might, therefore, best be translated "covenant loyalty." The term refers to the fidelity of God to covenants in which God has obligated himself or covenants in which another party (especially Israel) becomes Yahweh's spouse. In terms of the covenant with David established here, the interpreter will do well to read Psalm 89:2–4, which reasserts God's promise of an enduring dynasty to David on the basis of Yahweh's *ḥesed* (and in parallel, as often, *'ᵉmûnâ* [faithfulness]). While none of the translations renders the Hebrew term as "covenant loyalty," the traditional "steadfast love" comes closest to the meaning.

Verse 16 provides a fitting climax to the pericope and to the story itself, for here any doubt about the meaning of David's "house" is removed. Used all together like beads on a string are the words "house," "kingdom," and "throne." In fact, the verse reads like a poetic parallelism:

> Your house and your kingdom will be firm forever before you (me?);
> your throne will be established forever.

The promise to which Yahweh obligates only himself is called an "everlasting covenant" in David's last will and testament (23:5). There, too, the security of the dynasty's reign is emphasized. Further, in Psalm 45:6 (a royal psalm) the same evaluation of God's promise is affirmed by the words addressed to the king: "Your throne, O God, (is) forever and ever."

4. The Criticisms

While the basic promise and story probably originated during the time of David, other hands betray an editorial interest in the story over the centuries. We have seen above the use of the typical Deuteronomistic expression "rest from your enemies (round about)" in verses 1 and 11. We can also imagine verse 13 as a contribution of the Deuteronomistic redactors, for the prophecy that Solomon would succeed his father and build the temple was, of course, fulfilled in due course. That understanding of history as Yahweh fulfilling earlier prophecies characterizes the whole Deuteronomistic work from the books of Deuteronomy through Kings.

At least one other editorial hand seems to have been submerged in the original pie. The basic story seems to consist only of the twist on the "house" theme: David proposed building a house for Yahweh, but Yahweh insisted instead on building a house for David. That tradition is evident in verses 2–7, 11b, and 16. The intervening verses seem to move the emphasis from the dynasty to the successor, namely, Solomon, who now appears to be the founder of the dynasty. The contributor of this material probably worked after the Deuteronomist since D seems to know nothing of the change. Furthermore, one can imagine that Yahweh's promise to provide "a place for my people Israel and plant them, that they may dwell in their own place," is a message to people who have been disbursed, or more specifically exiled, to another land. The same language about Yahweh planting the people in Canaan is used for the time of Joshua (Ps. 44:2). Equally important is the planting of the people in their own land in a prophecy about restoration and the promise of no more exile (Amos 9:15, a passage often regarded as an exilic redaction to the book). Even more specifically, the same image is used precisely for the return of exiles at Jeremiah 24:6; 32:41 (differently used at 42:10). Realistically, the promise of 2 Samuel 7:10 does not fit the time of David so much as the period of the exile.

Tracing the *tradition* of this promise would require a volume of its own. Let it suffice here to say the following. God's promise to relate to the people of Israel through the Davidic dynasty provided not only a theology but an ideology that permeates the psalms and many prophetic utterances. Psalms about the Davidic king cover many instances of his public life (Pss. 18; 20; 21; 45) and his responsibilities through Yahweh's election (Ps. 72), to say nothing of providing the liturgy for his coronation (Pss. 2; 110) and the theological background for his power (Ps. 89). When things looked bleak for the people of Judah and Israel, prophets repeated this promise of a Davidic king and the ideology connected with it in terms of the coming Day of Yahweh (Isa. 9:2–7; 11:1–9; Jer. 23:5–6; 33:14–16; Mic. 5:2–4; Zech. 9:9–10). This future king of Davidic descent would, of course, be the Messiah who would rule over God's Kingdom with justice and righteousness, thus securing a reign of peace and harmony.

Within the expectations of this tradition the Gospel writers would one day tell their story of Jesus. The lectionaries list as the Gospel for the day Luke 1:26–38, a passage that is unambiguous about the need to establish the Davidic descent of Jesus. The author describes Mary as a woman "betrothed to a man whose name was Joseph, of the house of David" (v. 27), and the angel Gabriel promised her that "the Lord will give to him the throne of his father David" (v. 32).

5. Theologies of the Passage

At its most basic level, namely, the twist on the meaning of house and the original promise to David of a dynasty, the proclamation of the passage might be simply: *Rejecting David's good intentions to build a temple, the Lord promised to establish for David a dynasty and obligated only the divine side of the arrangement to continue it forever.*

On another level, when a Deuteronomistic editor expanded the original promise by referring to the Lord's gift of "rest from your enemies round about" and by including a prophecy about Solomon's building of the temple, the message takes on a different twist. *Just as the Lord fulfilled the earlier promise of rest from enemies, so the Lord offered new promises on which the people could count because the Lord's word effects what it says.* Such a message would have had particular meaning to the exiles in Babylon, for the history lesson could easily be applied to their own generation.

Still other expansions of the material also appear to address the exiles in Babylon with the message that Yahweh will again bring them into the land to plant them, provide rest and security, and rebuild the house where the people might worship once again. *To a people aware of the history of God's actions and promises but skeptical of God's faithfulness in the present, God reasserts the promises of old to provide hope and presence and faithfulness.*

When the preacher considers the annunciation to Mary (the Gospel reading for the day), the tradition of the messianic promise comes to the fore at the same time as the insistence of God on doing all that needs to be done. *To and through an unlikely servant — a teenage girl — God comes miraculously to fulfill the promise of a Davidic king through whom God's Reign would be accomplished on earth.*

The combination of these two lessons, the promise to David and the announcement to Mary, provides a powerful setting for the Sunday before Christmas and ample possibilities for preaching about the faithfulness of God and the ways that God works among us.

Isaiah 6:1–8 (13)

Revised Common Lectionary, Year B, Trinity Sunday
Year C, Epiphany 5

Lutheran Book of Worship, Year C, Epiphany 5

Book of Common Prayer, Year C, Trinity Sunday

I. Establishing a Working Text

The problems with the text center on the following points of comparison:

Verse 3:

RSV/NRSV:	"The whole earth is full of his glory."
NEB:	"The whole earth is full of his glory."
NIV:	"The whole earth is full of his glory."
NAB:	"All the earth is filled with his glory."
JB:	"His glory fills the whole earth."
Kaiser:	"His glory is the fullness of the whole earth."

The rendering by Otto Kaiser is identical to the construction and syntax of the Hebrew.[35] The translations of the others seem to indicate that God's glory is *in* the world, but the literal rendering of the Hebrew (followed by Kaiser) seems to announce that the world in some way *is* God's glory.

Isaiah's initial response to his vision of the enthroned God is generally stated as horror. Following the "Woe is me!" is the further expression "I am lost/ruined, doomed!" Only Kaiser translates "for I must be silent. . . . " The problem here lies in the identification of the Hebrew root, which will be discussed below.

Verse 5:

RSV:	"For my eyes have seen the King, the Lord of hosts!"
NEB/NRSV:	"Yet with these eyes I have seen the King, the Lord of Hosts."
JB:	"And my eyes have looked at the King, Yahweh Sabaoth."
NAB:	"Yet my eyes have seen the King, the Lord of hosts!"
NIV:	"And my eyes have seen the King, the Lord Almighty."
Kaiser:	"For my eyes have seen the King, Yahweh Sebaoth."

While here and in verse 3 Kaiser transliterates Yahweh Sebaoth rather than translates it as "the Lord of Hosts" and the NIV renders the title "the Lord Almighty," the major difference is the NRSV/NEB's "yet" rather than the usual "for." The translation "for" (Hebrew *kî*) explains the reason for Isaiah's devastation ("Woe is me!"), but the NEB/NRSV's "yet" indicates that Isaiah has seen the Lord in spite of his and his people's sinfulness.

Verse 8:

RSV/NRSV/NIV:	"And who will go for us?"
NEB:	"Who will go for me?"
JB:	"Who will be our messenger?"
Kaiser:	"And who will go from us?"

The obvious difficulty with the literal translation of the last word "us" is the identity of the audience about whom Yahweh is speaking. The NEB smooths out the difficulty by translating it in the singular.

2. Literary Matters

These eight verses may provide more significant testimony than any other such block of material in the Hebrew Bible. The passage is loaded with almost too much significance for a brief study such as this. For the sake of brevity and clarity, therefore, our treatment will fail to do justice to the full depth and breadth of the text. In our selectivity we shall, however, try to comment on issues that are especially important for preaching.

The authorship of this passage is universally assigned to the eighth-century prophet Isaiah. The autobiographical account is quite with the style and content of other Isaianic material. Furthermore, the passage even provides a precise date: "the year that King Uzziah died." Any history of Israel or commentator will explain the year was about 742 B.C. We are not told whether this call of Isaiah took place before or after the king's death in that year, but the superscription to the book at 1:1 (added by a later editor) gives the impression that some of Isaiah's ministry came *during* the reign of Uzziah. At any rate, Isaiah's prophetic experience began prior to the Syro-Ephraimite crisis of the following decade (see the discussion of Isa. 7:10–17 below). His call is included in the block of material from 6:1 to 9:7, which dates from the time of that crisis rather than at the beginning of the book, where we would expect to find such a call recorded (cf. Jeremiah's call at Jer. 1:4–10; Ezekiel's at Ezek. 1).

Verse 1: the vision took place in the temple. That it was indeed a "vision" relieves us of the necessity of determining how Isaiah had access to the throne of God, the Ark of the Covenant, within the Holy of Holies. We do not likewise need to concern ourselves unduly about identifying an annual festival event when Isaiah might have seen the Ark carried from the Holy of Holies to some other location. The vision could have occurred on any day in which Isaiah worshiped in the temple. What is interesting, at any rate, is that while Isaiah says he "saw" the Lord, the description he gives concerns everything around God rather than the deity.

Verse 2: that Yahweh is surrounded by creatures of the celestial court is attested elsewhere in the Hebrew Bible; see 1 Kings 22:19–23; Job 1.

Verse 3: the song of praise these strange-looking seraphim (whatever they are!) were calling to one another is a beautiful expression of God's "holiness" and "glory." These two words are important to understand, and a Bible dictionary can serve this purpose well. The biblical view of holiness means basically "separateness" (root *q-d-š*): that which is holy is set aside from profane use or set apart for particular, usually cultic, use. To speak of God's holiness is to bear witness to the Lord's transcendence, to the divine "otherness," from humanity and from the world. The word "glory" (Hebrew *kābôd*) means basically "weight, heaviness, power." It is used of people who are rich and influential, who "throw their weight around." Thus, glory has to do with a manifestation of someone's power or influence, that by which someone is known. The use of the word "glory" in reference to God has a particularly interesting development, especially in the works of Ezekiel and P. Yet God's glory is elsewhere associated with the temple and the Ark even before the days of Ezekiel and P (1 Sam. 4:21–22; Pss. 24:7–10; 63:2; 78:61), and so the emphasis on God's glory in Isaiah's temple vision is expected.

What is interesting in the hymn of the seraphim, however, is that while the first line testifies to the separateness of God's transcendence (holiness), the second line indicates that God's power and influence are manifested *as* the created world (glory). While God is invisible to human eyes (apart from visions), God's power and works are evident to people who are thus to worship the One Beyond. Attesting to the physical world as the visual demonstration of God's glory, this hymn might be one of the most powerful theological statements that can be made today concerning stewardship of the earth and its resources.

As for the origin and meaning of the title "the Lord of hosts," there has been much debate. It has been explained as referring to the Lord of the heavenly armies, of Israel's army, or of all divinities whom the pagans worship. Other scholars have argued that since the name Yahweh is never elsewhere used in the construction "Yahweh of" (Hebrew construct state), the word "hosts" must be in apposition to Yahweh: "Yahweh, the sum total of powers." Whatever the ultimate answer to this question, the title is usually related to the Ark of the Covenant (see especially 1 Sam. 4:4) and thus confirms the whole vision as taking place in the temple and looking toward the Holy of Holies where the Ark was housed.

Verse 4: the presence of smoke and the quaking of the earth are typical of "theophanies" (God-appearances). We shall return to this matter under our discussion of form criticism.

Verse 5: the distinction among the translations cited above has to do, first of all, with whether the Hebrew word is *dāmâ* (to cease, to destroy; and so in the passive [*niph'al*], "I am lost, destroyed, undone") or *dāmam* (to be silent). Clearly, the former root is that which appears in the Hebrew text as pointed by the Masoretes; the latter root (used by Kaiser) requires a very slight emendation. However, as it turns out in this case, even the latter word, when used in the passive (*niph'al*) stem, as it is here, means "to be made silent," that is, "to be destroyed." In either case, the meaning is basically the same.

What lies behind the whole meaning of Isaiah's "woe" is the notion that when a human being looks at God who is "other," the observer will die. There exists such a qualitative difference between the transcendent God and sinful humanity that humans cannot withstand the encounter (see Exod. 33:20; Judg. 13:22; and the surprise of Jacob that he remained alive at Gen. 32:30). With this understanding, the reading "*for* my eyes have seen" is to be preferred over the NRSV/NEB's "yet."

Verse 8: after God had cleansed Isaiah of his sin, the Lord asked, "Whom shall I send, and who will go for *us?*" The NEB's "for *me*" certainly avoids the problem, but it does some injustice to the literal "from *us*." To whom and about whom is the Lord speaking when God says "us"? Such statements from God occur also at Genesis 1:26: "Let *us* make humankind in *our* image"; Genesis 3:22: "Behold, the man has become like one of *us*"; and Genesis 11:4: "Come, let *us* go down and confuse their language." These divine plurals (my italics) in the first person have been interpreted in a number of ways: (1) as an editorial "we"; (2) as a plural of majesty; and (3) as a reference to heavenly beings of some sort who are present in the Lord's court. While the second possibility is very real, the third seems to be intended in our passage because such courtiers have already been mentioned: the seraphim. It has been pointed out above that at 1 Kings 22:19–22 and Job 1, God is indeed portrayed as surrounded by and addressing the celestial court. Moreover, the language of a number of psalms indicates that God rules over but is not alone in the heavenly court (Pss. 29:1–2; 82; 89:6–7).

Isaiah's response "Here I am!" is identical to the response of others who are summoned by God for a particular task. It is the response of Abraham when he is asked to sacrifice Isaac (Gen. 22:1), of Moses when he is about to be commissioned by Yahweh as the deliverer of the Hebrew slaves from Egypt (Exod. 3:4), and of Samuel when he is told to serve as a messenger to Eli (1 Sam. 3:2–14). In each of those cases, the person involved is addressed by name. In our pericope, however, the name is not used. It appears that God was searching for a volunteer. At worship that day was Isaiah, overwhelmed at the presence of a holy but forgiving God. He responded as though he were personally addressed by God's question. And indeed he was!

The passage is sometimes limited in lectionaries to verses 1–8 (e.g., *Revised Common Lectionary,* B Year, Trinity Sunday). However, the passage obviously continues as far as verse 13. In fact, the account is incomplete without that speech, for verses 9–13 give the content and the purpose of Isaiah's call: he is to speak God's word so that the people's hearts will be hardened and in this way bring God's judgment on Judah. Isaiah's call is one of the most difficult passages to comprehend, for he is called to be a failure: to speak God's word clearly and forthrightly so that the people will reject it and bring devastation upon themselves. In spite of its difficulty, the speech of God in verses 9–13 must be regarded within the scope of the passage, for without this speech God sends a prophet without a message to proclaim.

3. Setting in Life

The historical allusion to the year of Uzziah's death sets the passage at about 742 B.C. It was a time of impending disaster on the international scene, for Tiglath-Pileser III, king of the ever-expanding Assyrian Empire, had the kingdoms of Palestine in a state of fear. Takeover of the whole area by this brilliant military leader was inevitable, and the Assyrians were well known for their brutality and ruthlessness. As Isaiah's preaching developed, the Assyrian kings were interpreted as Yahweh's instruments of judgment upon Judah and Israel. The judgment that this prophet was sent to preach, though it was Yahweh's word and command, would come at the hands of the Assyrians (see especially Isa. 10:5–11).

The eighth century B.C. was also a time of prophetic denunciation of the evils of society, especially of the oppression of the weak by the strong and rich. This sociological situation was a theological problem for the redeemed and elected people of God, who themselves had been oppressed and weak when God sent Moses to deliver them from Egypt (Deut. 24:17–22).

4. The Criticisms

The passage can be classified according to several *forms*—depending upon which verses or characteristics are emphasized. To begin with, the passage in verses 1–8 is a narrative, and the first verse makes clear that the narrative is a visionary account. But since the vision is of God, the passage can be classified as a *theophany.*

The designation of the passage as a theophany brings to mind several other theophany texts in the Hebrew Bible: Exodus 19:16–19; 20:18; 24:9–11; Psalm 18:7–15; Job 37; Ezekiel 1:4–28. Characteristic of such theophanies is the presence of thunder and lightning, earthquake, and smoke. Strikingly, these theophanies never describe God; while the individuals or the people "see" the Lord, only the signs of God's presence are listed. In this respect, theophanies in the Bible differ from theophanies of other ancient Near Eastern peoples, who both described and portrayed their gods in physical terms. Moreover, in almost all such theophanies in the Hebrew Bible (with the exception of Exod. 24:9–11 and Ps. 18:7–15), the texts move directly from the descriptive signs of God's presence to God's address to the persons intended. The emphasis is *not* on the vision but on what God says. The vision paves the way for the address. The same is true of Isaiah 6:1–8. While the beginning of the passage portrays a theophanic description (court creatures, earthquake, thunder, and smoke) and describes Isaiah's awe before these signs (like the people at Exod. 19:16–19; 20:18; like Job at 41:6; and like Ezek. at 1:28), the passage moves on to its climax with the Lord's call of Isaiah and the message he is to speak.

Since the climax of the passage is the calling of Isaiah to be a messenger and the message he is to proclaim, the passage can more appropriately be called a *report of a prophetic call,* similar to those at Jeremiah 1:4–10 and Ezekiel 2:1–3:16. The purpose of these reports was to provide authenticity for the preaching of these individuals as messengers of Yahweh. While Ezekiel was a priest and Jeremiah of priestly origin and training, Isaiah's prior activity is unknown to us. In all cases, however, the report of their calls legitimizes their role as prophets since apparently none of them was officially installed as a cultic prophet (see also Amos 7:14–15).

In comparing and contrasting these three call reports, several emphases stand out in Isaiah's call that are not present in the other two: the incident takes place in the temple; the overwhelming divine presence causes Isaiah to confess his and his people's sin, from which he is forgiven; Isaiah volunteers for the task once he has been cleansed; and, above all, Isaiah's preaching is solely to hasten the judgment of God, for it is clear that God's mind is already made up. Employing the form of a prophetic call report, Isaiah has made some peculiar emphases that are important for the interpretation of this passage.

As for the *tradition-critical* aspects of the passage, there are two matters worthy of mention, and both have to do with the message that Isaiah was to proclaim. First, Isaiah was apparently using an old tradition that has been called the "hardness-of-heart motif." Gerhard von Rad demonstrated that this motif, as difficult as it is to understand, was inherited by Isaiah from old traditions in Israel and in the ancient world as a whole. Yahweh's hardening of human hearts is attested in such old traditions as 1 Kings 22:21; Judges 9:23; 1 Samuel 16:14, 18:10; 19:9; 2 Samuel 17:14; 1 Kings 12:15; and, of course, in the exodus story in reference to the heart of pharaoh. But Isaiah used this old motif to announce Israel's downfall (see also Isa. 29:9–14) and to point beyond the coming disaster to a saving event (see 6:13), both understood as the result of the creative word of Yahweh. Thus, in the use of this motif, as in several others, Isaiah reinterprets an old tradition to say something unique about God's activity with Israel.[36]

Second, the message that Isaiah was commissioned to preach to the people is used in several ways by New Testament writers. In the Synoptic Gospels (Matt. 13:14–15; Mark 4:12; Luke 8:10) the hardness-of-heart motif of Isaiah 6:9–10 provides the explanation for Jesus' use of parables in his teaching. The precise meaning of this explanation for parables has been debated, but it seems that the intention is to announce to the disciples that only those so elected can understand the meaning behind the parables; to others they remain only simple stories ("they hear but they do not understand"). At Mark 8:17–18 Jesus alludes to this passage from Isaiah in his address against the disciples, who did not understand the meaning of Jesus' act of feeding the multitudes. The use of the motif in connection with the failure to understand Jesus' acts as signs of something beyond the appearance can be seen also at John 12:36b–41, where the quotation speaks of the unbelieving multitudes. Finally, Paul, frustrated by the disbelief of the Jews in his message about the Kingdom of God and about Jesus, quotes the passage as having been fulfilled and thus uses it as the reason for his mission to the Gentiles (Acts 28:23–28).

It is clear, then, that the message of verses 9–13, especially that of verses 9–10, was more important in the tradition of the passage than the vision that preceded it. This use of the tradition confirms what was said earlier under the discussion of form: even in the so-called theophanies of the Hebrew Bible the emphasis is not on the vision but on the message to be proclaimed. Such a conclusion might encourage a lector to read beyond the designated pericope that ends at verse 8.

5. Context

The body of material in which the pericope stands (6:1–9:6) originates from Isaiah himself, and all of it dates from the same general period (742–34 B.C.). Further, while chapter 6 is an independent report, the message and the theology contained therein must be interpreted in light of Isaiah's preaching as a whole. For this overview of that prophet's theology, a good commentary or general introduction or even an article in a Bible dictionary will serve well.

6. Interpretive Rendering

The following is an interpretive rendering of the text:

> In the year that Uzziah died, 742 B.C., while I was worshiping in the temple at Jerusalem, the Lord appeared to me with all the signs of the divine splendor. The impact of God's presence drove home to me my own unworthiness and that of the people among whom I live. But the Lord, through one of the strange-looking courtiers, forgave my sin and then asked for a volunteer to serve him. I responded as a person does when summoned by the Lord and volunteered for service. Then the Lord told me what I was to say: "Speak my word clearly and forthrightly with the result that the people will reject my word and bring upon themselves the judgment I have already decreed." I was aghast at the thought of such a mission, and so I asked how long I must speak. The Lord answered that my mission would continue until utter devastation would wipe away the land. This is the story of how I came to be a prophet — not through the official laying on of hands in a cultic ceremony, not through familial tradition, but through the devastating and comforting presence of the Lord who gave me the message that I preach.

7. Theologies of the Passage

Although we are dealing here with a unit that probably goes back to the prophet himself with little, if any, editorial revision, there are several important proclamations that can be heard from this passage. In the first seven verses the proclamation seems to be: *In the presence of the holy God who drove Isaiah to his knees, that same God acted to forgive sin and bridge the gulf between them.* Such a proclamation, though it does not give full justice to the purpose of the account by Isaiah, is certainly consistent with the New Testament understanding of the power of God's presence and of God's will to accept us in spite of — not because of — ourselves.

As indicated above, however, the purpose of the account by Isaiah is to record his call to be God's messenger and, particularly, the content of the message he was to proclaim. In this way the theology of the text can be summarized as: *To Isaiah, who was judged and then forgiven by the presence of God and the word, God gave a mission to be a spokesperson of that word — no matter how incomprehensible and difficult that word was for the new prophet.* Again, from a Christian perspective such a proclamation is not only useful but imperative, for all who stand judged and justified by God's act on the cross are given precisely that scandalous message to proclaim.

Finally, but still not exhausting the pericope's possibilities, an emphasis in this report of Isaiah's call — unlike those of Jeremiah or Ezekiel — is that the summons occurs while Isaiah is at worship. This point can lead to the proclamation: *In the midst of liturgical routine God came to devastate, to comfort, and to lead Isaiah, who heard God's word addressing him.* This interpretation of the passage requires little imagination to see how it could be addressed to a Christian congregation for whom Christ is present in the words — all too familiar sometimes — of the liturgy, the reading of the biblical lessons, the sermon, and the sacraments.

Paired with this pericope on the Fifth Sunday after the Epiphany (Year C) is Luke 5:1–11, the call to discipleship of Peter, James, and John. Peter's response to the presence of Jesus, especially his confession of fear and unworthiness, is strikingly reminiscent of Isaiah's. The balance between the two might be seen in two ways. First, Isaiah's call occurs while he is worshiping in the temple, but Peter is summoned while he is participating in his daily work. The two call stories together enable us to discern the range of settings in which God commissions people to participate in the mission to the world. Second, while Isaiah's call is to preach the Lord's judgment on the people of Israel, Jesus interprets the call to Peter and the others as meaning that from now on they will be catching people alive. Together the two accounts provide us with the effects of God's word — judgment and grace — as it commissions the baptized to go out into the world. A possible sermon sentence developing out of the two accounts might be phrased something like this: *Whether we are at worship or at work, when we are least expecting it, God confronts us, making us aware of our unworthiness in the presence of the divine, and then, forgiving us, sends us forth as ambassadors of the word that both judges and saves.*

Isaiah 7:10–17

Revised Common Lectionary, Year A, Proper 19 [24]

Lutheran Book of Worship, Year A, Advent 4
Years ABC, Annunciation

Book of Common Prayer, Year A, Advent 4
Years ABC, Annunciation

I. Establishing a Working Text

Differences in the first four and a half verses among various English translations are merely stylistic. The problems occur, however, in the second half of verse 14 where the content of the sign is described.

Verse 14b:

RSV:	"Behold, a young woman shall conceive and bear a son."
NRSV:	"Look, the young woman is with child and shall bear a son, and shall call his name Immanuel."
NEB:	"A young woman is with child, and she will bear a son."
NIV:	"The virgin will be with child and will give birth to a son."
NAB:	"The virgin shall be with child, and bear a son."
JB:	"The maiden is with child and will soon give birth to a son."
Kaiser:	"If a young woman, who is now pregnant, bear a son . . . "[37]

The differences here are significant. The NIV and NAB regard the woman as "the virgin," while the others speak of her as being a certain age but without reference to her sexual experience (or lack of it). The RSV, NIV, and NAB view the conception as taking place in the future, while the NRSV, NEB, JB, and Kaiser indicate that some woman is already pregnant. The JB and NRSV seem to have in mind a particular pregnant woman, but Kaiser intends a general or collective situation in which any pregnant women might bear male children.

Verse 15:

RSV: "He shall eat curds and honey when he knows how to refuse the evil and choose the good."

NRSV: "He shall eat curds and honey by the time he knows how to refuse the evil and choose the good."

NEB: "By the time that he has learnt to reject evil and choose good, he will be eating curds and honey."

JB: "On curds and honey will he feed until he knows how to refuse evil and choose good."

NIV: "He will eat curds and honey when he knows enough to reject the wrong and choose the right."

NAB: "He shall be living on curds and honey by the time he learns to reject the bad and choose the good."

Kaiser: "Cream and honey shall he eat, when he knows how to refuse evil and choose good."

Only the JB considers the food as that which the young man will eat *until* he can make decisions regarding good and evil. The other translations simply indicate that *when* he reaches a certain age (when he can distinguish good and evil), his diet will consist of curds and honey. In this latter respect, the literal rendering is in agreement with the RSV, NRSV, NEB, NIV, NAB, and Kaiser.

At the end of verse 17, all the translations, except the NEB, retain the problematical "the king of Assyria," which appears in the Hebrew text. The NIV, however, inserts before "the king of Assyria" the words "he will bring."

2. Setting in Life

The passage 7:1–9:6 of the Book of Isaiah is almost universally agreed to be Isaianic in origin and to date from the period of the Syro-Ephraimite crisis, which occurred about 735–734 B.C.

The Assyrian Empire, under its powerful king Tiglath-Pileser III, was spreading westward with the intention of gaining complete control of Palestine, an important crossroad at the east end of the Mediterranean Sea. Ruling over the northern kingdom Israel at this time was a certain Pekah, who along with the king of Damascus, Rezin, decided to form a coalition to stop Tiglath-Pileser's move. Naturally, the two northern kings wanted the king of Judah — first Jotham and then his son Ahaz — to join the resistance. Out of fear of the Assyrians' power, Ahaz refused his northern neighbors. Therefore, Pekah and Rezin decided to move first against Judah, depose Ahaz, and put their own crony — an Aramean known only as the son of Tabeel (Isa. 7:6) — on the throne, so that Judah would become part of the alliance. Against Isaiah's advice that Ahaz trust in the Lord, Judah's king deemed it wiser to put his confidence and his tribute in the hands of Tiglath-Pileser, who would prevent the Syro-Ephraimite coalition from deposing him. Ahaz's plan did, in fact, work, but as a result he became eternally grateful for the Assyrian's help.

To understand Isaiah's plea to Ahaz that he do nothing in the face of this crisis, the interpreter must remember that Ahaz was a member of the Davidic dynasty. Yahweh himself promised that David's descendants would forever remain on Jerusalem's throne (see 2 Sam. 7). With this promise from the Lord as a background, it was utter rebellion on Ahaz's part to trust the power of a political alliance rather than the faithfulness of Yahweh.[38]

3. Literary Matters

The adverb "again" (expressed in Hebrew by a verb: literally, "he added to speak") at the beginning of verse 10 is significant because it obviously ties the speech of our text to a previous speech — apparently concerning the same issue. That previous speech in verses 1–9 reports that Yahweh, through his messenger Isaiah, promised Ahaz that the alliance formed to depose him would not be successful.

Isaiah's reference to "your God" in verse 11 might indicate a relationship between Yahweh and Ahaz that simply involved Ahaz being a member of the covenant community or might point specifically to the special relationship between Yahweh and the king on Jerusalem's throne (cf. Ps. 2:7). In any case, the use of the possessive pronoun shows that Isaiah is announcing that the authority of his message is based upon a word from the God with whom Ahaz has a special relationship. This word is neither from Isaiah himself nor from a strange deity but from "*your* God."

A word study of "test" or "tempt" (Hebrew *nissâ*) in verse 12 shows that Ahaz was acting in a somewhat commendable way, because elsewhere in the Hebrew Bible "testing the Lord" is considered a grave offense (see Exod. 17:2, 7; Num. 14:22; Deut. 6:16; Pss. 78:18, 41, 56; 95:9; 106:14). But one gets the impression in our text that the king is mouthing pious hypocrisy. His refusal to ask for a sign, while admirable from one point of view, can also be understood as his refusal to change his plans for seeking help from Assyria. Ahaz had his own — probably popular — plan to escape disaster. Since he already knew from the previous speech (vv. 1–9) that Yahweh's plan was different, he did not want a sign or anything else from Yahweh to confirm the message.

In verse 13 Isaiah's response, "Listen, O house of David!" calls attention to the dynasty of which Ahaz was a member and simultaneously highlights the problem: the threat to the Davidic dynasty. Moreover, the summons to hear, followed by a vocative, is reminiscent of an announcement of judgment (see, e.g., Mic. 3:9–12). Furthermore, the question that Isaiah puts to the king sounds like the "accusing question" that is common in judgment announcements (cf. Jer. 2:4–13, especially v. 5; Mic. 6:1–8). This question contains an interesting switch from Isaiah's previous sentence: in verse 11 he spoke to Ahaz about "your God"; now, after Ahaz's hypocritical response, Isaiah speaks of "my God."

As for the identity of the woman (*hāʿalmâ*) in verse 14, the definite article is used in Hebrew to designate something or someone known to everyone, or something or someone to whom the speaker can point. For example, when Obadiah is described as the one who hid and fed the prophets of Yahweh (1 Kings 18:4), the hiding place is designated as "the cave," that is, the well-known cave that comes to mind when Obadiah's name comes up. Likewise, the article used for "the young woman" might indicate "the well-known lady," maybe the queen. Or it might simply be used in a demonstrative sense to refer to a woman in the vicinity of the discussion, thus "that young woman."

As for the question of that female's sexual experience, a word study of *'almâ* seems to reveal neutrality on the issue. At Exodus 2:8 the word is used for Moses' young sister, about whom we know very little. At Genesis 24:43 the term is used for Rebekah, who is described in verse 16 as "a virgin, whom no man had known." However, the allusion to Rebekah's sexual inexperience uses the word *b^etûlâ*, not *'almâ*. It is questionable whether even *betûlâ* means "virgin," because, if it does, the expression "whom no man had known" is redundant. Finally, *'almâ* at Proverbs 30:19 seems to refer precisely to a woman who is in the midst of a sexual experience. The understanding of the woman of Isaiah 7:14 as a virgin seems to have originated only when the Hebrew text was translated into Greek; *'almâ* then became *parthenos,* which refers to an unmarried girl who apparently is a virgin.

In light of this understanding of *'almâ* and on the basis of the definite article, who is "*the* young woman" who is pregnant? Perhaps no question has enjoyed so much attention among biblical interpreters, but the three most likely candidates are as follows.

1. *Isaiah's wife.* The symbolic name Immanuel would be quite fitting for the prophet's child, especially since we are told explicitly that Isaiah did confer symbolic names on two of his sons: Shear-jashub (7:3) and Maher-shalal-hashbaz (8:3). Of course, it is interesting that, shortly after the statement concerning the birth of a son (7:14), we are told that Isaiah and the prophetess (his wife?) had a son. However, that child was named Maher-shalal-hashbaz and not Immanuel. That "Mr. and Mrs. Isaiah" would have had two children—Immanuel and Maher-shalal-hashbaz—in the brief duration of the Syro-Ephraimite alliance is hard to imagine. Thus, while it is possible that "*the* young woman" is Isaiah's wife, such an identification is not probable.

2. *Ahaz's wife.* "*The* young woman" could mean "*the* first lady," although it would be difficult to provide evidence for such a conclusion. At any rate, it is not unlikely that, when Isaiah approached the king with Yahweh's message the second time, others, including the queen, were present. The queen could, indeed, have been pregnant at this time. If she is the young woman in question, then the passage takes on messianic significance: the child she bore would belong to the Davidic line, and such a family tree was essential for royalty. Moreover, since the Messiah would be a *king* of this Davidic family, the child in the queen's womb would have to

be Hezekiah. It was he who succeeded his father in 715 B.C. Thus, Hezekiah would have been born with the symbolic name Immanuel and would have been hailed as the expected deliverer. Perhaps it is his birth that is announced so joyously at Isaiah 9:6–7. When it is realized that Hezekiah, during his reign, made some startling moves to free Judah from Assyrian domination and to purify the temple at Jerusalem (2 Kings 18:3–8), one can imagine the optimism and confidence of the people in their celebrated "anointed one" (Messiah).

However, there is one serious problem with this entire theory. The whole notion rests on the concept that Hezekiah was the child in the womb while the Syro-Ephraimite alliance threatened Judah in 734 B.C. According to 2 Kings 18:2, however, Hezekiah was twenty-five years old when he came to the throne. Since the year of his accession was 715, he must have been born in 740 B.C., six years before the circumstances of our text. It is possible that the Deuteronomistic historian who wrote 2 Kings 18:2 was wrong about the young king's age; he is known to have made errors elsewhere in his chronology. However, at the present time the evidence falls against the messianic/Hezekiah interpretation.

3. *Any unidentified pregnant woman in eyesight of the king and Isaiah.* "*The* young woman" could mean "that young lady over there who is pregnant."[39]

After all this discussion, it is clear that the young lady cannot be identified with any certainty. Further, unless the young woman is the queen, it does not really matter who she is. In other words, the child has messianic significance only if the woman is Ahaz's wife and the son-to-be-born is Hezekiah. Apart from that possibility, the emphasis lies on the birth of a child in the near future, whose name Immanuel signifies the presence of God in the midst of the people and the end to the present threat.

Verse 15: the phrase "curds and honey" in this verse and in the following is variously interpreted. Most commentators argue that it is a menu for basic sustenance, one that designates a time of poverty following disaster. Usually verses 21–22 are cited to show what people will eat after the destruction of the land described in verses 18–20. But once again, a concordance comes to rescue the passage from that interpretation. How are curds and honey used elsewhere in the Hebrew Bible? Apart from Isaiah 7:15, 22, this same combination of food items occurs elsewhere only at 2 Samuel 17:29 and at Job 20:17. In the former passage, curds and honey are among the items brought to David at Mahanayim. It could be argued that these foods for basic sustenance were delivered to David, who was "camping out" during his son's takeover of the palace; it could also be argued, however, that curds and honey were the delicacies brought to the king along with beds, basins, wheat, meal, grains, beans, and lentils (2 Sam. 17:28). Such a list of goodies does not indicate that David and his men were roughing it. At Job 20:17 the situation is clearer: curds and honey are signs of prosperity that are denied to godless people.

Apart from the combination, "curds" alone appears as a food of prosperity at Job 29:6; Genesis 18:18; Deuteronomy 32:14; and Judges 5:15. Furthermore, even Isaiah 7:2 speaks of an "abundance" that the remnant will have to eat. Thus, the use of a concordance leads to the conclusion that a time of prosperity will prevail by the time the child "knows to refuse what is harmful and to choose what is good." But when does a child make that distinction?

Verse 15–16: "what is harmful . . . and what is good." The combination of good and harmful can mean several different things: (*a*) moral alternatives (see Deut. 1:39; Ps. 34:14; Prov. 31:12; Amos 5:14–15; Mic. 3:2); (*b*) "everything" (see Gen. 2:9, 17; 3:5, 22); and (*c*) pleasant and unpleasant food (see 2 Sam. 19:35). Which of these possibilities is intended by the author is difficult to determine. The use of good and harmful as "everything" is possible if the child is the Messiah who would be endowed with special gifts of wisdom and understanding (see Isa. 11:2). Apart from a messianic interpretation of the passage, however, this meaning is not possible. If moral alternatives are intended, then the child would have to be at least several years old. But if the distinction between pleasant and unpleasant food is meant, then the child need be only hours old.

It seems that the time of prosperity to come (our conclusion upon studying "curds and honey") will occur shortly after the birth of a child who is already in the womb or a few years after his birth. Or, least likely, it will come when the heir to the throne succeeds his father. At any rate, the solution to the impending crisis is near at hand.

The preceding statement implies a positive, rather than a negative, interpretation of "days that have not come since the turning aside of Ephraim from Judah" (v. 17). Such "days" would then be the glorious days of the Davidic/Solomonic Empire *before* the northern kingdom broke away from Judah during the reign of Rehoboam.

"The king of Assyria," attached loosely at the end of this verse, makes no sense at all. The phrase should probably be omitted, as it seems to be a scribal error. The NEB, in fact, does omit the phrase entirely.

4. The Criticisms

The discussion of literary matters raises the question concerning the *form* of the passage, for several characteristics of the announcement of judgment are evident in this passage. The introduction, "Listen, O house of David!" is quite similar to the summons to hear in the judgment announcement at Micah 3:9. The accusation here, given as a reason for judgment, appears in the form of the question of verse 13. The messenger formula is obvious in the "therefore" of verse 14, and the announcement of judgment would be developed by the intervention of God ("The Lord himself will give you a sign") and by the results of intervention, which would consider "curds and honey" (v. 15) as a poverty diet and the "such days" of verse 17 as a disaster equal to the splitting of the monarchy under Rehoboam.

Thus, form-critically the passage seems to be an announcement of judgment. Such a classification conflicts, however, with the results of the word study on "curds and honey," which led to the conclusion that the pronouncement is one of salvation. How, then, is the passage to be interpreted? First of all, we must seek to discover how Isaiah himself uses "signs" elsewhere in his preaching. At Isaiah 37:30–31 the "sign" points to a period of famine that will be followed in the third year by a time in which the people flourish and harvest their own food. At Isaiah 7:1–9, Isaiah's son, Shear-jashub ("A remnant shall return"), is a positive sign, even as the Lord announces to Ahaz the coming failure of the alliance against him.

It may be, then, that the prophet Isaiah intended his message to be one of judgment *and* of salvation. He may have used the typical form of announcement of judgment to speak the Lord's displeasure at the king's lack of faith and the inevitability of disaster that follows. At the same time, he filled the form with a content that proclaimed days of prosperity for the people, the continuation of the dynasty, and a restoration of stability in the not-too-distant future. In this way God would remain faithful to the promise issued to David centuries earlier. Isaiah was proclaiming, in other words, that God's promise continues in spite of the shortcomings of human beings.

The *tradition* of Isaiah 7:10–17, especially verse 14, is precisely what has made this passage one of the most popular texts in the entire Bible. The use of 7:14 at Matthew 1:23 serves as a prophecy for the virgin birth of Jesus. Since this birth story immediately follows the genealogy of Matthew 1:1–17, which establishes the Davidic line of Jesus, the quotation points also to the messianic role that this Christ-child was to play. The use of the quotation by Matthew, however, is somewhat different from the use in Isaiah 7. In the Isaiah passage, "Immanuel" is to be the name of the child; at Matthew 1:23, the name is a symbolic messianic title applied to the child whose actual name is to be Jesus.

At any rate, on the basis of our exegesis of Isaiah 7:10–17, the passage does not predict the birth of Jesus seven hundred years off in the future. Rather it speaks of an immediate situation in the lifetime of Isaiah, one that will come to pass in the birth and maturity of a child who is already in his mother's womb. But because the name Immanuel means "God with us," and because the Septuagint version that Matthew used rendered *'almâ* as "virgin," the passage was understood as a prophecy of the coming Messiah. Thus, the prophecy was taken out of its context and original meaning and reinterpreted in light of the person of Christ.

5. Context

The passage must be interpreted in light of the preceding section in 7:1–9 and in the larger context of Isaiah 6:1–9:6, which originates both prior to and in the midst of the Syro-Ephraimite crisis. It is questionable whether Isaiah 9:1–6 (English vv. 2–7) is a celebration of the birth of the baby promised in 7:14 or a hymn celebrating the birth of any royal child into the Davidic family or a hymn reserved for the coronation of a Davidic king when the "anointed one" becomes God's son (Ps. 2:7). Therefore, the relationship of that hymn to our pericope is not certain in regard to the identification of the baby. It is, however, surely connected in terms of Yahweh's promise to David of an enduring dynasty.

6. Interpretive Summary

The following is an interpretive rendering of the text:

> Again the Lord spoke to Ahaz concerning the attempt of Ephraim and Syria to replace the king with the non-Davidic son of Tabeel. When Ahaz hypocritically refused the sign of God's faithfulness to the promise of an enduring Davidic dynasty, Isaiah rebuked him with judgment but gave the sign anyway. The sign was this: "That young woman standing near us, the pregnant one, will bear a son whom she will name 'God with us.' When he is old enough to distinguish unpleasant tastes from pleasant ones (or to make moral decisions), he shall be eating the food of prosperous times. For before he reaches that age, Ephraim and Syria, who have made you so anxious, will be devastated. The Lord will bring upon this land of Judah days of glory such as we have not seen since the majestic reign of Solomon."

7. Theologies of the Passage

In the light of the total situation in history, the form-critical analysis of the passage, and the word study on "curds and honey," Isaiah's proclamation might lead to a sermon based on this sentence: *In the midst of troubles from the outside and in spite of Ahaz's own stubborn attempts to establish security, God renewed the covenant promise that alone could make the nation secure.* When this theological statement comes into contact with that of the Christian interpreter, there is obvious both a continuity and a discontinuity between the witnesses of the two testaments. The nation of biblical Israel is neither the church of Jesus Christ nor all of humanity, and so the identity of the recipient of God's promise must be reinterpreted for Christian preaching. Further, the United States or any other modern country is not the covenant partner of God. Those discontinuities mean that the promise of God must be addressed to the people of the new covenant, the universal Christian church, and the only king of that people is God. On the continuous side, the Father of Jesus Christ comes judging us also when we, the redeemed people to whom have been given the promises, attempt to launch out on our own without God and without regard to God's faithfulness to us. It is precisely in our attempts to establish our own security that we can be convicted of works-righteousness, on the one hand, or libertinism, on the other. In either case we are asserting our independence of the God who came in Jesus Christ to do it all for us. And yet in spite of this asserted independence, in spite of our insistence on being prodigal children, God invites us to rely on the divine promises and to trust the ever-faithful word.

While the passage at Isaiah 7:10–17 is not a prediction about Jesus' birth, it does proclaim the faithfulness of God to the promise that we see fulfilled decisively in Christ: Jesus Christ is the continuation and the end of the Davidic dynasty. In this way the passage has importance for homiletics even if we do not use it as a prediction of the virgin birth, as Matthew did in the Gospel assigned for this Sunday.[40]

Isaiah 35:1–10

Revised Common Lectionary, Year A, Advent 3
Year B, Proper 18 [23]

Lutheran Book of Worship, Year A, Advent 3
Year B, Pentecost 16
Years ABC, St. Luke

Book of Common Prayer, Year A, Advent 3

I. Establishing a Working Text

Setting side by side various English translations of the passage shows that the differences are primarily stylistic rather than substantive. A few verses, however, stand out with differences that demonstrate some confusion in the Hebrew text itself.

In verses 1–2, the RSV, NRSV, NAB, and NIV state the mood of verbs in a firm and positive indicative, while the NEB and JB render according to the jussive in Hebrew: "Let the wilderness . . . be glad," and so on.

At the end of verse 1 the type of flora is rendered "as the jonquil" (JB), "like the crocus" (RSV, NRSV, NIV), "with fields of asphodel" (NEB), or more generally, "with abundant flowers" (NAB). Moreover, the position of the phrase is different in these translations.

The second half of verse 7, precisely because it is difficult to understand in Hebrew, is translated differently in the sources used here: the RSV/NRSV, NIV, and NAB consider the animals "jackals," while the NEB renders "wolves." But the Hebrew text of the whole line is the major problem.

The most difficult portion of the passage occurs near the end of verse 8. The NEB translates "It shall become a pilgrim's way" (adding a footnote to the effect that the Hebrew is unintelligible);

the NIV has "It will be for those who walk in that Way"; the RSV assigns "It and he is for them a wayfarer" to a footnote, but the NRSV renders "But it shall be for God's people; no traveler..." The NAB, like the RSV, omits it from the text. Truly the Hebrew text at this point "is unintelligible."

2. Literary Matters

It would be fruitless to attempt to solve all the problems with the text, precisely because the Hebrew is extremely difficult, if not corrupt, at several points. However, for the sake of methodology, note that the translations cited do not offer in the last half of verse 7 a synonymous parallelism, which is expected both of the poetic structure and the entire lists of contrasts in verses 1–2 and 5–7.

More important in this passage is the determination of authorship. Although the passage appears in the first thirty-nine chapters of the Book of Isaiah, the style, terminology, and content indicate that the author is not the prophet of the eighth century but Second Isaiah of the exilic period. Some of the reasons for this judgment are as follows: the use of the word *ʾap* (then) in verses 5 and 6 is typical of Second Isaiah (cf. 40:24; 41:20, 26; 42:13; 43:7, 19; 46:11); the Hebrew expression behind "springs of water" in verse 7 occurs elsewhere in the Hebrew Bible only at Isaiah 49:10; the announcement in verse 4 is quite similar to that of Isaiah 49:10 (and virtually identical to Isaiah 62:11, the author of which seems to be a student of the exilic prophet); the "highway" of verse 8 sounds like that of Isaiah 40:3; 43:19–20; and the notion that Yahweh changes the wilderness into a place of glory appears at Isaiah 41:18–19. In fact, virtually every verse in the chapter bears striking similarities with the anonymous prophet of the exile. Such an assignment of authorship dates the passage at the end of the exile (just before 540 B.C.) and sets the place and audience in Babylon.

Some key words appear here that deserve attention, for the interpreter must attempt to determine what "wilderness," "vengeance," "redeemed," "ransomed," and "save" meant for Second Isaiah and his audience. The exegete might begin by using a Bible dictionary at this point; particularly interesting points, or insufficient information, might then lead to the use of a concordance.

"Wilderness" (*midbār*) in the Hebrew Bible generally is a place of anxiety and loneliness where people might at any time be attacked by vicious beasts and snakes (see Num. 21:4–9; Deut. 8:15).

More important is how the word is used by the same author. Even a quick glance at a concordance reveals that the wilderness is a place of loneliness and desolation (Isa. 50:2) but that Yahweh comes to transform it into a place of joy (Isa. 41:18–19; 51:3) and there build a highway (Isa. 40:3; 43:19–20).

This use of "highway" (v. 8) in Second Isaiah might be a deliberate attempt by the prophet to employ a piece of Babylonian religion in a polemical way. At every New Year's festival in Babylon (the Akitu), the Babylonian deity Marduk was carried in procession, escorted by the king, down a stone paving called the Sacred Way. The prophet might be using this imagery of "the way of holiness" to announce that against the Babylonian claim, Israel's God Yahweh will use the highway to take the people home.

"Vengeance" (*nāqām,* v. 4) is used by Second Isaiah (and Third Isaiah as well) to point to something positive for Israel (61:2; 63:4) but negative for Israel's enemies (47:3; 59:17).

The "redeemed" (*geʾûlîm*) of verse 9 are those who have been released in a court case (i.e., set free from forced servitude) by the intervention of a kinsman known as the redeemer (*gōʾēl*). This concept of Yahweh as Redeemer (Kin) of the people occurs thirteen times in the work of Second Isaiah; the fact that it appears only five times elsewhere in the Hebrew Bible is indicative of the importance of the term in addressing exiles.

Standing in synonymous parallelism with "redeemed" are "the ransomed of Yahweh." That God pays a ransom to free Israel is attested at Deuteronomy 7:8; 13:6; Micah 6:4, and elsewhere in reference to the exodus from Egypt; from exile God ransoms the people at Jeremiah 31:11; Zechariah 10:8; and, most important, Isaiah 51:11, which is exactly identical in expression to 35:10.

As for the term "save" (*hôshîaʿ*) in verse 4, a Bible dictionary or a Hebrew to English lexicon will explain that "salvation" in the Old Testament really means "to give spaciousness to (someone)," thus freedom from constraint and confinement. Second Isaiah proclaims that no idol, no diviner, no one, in fact, can save the people (45:20; 46:7; 47:13, 15). Only Yahweh can save and has promised to do so (43:12; 49:25; see also 59:1). Since the word of God effects what it says, the deed is as good as done (Isa. 55:10–11).

Of particular interest in the study of terminology is the expression in verse 6 that "waters will burst open" (*nibqeʿû . . . mayim*). This precise combination of Hebrew words occurs at Exodus 14:21 to describe the act of God in dividing the Reed Sea to allow the Hebrews to pass through. The use of this phrase is not accidental.

That the return from exile in Babylon is conceived by Second Isaiah as a new exodus can be seen elsewhere at 40:3, 10, 11; especially 43:14–21; 48:10, 20–22; 50:2; 51:9–11.[41]

Finally, throughout the whole chapter is a consistent use of synonymous parallelism. The interpreter must bear this feature of poetry in mind for the purpose of understanding each line in light of the preceding or following line. In the second half of verse 6, for example, the announcement that "waters shall break forth in the wilderness" means the same as "and streams in the desert." Homiletically we need to beware of splitting such literary devices in order to make separate preaching points.

3. The Setting in Life

A reading of the passage indicates that the situation to which the text is addressed is one of fear and trembling, a state of despair and hopelessness. The text proclaims a coming day of joy, and to describe that coming event it contrasts that joy with what is apparently the situation at the present: one portrayed in terms of a bleak and parched desert, one filled with despair, blindness, deafness, and dumbness. All these are terms of confinement, all the opposite of *šālôm*. Moreover, the situation is one in which the people are prisoners; the people need to be redeemed in order to return to Zion.

Such a situation *could* be seen in the time of the prophet Isaiah, for in 721 B.C. the Assyrian army had devastated the northern kingdom Israel and had carried off the leaders of the people to exile (Who knows where?). Therefore, Isaiah *could* be addressing those exiles with the message that Yahweh would come to bring them to Mount Zion with all these signs.

However, on the basis of literary matters we have already discussed, the passage addressed those people of Jerusalem who had been exiles in Babylon for fifty years and who longed to "return" to Zion (in this situation "return" to Zion makes more sense than if the prophet Isaiah were preaching to northerners). The time of Second Isaiah was near the end of the Babylonian exile (ca. 540 B.C.) when the people had grown tired of hoping for deliverance, when God seemed to have either called off the covenant arrangement or been destroyed along with the temple in 586, when plainly the exiles were in a hopeless state before the overwhelming powers that constrained them. The more we can learn of the people's attitudes in this period, the more relevant and concrete the message of the text becomes for preaching today. The prophet announces that God comes to save, to turn the whole situation around, to turn hopelessness into joy, death to life. Therefore, he exclaims, fear not!

4. The Criticisms

The first concern is related to *form*. Verses 3–4 can be classified as an "announcement of salvation."[42] This form is directed to a situation of distress and announces, by the use of the future verb (Hebrew imperfect), something that is about to happen. It is an announcement of the end of the distress by a coming event of God. Verses 1–2 and 5–10 provide the structure and content of the form called "portrayal of salvation," which contrasts the external nature of the present condition to the external nature of the new situation to come. This definition of form does not add anything of substantive nature to what we have already said about the passage. However, in this case the meaning of the passage is made sharper by showing that this contrast between distress and salvation, present condition and future condition, is not accidental to the proclamation of the passage but integral to it. This contrast, essential to the theology of the text, must be taken seriously by the present-day proclaimer as a sermon is developed.

In terms of *tradition* criticism we need to mention again that Second Isaiah interpreted the release from Babylonian exile as a new exodus. In this respect the old tradition concerning the bursting open of waters (Exod. 14:21) is repeated at verse 6. Moreover, the whole description of the triumphal march through the wilderness to Jerusalem is quite reminiscent of the delivery of Israel's ancestors from Egypt. The prophet of the exile is emphatic about his concern that the old exodus tradition be remembered as the basis for hope in God's new act of salvation, the deliverance from Babylon (see especially Isa. 43:18–19). The old tradition became the basis for an announcement about the future.

The realization that this pericope belongs to the preaching of Second Isaiah enables us to see also that these transformations from brokenness to healing in the context of salvation are part of the prophet's announcement about the coming Reign of God. The prophet connects the return of the Lord and of the exiles to Jerusalem as the victory that inaugurates God's Reign. "Your God is king!" "Your God is king!" yells the messenger from the mountaintop opposite Jerusalem, and the acclamation resounds among the guards on the walls and through the ruins of the city (Isa. 52:7–10). The coming Day of the Lord, which begins God's Reign, is the time when the transformations of life will begin.

5. Context

If the author of the text is indeed Second Isaiah, an interpreter might conclude that the immediate context of Isaiah 35 is not important for understanding the original piece. After all, who knows where it stood originally? What was the context in which it stood?

However, someone — a later redactor — saw some reason to insert the sermon at this point. In its present position it follows an announcement of judgment against Edom; in the description of the results of God's judgment there appears some terminology that is similar to some expressions in chapter 35 (for example, "the haunt of jackals" [34:13; 35:7]). In all probability, however, the final compiler who combined Isaiah 1–39 with 40–66 uses the sermon of chapter 35 as a transition from the one prophet to the other. In spite of a continuing number of chapters that deal with the life and times of Isaiah and Hezekiah (36–39), chapter 35 is the last sermon attributed by the final redactor to the prophet Isaiah. This position leads directly to chapter 40 and the call of the prophet Second Isaiah to "comfort my people." The vision of the salvation has already been portrayed before the prophet receives his call to announce the coming of God to save and the subsequent dawning of God's Reign. Perhaps it is only on the basis of such a vision that any of us can preach in a hostile world.

6. Interpretive Summary

On the basis of the prior investigation, one might paraphrase verses 1–2: "God-forsakenness and desolation shall be turned into the joy of divine presence." Verses 3–4: "Spread the news to the anxious and fearful: 'God is coming! Yahweh will bring comfort to you and disaster for those who oppress you. Yahweh will come with benefits to give you freedom from your confinement.' " Verses 5–7 seem to say: "All the unpleasantness you have suffered will become ecstasy; even nature will be transformed into its opposite when God comes." Verses 8–10 seem to mean: "You all know about that Sacred Way on which Marduk travels every New Year's day! Well, watch closely! Yahweh, our God, is coming down that Way to lead us home in joy."

7. Theologies of the Passage

The passage seems to be a unity — one sermon — that proclaims: *The Lord promises to rescue the people from their confinement of despair, hopelessness, and God-forsakenness and to transform their condition to the joy of freedom in the Kingdom.* That God comes in Christ, through the proclaimed word, to bring home a hopeless and despairing people is a message essential to our day when our self-made attempts to find meaning lead people even further into the exile of our times.

The lectionaries assign the pericope to the Third Sunday in Advent (Year A), when it is paired with Matthew 11:2–11. The Gospel lesson tells about the imprisoned John the Baptist sending his own disciples to Jesus to ask: "Are you he who is to come, or do we look for another?" Jesus did not answer the question directly with yes or no. Rather, he instructed John's disciples to go back to him with a report of what they had seen and heard: "The blind receive their sight, the lame walk, the lepers are cleansed, the deaf hear, the dead are raised, and the poor have good news preached to them" (v. 5). On the basis of the prophecies of Isaiah 35, Daniel 12, and Isaiah 61, these miracles that Jesus is performing and the message he is speaking are signs of the inbreaking of God's Kingdom.

If John's question "Are you he who is to come?" meant "Are you Elijah who is to come to prepare for the Day of the Lord?" (see Mal. 4:5–6), then Jesus' answer is a resounding no! In fact, according to Jesus, John "is Elijah who is to come" (11:14). What Jesus demonstrates in his miracles of healing and in his announcement of good news to the poor is that the eschatological transformations of God's Kingdom are already taking place. Jesus is, therefore, not the precursor of the Kingdom. Rather in Jesus Christ the Kingdom has begun.

Understood in connection with the Gospel for the day, the pericope from Isaiah 35 would then offer the following proclamation: *Having promised to the despaired and vulnerable that a new day of healing and harmony is coming, God fulfills that promise in the ministry of Jesus, in which God's Reign was already dawning.*

Verses 4–7a of the pericope are paired also with Mark 7:24–37 for Proper 18 (Year B). The story from Mark's Gospel reports two healing miracles of Jesus. The first is the exorcism of the demon from the daughter of the Syro-Phoenician woman (7:24–30), and the second is the healing of the man who was deaf and afflicted with a speech impediment (7:31–37). The reports here do not specifically relate the miracles to the Reign of God, but in light of Jesus' summary sermon in Mark (namely, "The time is fulfilled; the Reign of God is at hand"), it is difficult to read these stories apart from the eschatological promise of God in Isaiah 35 and other prophecies.

Isaiah 40:1–11

Revised Common Lectionary, Year B, Advent 2
Lutheran Book of Worship, Year B, Advent 2
Book of Common Prayer, Year B, Advent 2

I. Establishing a Working Text

Comparing six major translations does not reveal any divergences that change essentially the meaning of the passage. However, minor differences in the rendering of some words and phrases, possibilities allowed in footnotes, and differences in punctuation—all indicate the translation of the pericope is not as simple as it first appears.

In verse 2, for example, five of the six translate *dabbᵉrû ʿal-lēb yᵉrûshālaim* as "speak tenderly to Jerusalem" while the JB alone renders the expression "speak to the heart of Jerusalem." The divergence raises the question whether *ʿal-lēb* is simply an adverb qualifying the nature in which the speakers are to carry out their mission, that is, "tenderly," or a prepositional phrase indicating the address is to appeal to Jerusalem's heart. The former seems to point to speaking *from* the heart to comfort the people; the latter refers not to the nature of the speaking but to the content of the message, that is, appealing *to* the heart of Jerusalem.

Further in verse 2, the RSV renders *ṣᵉbāʾāh* as "her warfare" but admits in a footnote that an alternative would be "time of service." All of the other translations follow the RSV's suggestion in the footnote at this point, and so there is little to commend the earlier rendering.

In verse 3 only the NIV allows as an alternate reading, "A voice of one crying in the desert: / "Prepare the way for the Lord," and adds in a footnote that the LXX reads the next line as "make straight a highway for our God" with no mention of "in the desert." The LXX reading here is identical to Mark 1:3 and parallels. The other translations follow the Hebrew without allowing the LXX as an alternative, indicating the voice cries, "In the wilderness prepare,...make straight in the desert."

In verses 6–8 the greatest difficulty lies in the placement or nonplacement of quotation marks. Clearly one voice says, "Cry out!" and the prophet answers, "What shall I cry?" Then the problem begins. The RSV and NRSV use no further quotation marks to introduce the words "All flesh is grass....The word of our God will stand forever." The impression given is that the words are an editor's comment or that they are the words of God, who uttered without quotation marks in verse 1, "Comfort, comfort my people." The JB, NIV, NAB, and NEB introduce with quotation marks "All flesh is grass" and continue the same quotation down through the end of verse 8. The impression here is that the speaker of verses 6b–8 is the same as the one who summoned the prophet to "Cry out!" and that this speech is the direct response to the prophet's question, "What shall I cry out?" The ambiguity lies in the nature of Hebrew itself, in which there are no marks indicating the beginning and end of direct discourse. An interpreter must find some other way to decide who said what.

Without such marks the interpreter is left to agonize as well over the identity of the speaker in verses 9–11. Only the words "Here is your God!" are identified as direct discourse, and the speaker is the messenger who ascends to the mountaintop.

The greater difficulty in verses 9–11, however, centers on whether Zion is the messenger or herald of good tidings (RSV, NRSV, NAB) or the recipient of the message (JB, NIV, NEB). In other words, is Zion addressed in these verses to go up and announce, or is someone else (the prophet?) to ascend the mountain and address Zion?

2. Setting in Life

Chapters 40–55 of the Book of Isaiah belong to the preaching of the prophet known to us anonymously as Second Isaiah. The prophet lived and preached among the exiles who had been carried off from Jerusalem to Babylon in two waves, first in 597 B.C. and then in 587. According the internal evidence in the sermons recorded in these chapters, the prophet preached toward the end of the exile (538 B.C.), for he mentions by name Cyrus, king of Persia, who would accomplish the defeat of the Neo-Babylonian Empire and ultimately allow the possibility that the exiles might return home to rebuild their city (see 44:28; 45:13).

After so many years in Babylon a new generation had been born and grew up, one that knew little of Jerusalem or its temple or its liturgies. One must wonder how much they knew about their God, the one named Yahweh, for the Babylonian deities seemed to be riding on top of the world, controlling history, parading in celebrative processions, and enticing the exiles to worship them. Second Isaiah, called to announce the victory of Yahweh and the subsequent return home, needed to convince his listeners that Yahweh was the only God who deserved their adoration, their obedience, and their trust.

His task was complicated by the feeling among the exiles that God had forgotten them. Unlike many prophetic sermons where we need to imagine what the problem was on the basis of the answers given, this prophet provides us with the results of "interviews on the streets":

> Why do you say, O Jacob, and speak, O Israel,
> "My way is hid from the Lord,
> and my right is disregarded by my God"? (40:27)

This feeling of divine abandonment is expressed again at 49:14:

> But Zion said, "The Lord has forsaken me,
> my Lord has forgotten me."

These laments sound like the pitiful description of Ezekiel's vision of the dry bones: "These bones are the whole house of Israel. Behold, they say, 'Our bones are dried up, and our hope is lost; we are clean cut off' " (Ezek. 37:11).

Beyond the sense of abandonment, the exiles had little confidence that Yahweh could do much even if he finally did show up one day, for the Babylonians deities seemed to be the ones with the power. Aware of their fear of divine impotence, Yahweh asked bluntly:

> Is my hand shortened that it cannot redeem?
> Or have I no power to deliver? (50:2)

The rhetorical question sums up the attitude of the exiles. Feeling forsaken by God and in doubt about God's ability to deliver on any promises of salvation, the people turned to the idols of

Babylon. Whether or not Yahweh had forgotten them, they had forgotten Yahweh.

3. Literary Matters

The call to some unknown group to "comfort, comfort my people" in verse 1 reflects the work of God, even if at long last. The people sorely needed the comfort of God after sixty years of exile. The prominence of comforting at the beginning of the prophet's collection of sermons calls the interpreter to seek the word later in the collection. The same term, *nācham,* appears at 49:13:

> Sing for joy, O heavens, and exult, O earth;
>   break forth, O mountains, into singing!
> For the Lord *has comforted* his people,
>   and will have compassion on his afflicted.

The verb appears again in the perfect tense at 51:3:

> The Lord *has comforted* Zion;
>   he has comforted all her waste places.

The word occurs in participial form at 51:12: "I, I am he that keeps comforting you." On the basis of these verses we can conclude that the call to "comfort, comfort my people," at the beginning of our pericope is nothing less than the work of God, already enacted but now to be experienced by the people through the announcement of the prophet.

Interestingly, the call of the prophet Third Isaiah (chaps. 56–66) contains among other contrasts the command to "comfort all who mourn" (61:2), and other material indicates that for that prophet, too, comforting is God's work (57:18; 66:13).

As for the translation "tenderly" or "to the heart of" in verse 2, it appears to me that the JB alone has translated the meaning correctly. It is true that even lectionaries translate *'al-lēb* as "tenderly" or "kindly" and cite passages in addition to our own as evidence of its use. However, an examination of those passages challenges the lectionaries themselves. At Genesis 34:3 when Shechem raped Dinah and then realized his love for her, he "spoke to the heart of the young woman"; that is, he appealed to her heart rather than spoke from his own. Likewise, when Joseph explained to his brothers the work of God that came out of their deceitful actions years earlier, "he comforted them and spoke to their heart" (Gen. 50:21). The same is true at Judges 19:3; 2 Samuel 19:8; 2 Chronicles 30:22; Hosea 2:16; and Ruth 2:13. In each case the expression does not define *how* one spoke but what effect the speech had on the hearer. Therefore, if "speak tenderly to Jerusalem" is understood in terms of how one is to address the exiles, the point is lost. Those who are commanded to "speak to the heart of Jerusalem" might even be called to express the good news of their deliverance in harsh tones. It is the content of the message rather than the style of delivery that will comfort the hearers.

In verse 3 the words *pānû derek* (prepare the way) indicate that God's work of salvation will not occur in a vacuum, but rather when the event occurs, the people will know that it was Yahweh who announced it in advance. That ability to announce in advance what will happen in history is what distinguishes Yahweh from the idols of Babylon (see the discussion of form criticism of Isaiah 44:6–8 below). Further, the same expression appears in Third Isaiah's sermons. At 57:14 and 62:10 "prepare the way" refers not to a passageway for the Lord but to one for the people so that they might enter the presence of God. However, at Malachi 3:1 the task of "my messenger" (*mal'ākî*) is to *pānû derek* before the Lord who comes to the temple. The use of the same expression in Malachi is perhaps the reason for the confusion at Mark 1:2–3, where the prophet Isaiah is mentioned but Malachi is quoted first.

In verse 5 we realize that the salvation that will bring Israel from its captivity in Babylon is not merely a local event but one that will have cosmic significance: "All flesh shall see" the revealing of the Lord's glory. Earlier in the exile Ezekiel had used the same expression for the judgment that brought Israel to exile (Ezek. 20:48), and now the salvation event will also be witnessed by "all flesh." One can only wonder whether the words of the psalm celebrating Yahweh's victory over some unknown enemy ("All the ends of the earth have seen the victory of our God" [Ps. 98:3]) have contributed to the eschatological consciousness of the prophet, especially since those precise words were quoted by our prophet at 52:10 to speak of the return of the exiles to Jerusalem.

The confidence that exudes from the words "for the mouth of the Lord has spoken" (v. 5) reflects the most important aspect of Second Isaiah's preaching: the effectiveness of God's word. In verse 8 the enduring quality of God's word is announced, and that stability stands in sharp contrast to the natural and human worlds. At the end of this prophet's collection of sermons, the same emphasis is given to the word of God (Isa. 55:10–11) but there to its ability to accomplish whatever the word sets out to do.

In our discussion of translations above, we indicated the even split regarding whether or not Zion in verse 9 is the herald of tidings or the recipient of the herald's message. The Hebrew word for the messenger here is *m^{e}basseret,* a feminine single participle of *bsr.* In the view of some translations Zion is the messenger, apparently because names of cities and countries in Hebrew are usually feminine. Further, Zion/Jerusalem is the name by which God addresses the people and commands them to take action at 51:17; 52:1. Likewise, Zion is here called to announce the message not only to herself but to all the cities of Judah. The implication, then, is that the Zion/Jerusalem called here to act as the "herald of good tidings" is the group back home who wait for the return of the exiles. What they are to announce from the mountain height, however, is the returning of God to Mount Zion. Apparently the exiles follow Yahweh's lead like the booty won in a far-off land.

The other translations consider the messenger to be someone else, an individual who ascends the mount in order to announce to the exiles the coming of Yahweh or to the people back in Jerusalem that God is coming home again. Indeed, such a messenger to the exiles of Zion appears at 41:27, but there the participle appears in the masculine form. While a definitive solution to the problem is not possible, the question deserves some attention on the part of the would-be preacher because the sermon might focus on the identification of the messenger as Zion or one to Zion. Will the audience of such a sermon be called to announce the good news or hear it? Or both?

Perhaps more essential for preaching than the "who's who" issue is the meaning of the word *m^{e}bassēr* (herald of good tidings). Often one can interpret the theological usage of a word only by asking about its everyday meaning in the lives of people who lived at the time. In nontheological use the term defines the one who runs from the field of battle to announce the news of victory to the waiting king (see the frequency of this use in 2 Sam. 19:19–31). Further, the word is used to announce to a waiting father the birth of a baby (Jer. 20:15; this usage of *bsr* is also attested in Ugaritic literature). In either case, a messenger comes to another who is waiting anxiously about the outcome of an event and delivers good news. The result of the message is both celebration and relief, for the announcement begins a new time after a period of anxiety has been completed. For the king the message means his reign can continue; to the father the word of "Congratulations! You've got a son!" means the joys and responsibilities that come with a child. It is no wonder, then, that the Greek equivalents (verb *euaggelizesthai;* noun *euaggelion*) are used in the New Testament to announce the coming of God's Reign (Mark 1:14–15) and also the birth of Jesus (Luke 2:10).

4. The Criticisms

The pericope as a whole appears to mix together several forms. The message itself, with which the passage begins, focuses on the imminent act of forgiveness and salvation that Yahweh is coming to accomplish; that is, it is an oracle of salvation. That message, however, is to be delivered by this anonymous prophet who is here being called to that task. Therefore, the pericope contains within it a prophetic call report. (See the discussion above about the call in Isaiah 6:1–8.) Finally, the pericope ends with the salvation oracle couched within a psalm of praise.

Like the call of Moses in Exodus 3:1–15, this one carries as its central message the coming action of God. There God announces that, after hearing the people's cries for help, God has come down to deliver them (3:7–8). Here God announces to someone, obviously in the hearing of the prophet, that God has pardoned the iniquity of the people and has begun the divine act of comforting.

Like the call of Isaiah of Jerusalem (see the discussion of Isa. 6:1–8 above), which occurs in a vision of the heavenly court, this one also seems to take place in the company of God's attendants. As such, the report is also a vision of the heavenly domain. Such an understanding helps to identify who some of the hearers and speakers in the drama might be. God calls the heavenly court (the opening verbs are plural) to comfort the people on the basis of the divine pardoning of their sins. One voice in the crowd announces the need to prepare the way for the Lord's coming and the worldwide results of the divine act (vv. 3–5). Another unknown voice issues the call to prophesy: "Cry out!" or better "Proclaim!"

Now the prophet enters the conversation. Contrary to the usual end quotes after his initial "What shall I proclaim?" the prophet's speech continues through the end of verse 7. These words are the objection to the call. Moses asked, "Who am I that I should go?" and went on later to argue that he was not accustomed to speaking in public. Gideon raised the issue of his tribe's insignificance, and Jeremiah used his lack of maturity and experience as an excuse. For Second Isaiah the objection focused on the fruitlessness of the task: "All flesh is grass,... withers,... fades." In expressing his objection in such terms the prophet is merely using language familiar to his generation, the language of laments. His expression sounds like those used in some psalms to portray the vanity of human life. For instance, Psalm 39, especially verses 5 and 11, says: "Surely every human stands as a mere breath"; Psalm 90, especially verses 5–6, proclaims:

> You sweep them (mortals) away; they are like a dream,
> like grass that is renewed in the morning;
> in the morning it flourishes and is renewed;
> in the evening it fades and withers.

Thus the prophet's objection to his call lies in the frailty of human life. "What's the point of proclaiming?" he cries out.

Now we return in verse 8 to a speaker other than the prophet, perhaps the one who in verse 6a commanded the lamenting mortal to proclaim. The voice from the heavenly realm agrees with his analysis of the human condition and then refutes it as a basis for objecting. "Yes," he says,

> the grass does wither, the flower does fade;
> but the word of our God will stand forever.

The word of God that speaks and accomplishes its message (v. 5c) endures forever — unlike flowers, grass, and mortal beings. That everlasting quality of the word provides reason enough for fulfilling the mission to which the prophet is being called. That the eternal word promises comfort and deliverance now in this time and place is the motivation for fulfilling the messenger role immediately.

Verses 9–11 sound like the psalms of praise throughout Second Isaiah that Israel is to sing on the basis of confident belief in the Lord's promise to come and save (see, e.g., 44:23; 48:20; 55:12–13). In terms of their specific content the verses announce to the waiting city and environs back home the promise of salvation and the restoration to the land of God and of the people. The announcement of good news even in advance of the event demonstrates the faith of the people in accepting God's promise even when they are still in the pits of life.

God's announcement of salvation with which the pericope begins is heard and acted upon first within the heavenly court

(vv. 3–5), then in the person of Second Isaiah, who is called to proclaim it to the people (vv. 6–8), and third by the people back home who have been waiting for almost sixty years for the homecoming of Yahweh and the people (vv. 9–11).

A similar announcement at 52:7–10 shows also the crescendo of voices from a single "herald of good tidings" on the mountaintop to the watchmen on the walls of Jerusalem to the culmination of praise among all the surrounding towns. The message that they share is not only that Yahweh is coming home but that the homecoming represents the eschatological Reign of God: "Your God is king!"

5. Context

The pericope represents the editorial beginning of the sermons attributed to Second Isaiah. This oracle of salvation that is based upon the reliability of God's spoken word (vv. 5, 8) and results in a song of praise is not only the first of the recorded sermons. It is also the beginning framework of content and style that culminates in 55:10–13. There the collected sermons end the way they begin, namely, with an announcement about the effectiveness of Yahweh's word and the praise-filled exodus from the bondage in Babylon.

Between these two bookends lies the embellishment of the content and message about God's word of restoration and the praise that already accepts the promise before it is realized. The embellishment will call the exiles to begin that praise by recognizing the exclusivity of Yahweh's claim and the deception of Babylon's gods. (See the discussion of Isa. 44:6–8 below.)

6. Interpretive Summary

The following is an interpretive rendering of the passage:

> After some sixty years of the exile in Babylon, God sent the Persian king Cyrus to serve as "the anointed one" to free the Israelites from their bondage and send them home. Prior to the actual event God announced the forgiveness of Israel's sin and the end of its period of punishment. Upon hearing that announcement and accepting the call to comfort the people,

members of Yahweh's heavenly court burst out in acclamations. One such courtier announced the need to prepare the way for the Lord through the wilderness and indicated, first, that the whole world would see the results, and, second, that the deed was as good as done because Yahweh had spoken.

At first an anonymous man was enjoying this peek into the heavenly realm. Then one of the courtiers shouted at him, "Proclaim!" He responded in typical fashion by objecting to the call on the grounds that such a task had no purpose. Among other things he had learned as an exile was the meaningless and frailty of human life. The voice that called him to proclaim agreed on the evaluation of life's frailty but refuted his objection to prophesy on the grounds that God's word stands forever, and that is the message he is to announce.

Then the prophet heard the commissioning of Jerusalem/Zion to begin back home announcing the coming of God in power and in compassion. That announcement in advance demonstrates the confidence with which the prophet in Babylon could hear and preach God's message of salvation.

7. Theologies of the Passage

As a single sentence involving the action of God and the situation in which God is acting, the following might serve as the focus of a sermon: *To those exiles who experienced only the pain of God-forsakenness and the resultant feeling of unworthiness, God sent a messenger with the assurance that the word of God endures and that the word promises their salvation.*

Perhaps no period in the biblical era matches the dynamics of our day better than the exile of the sixth century B.C. The apparent God-forsakenness felt by many in a society that seems to have no values or rootedness or future fits that ancient situation as well as it does our own. The preaching of Second Isaiah to those bereft of all the supports that had held the people of God together for more than three centuries can offer to us insights about the theological response we can provide for people today.

The emphasis on forgiveness and the word of God that effects that pardon enables us to focus our preaching on the need for those forces of healing today. When so many people feel the agony of loneliness and forsakenness, of grief and of terminal illness, of fear of violence random and targeted, the situation is ripe for interpreting such ills as the result of human sinfulness and for announcing the forgiveness of God to our listeners and through them to others.

That this pericope is assigned as the first reading for the Second Sunday in Advent raises the issue of expectation, preparation, and response. In the Christian experience we identify with the exiles of ancient Israel as we await the coming of God and the dawning of God's Reign. We can see the need for preparation that is announced in the appearance of John the Baptist (the Gospel for the day is Mark 1:1–8). In sure and confident expectation that God's promise of God's coming can be trusted, we live not in dismal anxiety but in hopeful worship and celebration. For Christianity the dawning of God's Reign is identified not with the historical return from the land of Babylon but with the coming of Jesus Christ into our midst, his death to effect the forgiveness of our sin, and his resurrection as the firstfruits of the resurrection of us all.

Isaiah 44:6–8

Revised Common Lectionary, Year A, Proper 11 [16]

Lutheran Book of Worship, Year A, Pentecost 9

1. Establishing a Working Text

A comparison of six modern translations reveals only three major differences in this pericope. First, at the beginning of verse 7, following the challenging question "Who is like me?" the JB, NAB, and NEB read with the LXX "let him stand up." The NEB alone notes that in this expression it is following the LXX and that the words are omitted in the Hebrew.

Second, further in verse 7 the NIV alone includes as part of the text the words "what has happened since I established my ancient people." The RSV/NRSV supplies as a footnote: "Heb *from my placing an eternal people and things to come,*" while the NEB in a footnote gives: "since my appointing an ancient people and . . . " Neither the JB nor the NAB mentions the additional words in the Hebrew text.

Third, in the final line of the pericope (v. 8) the NEB reads "creator," while the others translate Hebrew *ṣur* literally as "rock." Of less significance is the NEB's translation in verse 6 of the Lord's epithet as "his ransomer," while all the others render "his redeemer."

2. Literary Matters

Consistent with his purpose (see section 2 in the discussion of Isa. 40:1–11) Second Isaiah used the following terms and expressions.

In verse 6 the Lord is called "the king of Israel." While the Hebrew Bible frequently uses the verbal form "the Lord is king" (*yimlōk;* e.g., Exod. 15:18) and "will reign" (*mālak*) on the Yom Yahweh ("the Day of the Lord"; see, e.g., Isa. 24:23; 52:7), the title *melek yisrā'ēl* (the king of Israel) occurs only here and at Zephaniah 3:15. The title must have been considered appropriate to the claim of Yahweh on the people of Israel, even here in a foreign land where other kings and gods vied for their loyalty and service. Immediately following the king's title is another epithet for Yahweh, "his redeemer" (*gō'^{a}lô*). The word describes both Yahweh's relationship to the people and his function in this foreign land. In nontheological usage a *gō'ēl* is one's next of kin who bears the responsibility of paying damages so that the indebted or accused relative might go free. Thus, the term defines Yahweh as Israel's nearest Kin and as the one who is fulfilling the obligation of the *gō'ēl* to free the people from their servitude. The word is used of Yahweh randomly in such widely scattered passages as Job 19:25; Psalm 19:14; Proverbs 23:11; and Jeremiah 50:24. That it occurs ten times in the preaching of Second Isaiah (41:14; 43:14; 44:6, 24; 47:4; 48:7; 49:7, 26; 54:5, 8) and three times in Third Isaiah (59:20; 60:16; 63:16) shows its importance for the prophet during the exile and immediately afterward.

Finally, still in verse 6, is another epithet: *Yahweh ṣ^{e}bā'ôt* (the Lord of hosts). The title appears six times in the preaching of Second Isaiah (44:6; 45:13; 47:4; 48:2; 51:15; 54:5). It probably refers to the armies that Yahweh brings to accomplish the necessary victory, and in so applying the warlike image to the imminent battle (note 40:9–11), this prophet follows the example of his namesake (the eighth-century Isaiah of Jerusalem), who used the title forty-seven times to announce the power of Yahweh against the Assyrian invasion that threatened Jerusalem in his day.

The difficulties in verse 7 regarding the Hebrew "from my establishing a people of eternity and things to come" can be removed by following the proposal in Rudolf Kittel's *Biblia Hebraica,* an emendation involving basically a different division of the Hebrew consonants into words: "Who has announced from of old the things to come?" The translations that have followed that suggestion appear to be on the right track, especially since the rhetorical question of verse 8 provides the contrast between the impostors and the true God: "Have *I* not told you from of old and declared it?" The same contrast occurs in the speech at 58:3–8, especially v. 5, where the Lord indicates that giving the announcement prior to the events was to ensure the people would not credit the deeds to the idols.

In verse 8 the Lord identifies the people in exile as "my witnesses" (*ʿēdāy*). The same term is used at 43:10, 12, where God indicates that against "the nations" who have no one to declare "the former things" and no witnesses to say, "It is true," the Lord has Israel to serve as witnesses. They are to indicate in the assembly of nations that only the Lord is God, and their testimony is based on the fact that the Lord spoke in advance what was to come and then made it happen.

Earlier in the same verse God comforts the people with the words, "Fear not and do not be afraid" (Hebrew *ʾal-tipḥᵃdû wᵉʾal-tirhû*). Part of the expression or a synonym occurs ten times in Second Isaiah (40:9; 41:10, 13, 14; 43:1, 5; 44:2, 8; 51:7; 54:4). The comfort lies in the accompanying promise of God's help and deliverance from the exilic bondage, often specifically phrased in terms of the word "redeem" or the title "Redeemer" (see 41:14; 43:1; here at v. 6).

"Rock" (Hebrew *ṣûr*) appears in verse 8 as an epithet for God, as it does at Deuteronomy 32:18. There in the Song of Moses the term appears in a synonymous parallelism:

> You were unmindful of the Rock that bore you,
> and you forgot the God who gave you birth.

Perhaps it is that allusion to the birth of Israel that led the NEB to translate the word in our pericope as "creator." Several times in the vicinity of our passage Yahweh is described as the one who "formed you, O Israel" (43:1), indeed "who formed you from the womb" (44:1, 24). Yahweh is Israel's "creator" (43:1, 15), although the term used in both places is *bôrēʾ* (cf. Gen. 1:1). At Isaiah 31:9 *ṣûr* seems to apply to the pagan deity who will flee at the sight of Yahweh when the Lord defends Jerusalem from the Assyrian attack at the end of the eighth century B.C.

3. The Criticisms

Perhaps the most important issue in this pericope is the consideration of its *form*. We encounter here a form that was probably the creation of Second Isaiah, namely, the "trial speech." In the context of exile the people of Israel faced daily the question about which god(s) had the authority to be worshiped and to exert their claim on the people. The exclusive worship of Yahweh had been the claim of Israel's God from the beginning, and so we would expect Yahweh to make a burning issue out of the temptation to idolatry in the foreign land. In several passages in the preaching of Second Isaiah, Yahweh calls to civil court the nations and their gods, bringing suit against the idols as impostors: they claim to be gods, but they are not (see also 41:1–5, 21–28; 43:8–15; 46:5–11).

The trial speech consists of a summons to court issued by the Lord to the nations and their gods, the direct challenge to the gods to prove themselves, and the calling upon Israel to be character witnesses to the "godness" of Yahweh as direct support to Yahweh's claim to be the one beside whom "there is no god."

The proof of divinity lies in the ability to speak beforehand what will be and to bring it to pass. The idols, of course, do not and cannot speak at all, and the call to the nations to bear testimony to their gods' ability to speak effectively (i.e., to accomplish what they say) leads only to silence:

> Tell us what is to come hereafter,
> that we might know you are gods. . . .
> There was none who declared it,
> none who proclaimed,
> none who heard your words. . . .
> Behold, they are all a delusion;
> their works are nothing;
> their molten images are empty wind.
> (Isa. 41:23, 26, 29)

Against their dumb presence in the courtroom, Yahweh asserts divinity by reciting the ability to bring words to effect.

> I first have declared it to Zion,
> and I give to Jerusalem a herald of good tidings. (v. 27)

> I declared and saved and proclaimed. (43:12)

> Have I not told you from of old and declared it? (44:8)

> I am God, and there is none like me,
> declaring the end from the beginning
> and from ancient times things not yet done. (46:9–10)

During the exilic period this theology of the effective word of God defined the nature of Yahweh. In this time, it appears, the creation account of Genesis 1:1–2:4a came to its final form at the hands of the Priestly school: each piece of the universe was created by the divine fiat. Somewhere in the middle of the exilic period the Deuteronomistic historian appears to have finished his work in which the theological lesson is that history has unfolded due to the prophetic word of God spoken and fulfilled. The prophet-priest Ezekiel announced to exiles that their dried bones would spring to life upon hearing the word addressed to them (Ezek. 37:4, 7–9). And Second Isaiah announced that the word of God endures forever (Isa. 40:8) and accomplishes whatever it sets out to do (55:10–11).

Perhaps Second Isaiah was aware that in the epic used at the celebration of the Near Year in Babylon (the *akitu*), the god Marduk demonstrated the ability to make a piece of cloth vanish and then reappear just by speaking his divine word (*Enuma elish* 4.20ff.). But the prophet must have considered that act trivial compared with the power of Yahweh's word to bring creation into being and to direct the course of history, even effect the judgment that brought the people to Babylon and now accomplish salvation for the exiles — merely by uttering the word.

What distinguished Yahweh from the gods of Babylon was the word of God that existed from before the beginning of history and will continue even after history has been fulfilled. That enduring and effective word of Yahweh is the proof of the claim that "there is no god besides me."

The connection between the trial speech and the promise of salvation becomes even clearer in our passage when we recognize that the opening words, "Thus says Yahweh . . . ," make up the characteristic messenger formula that introduces an oracle of judgment or of salvation. Since the message of Second Isaiah is to "comfort my people" and since he was preaching to a people already experiencing the judgment of God for their sins, his speeches are oracles of salvation (see the introductions to salvation oracles at 43:1; 44:2). In light of that connection of the trial speech to an oracle of salvation, some interpreters consider the pericope to continue at verses 21–22. The argument is that the intervening prose material at verses 9–20 has interrupted the salvation oracle introduced in verse 6a; it concludes with the promise of forgiveness and redemption and the call to the people to return to Yahweh in verses 21–22.[43]

4. Theologies of the Passage

In light of the results of literary matters and the form-critical analysis of the passage as a trial speech, the sermon of Second Isaiah might be summarized as follows: *In response to the people's idolatry, Yahweh files suit and tries the idols as impostors, claiming that only the one who can speak in advance what will happen has a right to be called God.*

When one combines the trial speech form with that of the oracle of salvation, especially in light of the entire purpose of Second Isaiah, the summary might look more like this: *Against the gods of the surrounding society who demand worship but can offer nothing of ultimate value, Yahweh promises that the word of salvation can be trusted because Israel knows the effect the word has had in the past.*

The entire theology of the word of God is essential for the Christian faith, for the word as gospel is "the power of God for salvation to every one who has faith" (Rom. 1:16; see the discussion on the power of the word in chapter 1). Further, that the word is that which existed from the beginning, not only with God but as God, became flesh and dwelt among us, attests to the dynamic nature of the word in the person of Jesus Christ.

Christologically the notion of the effectiveness of the word occupies a prominent place in the Gospels. Jesus speaks the word "with authority" in contrast to the scribes and Pharisees, who are authorities *on* the law (Matt. 7:29). Indeed, the entire Sermon on the Mount asserts the authority of Jesus as he repeatedly announces his word that supersedes that of the old law of Moses (Matt. 5:21, 27, 31, 33, 38, 43). The effectiveness of Jesus' word might be seen also in the report of the angel to Mary Magdalene and the other Mary at the empty tomb: "He is not here; for he has been raised, *as he said*" (Matt. 28:6). Jesus' rebuking word effects exorcisms (Mark 1:25) and calms the storm (Mark 4:39). Repeatedly he heals people of diseases merely by announcing the cure and proclaiming the forgiveness of sins.

For the apostle Paul, the word that Jesus *is* makes that authority essential for our salvation (Rom. 10:8–13). That word is near us at all times, and the content of that word is the confession that Jesus is Lord and that God raised him from the dead.

Pairing the lesson from Isaiah 44:6–8 with Matthew 13:24–30 (36–43) for the Ninth Sunday after Pentecost (or Proper 11, Year A) does little to enhance the meaning of Isaiah's powerful sermon. Jesus' parable about the sower and his allegorical explanation of its meaning stand on their own as a profound teaching about the Kingdom of God among us: weeds and wheat growing together. Perhaps the preacher will do well to choose one or the other as the pericope on which to base a sermon.

Isaiah 61:10–62:3

Revised Common Lectionary, Year B, Christmas 1

Lutheran Book of Worship, Years ABC, Christmas 2

Book of Common Prayer, Year A, Christmas 1

I. Establishing a Working Text

In the third and fourth lines of 61:10 the translations appear at first glance merely to use synonyms in their rendering, but the impact of the words selected might lead to different understandings of the verse. The RSV, NRSV, and NIV render the clothing in the bicolon as "garments of salvation//the robe of righteousness." The NEB and JB retain "salvation" in the third line but change "righteousness" to "integrity" in the fourth. The NAB likewise uses "salvation" in the third line but sets in parallel "justice." A comparison of the translations thus raises the questions whether the words "righteousness," "integrity," and "justice" are really synonyms and whether they are adequate translations of the Hebrew word.

In 61:11 some of the same differences occur. The RSV, NRSV, NEB, and NIV translate "righteousness and praise," while the NAB renders the combination "justice and praise," and the JB offers "integrity and praise."

At 62:1 the speaker vows to speak on behalf of Zion/Jerusalem until there breaks forth "vindication//salvation" (RSV, NRSV), "vindication//victory" (NAB), "righteousness//salvation" (NIV), "right//deliverance" (NEB), or "integrity//salvation" (JB). Once again the renderings of the Hebrew words raise the question whether all these are synonyms or intentional variations in meaning.

The dilemma continues in 62:2 where the nations will see "your vindication" (RSV, NRSV, NAB), "your righteousness" (NIV), "your integrity" (JB), or "the triumph of your right" (NEB).

2. Setting in Life

Chapters 56–66 of the Book of Isaiah are assigned to still another anonymous prophet, one we call Third Isaiah. The situation gleaned from these chapters is neither that of the eighth century (the time of Isaiah of Jerusalem) nor the exilic period (the time of Second Isaiah). Rather we have in these chapters a series of proclamations to the people who had returned to Jerusalem after the Edict of Cyrus in 538 B.C. and also to the people who had been living in Jerusalem and its surroundings during the time the others had been in exile.

Within these eleven chapters, 60–62 are generally agreed to provide the nucleus of the preaching of Third Isaiah. There is less scholarly agreement on the material surrounding that core of three chapters. When did the preaching of this nucleus material occur? What were the circumstances that prompted it?

Very shortly after the Edict of Cyrus some of the exiles returned to Jerusalem and quickly began the reconstruction of the temple. After they laid the foundation, however, the work stopped, primarily for economic reasons (see Ezra 5:14–17). Thanks to the ascendancy of Darius as king of the Persian Empire, work on the temple was resumed in 520 and completed in 515 B.C.

According to Isaiah 60:13, the temple had not yet been built when that text was composed. The lumber for its construction was yet to be transported from Lebanon. That little note helps us set the nucleus of Third Isaiah somewhere between 537 and 520 B.C.

The historical and economic situations of the time were dismal, to say the least. The walls of the city were not yet rebuilt; the temple where many had been employed in the good old days was still a heap of ruin. The folks returning from exile had anticipated living in their ancestral homes, but they found that others had occupied those homes during the long sojourn in Babylon. Unemployment percentages went off the scale, and in order to survive and keep their families alive, people resorted to theft and, as a result, ended up in prison.

The theological dilemma behind all that instability was the question about the promise of God. Second Isaiah had told them back in Babylon that Yahweh's return (and theirs) to Jerusalem would signal the beginning of the Reign of God (see Isa. 52:7–10). The expectations connected with that Day of Yahweh pointed the people's hearts and minds to a time when suffering would be turned to its opposite (see the discussion of Isa. 35 above). Their experience of returning home, however, brought everything the Reign of God was not supposed to be: homelessness, poverty, illness, imprisonment, starvation, insecurity.

Into this situation of despair Yahweh called the prophet Third Isaiah. His call was to bring good news to the poor, healing to the brokenhearted, liberty to the captives, release to the prisoners, and comfort to those who mourn. In essence, he was indeed to proclaim the Day of the Lord — not as accomplished but about to appear (61:1–4). His message was that all the signs of despair would be turned into their opposites. His message was filled with "instead of" and "no more" suffering and oppression. In their places Yahweh would provide peace and security. Third Isaiah's purpose in announcing those transformations was to provide the people with hope, and so his preaching, like that of his predecessor, Second Isaiah, consisted of one message of salvation after another.

3. Literary Matters

The difficulties raised in the comparison of translations above are not easily solved. Essentially, the problems center on the translation of the word *ṣedeq/ṣᵉdāqâ*. In these verses it is rendered as "righteousness," "vindication," "right," "integrity," and "justice." The word is used in synonymous parallelism twice with "salvation" (*yeshaʿ/yᵉshûʿâ*), once with "glory" (*kābōd*), and once in combination with "praise" (*tehillâ*).

The interpreter would benefit from a reading of Gerhard von Rad's discussion of "righteousness" in his *Old Testament Theology.*[44] For von Rad, *ṣᵉdāqâ* is essentially the fulfillment of the obligations of a relationship. That fulfillment takes specific actions of loyalty, and so in reference to God the word often refers to an act of salvation. Indeed, in the preaching of Second Isaiah, the word comes to mean "victory" and is often so rendered in synonymous parallelism with *yᵉshûʿâ* (salvation).

Likewise the discussion of the terms *mišpāṭ* and *ṣᵉdāqâ* by Klaus Koch[45] will further assist the interpreter in understanding the relationship between the two words usually translated "justice" and "righteousness," respectively. In a nutshell Koch suggests that *mišpāṭ* means "the positive order of existence *per se,*" while *ṣᵉdāqâ* means "the spontaneous act in favor of an ordinance of *mišpāṭ.*"

The use of "justice" by the NAB to render *ṣᵉdāqâ* gives the impression that the Hebrew word is *mišpāṭ,* and so that rendering has less appeal than the others. However, the translations "righteousness," "vindication," "triumph of your right," and "integrity" are serious attempts to translate the word in ways that are appropriate for Yahweh and for the people. What is important, no matter which words are selected, is to realize that the salvation and righteousness of which the passage speaks are derived terms: that is, Israel has salvation and righteousness/integrity/vindication only by the action of Yahweh. It is only because Yahweh has acted or will act that Israel can experience integrity and vindication.

The imagery of "bridegroom" and "bride" in 61:10 might point to the marriage analogy used often in the Hebrew Bible to describe the covenant relationship between Yahweh and Israel (especially prominent in Hosea and Jeremiah; also used eschatologically at Rev. 21:2, 9, where the bride is the heavenly Jerusalem). In any case, the wedding adornment here portrays the utter joy at being clothed by Yahweh in salvation/righteousness. In its present context the imagery also points forward to 62:4, where the new name by which Israel's land will be called is "Married," and to 62:5, where the Lord will rejoice over Israel as a bridegroom exults over his bride.

4. The Criticisms

Part of the difficulty in examining this pericope is the division of the material between 61:10 and 62:3. The first part (61:10–11) is a brief song of praise that an interpreter would expect to conclude the previous unit. In Second and Third Isaiah such little statements of praise generally represent a believer's acceptance of the message proclaimed immediately prior to it. To begin the pericope with such a song places at the forefront the believer's acceptance rather than the announcement of God's promised action. The issue becomes even more complicated when the interpreter tries to determine the function of 61:11, for the promise about the people seems to connect the verse to 61:9.

As for the selection of the first three verses of chapter 62, the interpreter is left somewhat frustrated by the fact that the images in these verses cease abruptly at the end of verse 3, and the expected continuation of thought disappears. In verse 2, for example, the people are promised a "new name." Yet without verse 4 we do not know that the name will be "My delight" and that the land will be called "Married." Further, the first person refusal to "not keep silent" and "not rest" of verse 1 loses something of its impact without the corresponding insistence by the "watchmen" and the "remembrancers" of verses 6–7.

Form-critically, the passage beginning at 62:1 appears to be a proclamation of salvation, and the terminology and structure used here call to mind a community lament that is being transformed or reversed.

During the exilic period the community lament played a particularly significant role in the life of the people. It was a form in which the people could offer to Yahweh their despair, their feelings of God-forsakenness, their dwindling hopes, and yet their expectation that Yahweh should and could do something to relieve them of their oppression. The laments, such as Psalms 74 and 89, set the case before Yahweh; asked the customary "Why?" and pleaded to know "how long" God's silence would continue; and prodded God to "remember" and "not forget" the people and their past history as God's people.

While the time of exile was one of Yahweh's silence (even by God's admission at Isa. 42:14), the new period will be one in which the prophet, the watchmen, and the remembrancers will not allow God to remain silent. They themselves will not keep silent, not allow God any rest, "until" (the reverse of "How long?") God keeps the promises. So certain is the prophet that God will eventually weary of their protest and respond accordingly that he announces beforehand *God's* righteousness and salvation and the results for the people — new name, crown of beauty, praise, and celebration.

The sequence of the protest rising from the individual prophet to the watchmen and on to the remembrancers calls to mind the sequence of the acclamation "God is king!" at 52:7–10. There the "messenger" with the beautiful feet begins on the mountaintop, followed by the "watchmen" on the walls, and then the crescendo bursts open from the "waste places" of Jerusalem. There "all the ends of the earth shall see the salvation of our God" (52:10), while in our pericope "the nations shall see your righteousness, and all the kings your glory" (62:2).

5. Interpretive Rendering

The following is an interpretive rendering of the passage:

> In my utter confidence in the Lord's promises I will sing in advance joyful songs. Indeed the Lord has already clothed me with victory and the act that will accomplish that victory; I feel like a couple on their wedding day, dressed up in anticipation of the vows of commitment.
>
> For years in exile we sang our songs of lament, asking God why we suffer in silence and wondering how long we must bear God's absence. Now, though we have been delivered from Babylon, God's promise still eludes us. And so if God is silent, I will not be. I will hound God day and night for the sake of Jerusalem until we experience the fulfillment of that promise when we are no longer Forsaken but Wed to God forever. When that happens, the whole world will know what God has done for us. Maybe they'll even throw rice.

6. Theologies of the Passage

Concentrating on the initial verses of chapter 62 in light of the entire chapter and considering the "situation of the people" in which God acts or will act, the summary might be expressed as follows: *In complete confidence in the Lord's promise to bring salvation and righteousness for the people, the prophet commits himself and others to unceasing intercession until the Lord fulfills the promise of the coming Reign.*

Such a summary sentence, to be sure, does not use God as the subject of the sentence, and in that respect conflicts with the formula I have suggested throughout this book. Yet, to be honest to the pericope, the "I" is not God but the prophet, and as announcer of the coming action of God and simultaneously as God's petitioner, the prophet is the major speaker in these verses.

His message is founded, however, not on his own wishful thinking; neither is the hope he offers to the people the machination of his own mind. Rather God's promise of a divine Reign of peace and security compels him at this point to take up his position not as God's spokesperson to the people but as the people's spokesperson to Yahweh. The role of intercessor is throughout the Bible a major function of a prophet (see above all Gen. 20:7; Jer. 14:19–22; Amos 7:1–3).

In the *Revised Common Lectionary* the pericope is linked with Luke 2:22–40, the story of the infant Jesus in the temple before Simeon and then Anna. Simeon had spent his life "looking for the consolation of Israel," and Anna "spoke of him to all who were looking for the redemption of Jerusalem." The words of Third Isaiah "*until* her righteousness goes forth as brightness" and "*until* he establishes Jerusalem" chime loudly here, for the prophet's expectant "until" has become in Jesus "now."

The *Book of Common Prayer* and the *Lutheran Book of Worship* use John 1:1–18 as the Gospel corresponding to our pericope. The entire message about the eternal word of God becoming flesh and dwelling among us seems to provide the Gospel's "now" for the "until" of the prophecy. In addition, however, such themes as light/brightness and glory might also provide connections for preaching from these pericopes.

In any case, the lesson from Isaiah 61:10–62:3 focuses our attention on the utter confidence, even brazenness, believers can have in the promises of God. While we always need to distinguish between what God actually promised and our own needs and desires, the commitment of God to bring salvation and peace can offer comfort to people of any time and place, including our own.

Jeremiah 20:7–13

Revised Common Lectionary, Year A, Proper 7 [12]

Lutheran Book of Worship, Cycle A, Pentecost 5

Book of Common Prayer, Year A, Proper 7

I. Establishing a Working Text

Differences among the translations of this pericope indicate degrees of intensity and passion rather than substance. The major divergences occur in the first verse where Jeremiah laments the action of Yahweh that has led to the prophet's rejection and despair. In verse 7 the RSV and NIV agree on "You have deceived me, and I was deceived"; the NEB and NAB translate "duped," as though the Lord operated a sting; the NRSV moves toward an allurement with "enticed," and the JB blurts out "seduced" as though Yahweh were guilty of statutory rape on this young man.

In verse 9 an interesting difference occurs in Jeremiah's admission of wanting to cease prophesying. The RSV, NRSV, NIV, and NAB translate in such a way that the desire to desist continues: "If I say" or "I say to myself." However, the JB and NEB give the impression that having had that wish in vain, Jeremiah has come to accept the task Yahweh has laid on him: "When I said" (NEB) or "I used to say" (JB).

The report of the enemies' disparaging words as "Denounce him! Let us denounce him!" in verse 10 is agreed on by most all translations except the NIV, which renders more politely "Report him! Let's report him!" Further in the same verse where the enemies express their plan for the prophet's downfall, they suggest perhaps he will be "deceived" (RSV, NIV), "enticed" (NRSV), "seduced into error" (JB), "trapped" (NAB), or "tricked" (NEB). The first three possibilities indicate correctly that the Hebrew verb used here is the same as that at the beginning of verse 7. The NAB and NEB lose that connection by translating the verb differently.

The description of Yahweh in verse 11 varies from "a dread warrior" (RSV, NRSV) to "a mighty warrior" (NIV), "a mighty hero" (JB), "a mighty champion" (NAB), and on to a more blood-curdling "strong and ruthless" (NEB). In verse 12 Yahweh is defined further in the second person as "you" who "triest the right-eous, who seest the heart and mind" (RSV; also see NRSV), "test the righteous and search the depths of the heart" (NEB), "test the just, who probe mind and heart" (NAB), "examine the righteous and probe the heart and mind" (NIV), and "probe with justice, who scrutinize the loins and heart" (JB). An interpreter does well to pay attention to such differences in the ways in which God is described, because answering the question "What is God doing here?" might well depend on the precise words used for God's nature and action.

Finally, in the brief song of praise that concludes our peric-ope (v. 13) we are left with the question whether Yahweh "has delivered/rescued" (RSV, NRSV, JB, NAB) or whether Yahweh con-tinually "rescues" (NIV, NEB) the poor from their affliction. Is the song, in other words, praising Yahweh for having delivered this particular petitioner (Jeremiah) from his distress or for delivering anyone in such circumstances?

2. Setting in Life

Jeremiah was called to be a prophet early in life (1:6). If we can trust the superscription to the book, this call occurred in the thir-teenth year of the reign of Josiah over Judah. That detail would place the prophet's call at about 627 B.C. The superscription indi-cates further that Jeremiah's ministry continued through the reign of Jehoiakim (609–598 B.C.) and up until the eleventh year of Zedekiah (i.e., 587 B.C.).

From the time of Jeremiah's call until the death of Josiah in 609 B.C., the hopes of the people in the land were riding high. Josiah was carrying out religious and political reforms that seemed headed toward reestablishing the glories of the Davidic-Solomonic period. The diminishing of the strength of Assyria during those earlier years and its demise in 612 B.C. contributed to Josiah's early successes, but his own purification of the temple and the centralization of worship there attest to his leadership ability.

Josiah's sudden death at the hands of Pharaoh Necho in Megiddo dashed the hopes that were skyrocketing over Judah. Jehoiakim was not the equal of his father, and instead of Assyrian supremacy over their lives, Judah had to contend with the power of Egypt (until 605 B.C.) and then with the might of the Neo-Babylonian Empire.

Part of the legacy Josiah left behind was the renewed confidence in the Jerusalem temple. The old tradition about Zion's invincibility played an important role in the preaching of the prophet Isaiah a century before Jeremiah.

The confidence in the city and its temple engendered during Josiah's reforms left no room for the kind of preaching to which Jeremiah was called: "to pluck up and to break down, to destroy and to overthrow, to build and to plant" (1:10). Jeremiah's plucking sermons delivered in the temple precincts (chaps. 7 and 26) and other proclamations around town did not exactly qualify the prophet for the Mr. Congeniality contest. In fact, they led to his being ostracized from the community and eventually to an attempt to execute him.

3. The Criticisms

The difficulty in setting this pericope into the life and times of Jeremiah lies in its *form* as an individual lament. One need only study such laments (e.g., Pss. 4; 5; 6; 10) to realize there is nothing particularly unique in these verses to attribute them specifically to Jeremiah's situation. Such a realization warns us to take care that we do not psychologize the prophet on the basis of these stereotypical expressions. Therefore, while we discuss the pericope as a saying of Jeremiah, we do so with the precaution that he might not have uttered these precise words.[46]

On the other hand, the narrative material in the book describes the utter contempt the people had for his preaching. He had, after all, attacked the "sacred cow" by announcing the judgment of God and the ensuing destruction of the city and its temple. He was convicted on trumped up charges and sentenced to death, only to be rescued to a dungeon. In light of his experience one could imagine he uttered laments, probably those known to him from the Psalter, although he might have known or composed others, including this one.

Like many such laments, our pericope ends with a song of praise for the deliverance Yahweh has accomplished for the afflicted one. The bursting into song at the end of a lament reflects the bold confidence that the believer holds in the faithfulness of God; such singing will ultimately be the expression of thanks and praise when the deliverance has been achieved. For such joyful expressions within songs of lament see Psalms 7:17; 10:15–18; 22:22–31.

4. Literary Matters

The opening words, as noted above, are rendered differently among the major translations. The Hebrew *pittîtanî YHWH wāʾeppāt* is probably best translated "You seduced me, O Lord, and I was seduced" (so JB). While the verb means essentially "to be simple," in the *piʿel* form here it can mean "deceive" (2 Sam. 3:25; Prov. 24:28) or "entice" to sin (Prov. 1:10; 16:29). Most dramatically, however, the word can mean "seduce" sexually (Exod. 22:15; Judg. 14:15; 16:5), and indeed is so used figuratively of Yahweh in the description of Yahweh's honeymoon with Israel (Hos. 2:16). Because of the following words, "You have overpowered me," some scholars actually understand the whole expression to describe a rape (metaphorically, of course!). While the idea of Yahweh raping Jeremiah even metaphorically might not appeal to more sensitive ears, Jeremiah himself was not so concerned about offending the Lord with his accusation. Obviously he felt overpowered! Ravaged! His privacy invaded! It would take a lifetime to recover, and he wanted Yahweh to know how he felt.

The complaint that "everyone mocks me" (Heb. *lāʿag*) also occurs in similar circumstances at Psalm 22:8. Like the pericope here, that psalm is an individual lament and reflects the same kind of outrage at Yahweh for the treatment suffered at the hands of those around the afflicted one. The JB's translation of this part of the verse is delightfully descriptive of the attitude behind the lament: "I am a daily laughingstock, everybody's butt."

Jeremiah says his troubles come from proclaiming throughout the city, "Violence and destruction!" (v. 8; Heb. *ḥāmās wāšōd*). Such indeed is the word from the Lord he preached as a warning to Jerusalem (see 6:7). In Habakkuk, too, contemporary of Jeremiah, the expression depicts the coming wrath of God (Hab. 2:17). More than a century earlier Amos cited such "violence and destruction" not as the result of Yahweh's judgment but as the reason for the impending divine doom (Amos 3:10). The combination *ḥāmās wāšōd* describes the activity for which the people will receive judgment at Isaiah 59:6, 7 and that they are called to put aside in favor of justice and righteousness (Ezek. 45:9). Finally, such "violence and destruction" are the conditions that prevail because Yahweh has not yet come to save (Isa. 60:18; Hab. 1:3). When taken all together, what Jeremiah is proclaiming among the people in Jerusalem is the polar opposite of salvation and security.

Strikingly, not only Jeremiah's enemies cause him grief. It is also "every man of my well-being" (v. 10; Heb. *kōl ʾenôš šelômî*). The same expression appears in synonymous parallelism with "allies" and "confederates" at Obadiah 7, where it appears to mean "trusted friends." The rejection of even one's closest friends occurs in the lament of Psalm 41 (v. 9) and later in Jeremiah at 38:22. The frequency of betrayal by one's closest friends in expressions of lament enables us to see the inevitability of desertion by those closest to Jesus, especially when a psalm of lament, Psalm 22, played such an important role in the narratives about the passion of Jesus.

As for the difficulty of knowing whether Jeremiah is still tempted to forget Yahweh and the call to prophesy or whether he "used to" do that, the answer does not come easily. The Hebrew verb form could indicate the problem is a present one, but Hebrew tenses have more to do with whether or not an action is completed. Therefore, what would appear to be a verb indicating present time might simply be describing an incomplete action in the past, thus "I used to . . . " Perhaps more relevant than the tense of the verb here is the recognition that in an individual lament, like that of Psalm 22, the problem that afflicts the person is still present. Otherwise there is no need for the lament. The context of the expression in this form, therefore, leads me to prefer the ongoing nature of Jeremiah's complaint: "I say to myself . . . "

In light of this judgment on the basis of form, we might also recognize the tense of the verb in the song of praise of verse 13. Since the user of the lament sang this song in advance of his/her deliverance and would use it again when the crisis had passed, the announcement "He has delivered" seems more appropriate than the generic statement "He rescues the life of the needy."

That God is called in verse 11 a "ruthless warrior" (Heb. *gibbôr ʿārîṣ*) causes several of the translations above to soften the blow by rendering the adjective "mighty." The lighter touch is understandable because the word *ʿārîṣ* is commonly used as a synonym for "wicked" and describes people who fit the billing, not Yahweh. Yet on numerous occasions Yahweh is called a "warrior" (Isa. 10:21; Jer. 32:18), and sometimes the descriptions of God run in a string: "the great God, warrior and awesome" (Deut. 10:17; Neh. 9:32; Heb. *'ēl haggādōl haggibbōr wāhannôrā'*). The final term in the string derives from the verb *yārē'*, meaning "to fear, to be in awe of." Likewise, the verb from which the adjective *'ārîṣ* (ruthless) derives, namely *'āraṣ*, means "to inspire awe." At Psalm 89:8 the two terms for "awesome" appear in synonymous parallelism:

> a God feared (*na'ᵃrāṣ, niph.* participle of *'āraṣ*) in
> the council of the holy ones,
> great and awesome (*wᵉnôrā', niph.* participle of *yārē'*)
> above all that are round about him . . .

The parallelism shows that the words can be identical in meaning and might enable us to translate in our pericope, "The Lord is with me as an awesome warrior." The NEB's "ruthless" might be the most literal translation of the adjective *'ārîṣ*, but in reference to God the term "awesome" might better reflect the awe and dread that accompany the divine presence.

5. Interpretive Rendering

An interpretive rendering of our text might run as follows:

> Lord, I knew when you called me years ago that I was headed for nothing but trouble. You told me then that you would be with me to deliver me! Well, where have you been? I feel like I have been raped by your promise of protection, and like other such victims I don't know if I'll ever get over the trauma and the deceit. You told me to tell everyone in town that you were coming to destroy the city. For a while they were scared. But you never showed! Now they laugh at me, even my best friends, and no one will take me seriously.
>
> I realize that you will have the last word, and that you will be absolutely awesome when you show up to put my persecutors in their place. You have answered my petitions in the past, and so once again I commit my cause to you. So certain am I of your deliverance that I will lead everyone around to join me in singing your praises.

6. Theologies of the Passage

While the pericope is a lament uttered by a human being rather than an address or explicit action of God, the passage — like most laments — assumes a certain understanding of God and expresses it in words of confidence. While at the outset Yahweh is accused of seducing the afflicted one, at the end Yahweh is praised in advance for certain deliverance of the complainant as one of "the needy" (v. 13).

Perhaps such laments or complaints directed to and against God offend modern, sensitive ears. Yet within the life of biblical Israel these laments played such an important role in the life of the people — as community and as individuals — that there are more laments than any other kind of psalm in the Psalter. Their predominance demonstrates the freedom of the people of Israel to lay before God their most intimate thoughts, disappointments, and anger. Is this merely "Jewish argumentation"? Or is it deeper than that? And how does God feel about it?

No one, of course, can psychoanalyze God in order to know whether such complaining offends God or is welcomed. But if we consider what laments such as this one demonstrate, we can imagine how they sound in the ears of God. The complaints couched in the laments indicate clearly how important God is in the lives of people. When the community or the individual howls over God's apparent forsakenness, they are demonstrating how essential God is in their lives. When the complaining party cries out, "How long, O Lord?" he or she is admitting that any length of time without God is unbearable. When worshipers scream that the Lord has seduced them, they are admitting that God has taken over their lives. We can only imagine that God would rather have us complain than live life as though God's absence did not matter.

Further, the Bible records no instance where Yahweh struck down a person who offered a lament. On the contrary, the use of the psalm of praise at the conclusion of most laments leads us to believe that Yahweh has indeed delivered the afflicted one from the crisis. Or at least Yahweh has so consistently delivered lamenters in the past that one in the present can offer such a lament with confidence in God's saving action.

On the basis of these considerations, one way to summarize the passage theologically is as follows: *God responds to the cries for help from the righteous, even when the petitioner considers the major source of the trouble to be God.*

All that has been said above is true no matter who uttered the lament that makes up our pericope. In the context of the Book of Jeremiah, however, the issue about God's role becomes even more pointed. In the first chapter God called Jeremiah to be a prophet, that is, a spokesperson for God to the people of Israel and to the nations round about. Knowing that such a call would only lead to trouble, Jeremiah offered the typical objection. The Lord would not accept the excuse of the youthful man any more than that of Moses or Gideon or anyone else. At the same time, the Lord never said the call would be without trouble. What God promised was obviously not a rose garden but the divine presence: "I will be with you."

The theme of God's call to faithful proclamation without guarantee of personal safety is especially highlighted by the use of Matthew 10 as the Gospel for the day. Having commissioned the twelve disciples to (1) announce the nearness of the Reign of God by (2) casting out spirits and (3) healing every disease and infirmity, Jesus made no bones about the difficulties that awaited them in the hostile world. Since disciples are not above their teacher, they could expect the same kind of abuse that Jesus knew. Yet Jesus promised God's care of them while they underwent the suffering, and so they were to "fear not." In addition, Jesus would be their advocate on the day of judgment.

In light of the troubles that awaited Moses, Gideon, Jeremiah, and the disciples of Christ, one might summarize the passage in this way: *Though God does not promise exemption from suffering to those who are called to God's mission, God does promise through Jesus Christ the presence and care of God through the worst of times, through the rupturing of close human relationships, and through the onslaught of forces hostile to God's Reign.*

Finally, to pick up the theme of the Gospel lesson that "a disciple is not above the teacher," we might also consider Jesus' own use of an individual lament from the cross. Jesus' cry, "My God, my God, why have you forsaken me?" calls to mind the entire psalm of lament (Psalm 22). While Jesus might indeed have had the end in view—the deliverance, the celebration, and the praise—he did at that moment identify with all those who have felt in their suffering that God had deserted them. As Jesus so identified with us in the times of our apparent God-forsakenness, so we come closest to the crucified Christ when we cry out our laments to God about the absence of God in our times of need.

As we identify with Christ's death, so shall we be raised with him to life, and that promise of God is worthy of a song of praise, even here and now.

Ezekiel 18:1–4, 25–32

Revised Common Lectionary, Year A, Proper 21 [26]

Lutheran Book of Worship, Year A, Pentecost 19

Book of Common Prayer, Year A, Proper 21

I. Establishing a Working Text

A comparison of the major English translations reveals some slight variations, some of which affect the understanding of the pericope. In verse 1 only the NAB translates the question Yahweh puts to Ezekiel as implying that Yahweh does not know what the proverb means and is asking for information: "What is the meaning of this proverb . . . ?" All the other translations place the emphasis on Yahweh's bewilderment that the people of Israel keep reciting this proverb: "What do you mean by repeating this proverb . . . ?" The following verses indicate that the NAB's rendering gives a wrong impression.

In verse 4 occurs a variation that may be due simply to style but that can lead readers to quite different impressions.

RSV: "Behold, all souls are mine; the soul of the father as well as the soul of the son is mine; the soul that sins shall die."

NEB: "Every living soul belongs to me; father and son alike are mine. The soul that sins shall die."

NIV: "For every living soul belongs to me, the father as well as the son — both alike belong to me. The soul who sins is the one who will die."

JB: “See now: all life belongs to me; the father’s life and the son’s life, both alike belong to me. The man who has sinned, he is the one who shall die.”

NAB: “For all lives are mine; the life of the father is like the life of the son, both are mine; only the one who sins shall die.”

NRSV: “Know that all lives are mine; the life of the parent as well as the life of the child is mine; it is only the person who sins that shall die.”

The use of the word “soul” in the RSV, NEB, and NIV can lead to the impression that the biblical witnesses believed in the view that a soul inhabits each of our bodies, that is, a body-soul dualism. It is possible, perhaps even likely, that the translators of these editions were using the word “soul” to mean “person,” as in “every last soul at the party had a wonderful time dancing.” The other translations render the Hebrew word to mean “life,” “man,” “person,” “one.”

The accusation against the people in verses 25 and following is that they say the Lord’s ways are “not just” (RSV, NIV), “unjust” (JB), “not fair” (NRSV, NEB), and “without principle” (NEB). The interpreter needs to ask if all these words convey the same meaning in terms of how they are heard by a present-day audience.

In verse 26 the RSV, NRSV, NEB, and NIV render similarly “when a righteous man turns away from his righteousness,” while the JB renders “When the upright man renounces his integrity,” and the NAB offers “When a virtuous man turns from virtue.” The latter two attempt to move away from the word “righteousness” to substitute more contemporary words.

Yahweh orders the people to several actions toward the end of the pericope. One of those is to “get yourselves a new heart and a new spirit” (RSV, NRSV, NIV, NEB). The JB and NAB offer “make (for) yourselves a new heart and a new spirit.” The difference is that the former translation simply asserts the need for the people to *have* new mental and spiritual machinery, but the latter assumes the people of Israel have the ability to *make* it on their own.

2. Setting in Life

According to information supplied in the first paragraph of the Book of Ezekiel, the priest Ezekiel was called by the Lord to be a prophet in 593–592 B.C., the fifth year of the exile of King Jehoiachin. Ezekiel himself was one of the exiles living in the outskirts of Babylon in a community called Tel Aviv (not the present city in Israel). Following the bizarre vision connected with his call, Ezekiel heard Yahweh address him in clear words. The call was to proclaim God's word saying, "Thus says the Lord God" (2:4). Like all other calls to God's mission, this one would not be easy, for the people are "stiff of face and strong of heart," that is, stubborn and adamant.

One of the difficulties Ezekiel had to face among his fellow exiles was the question about why they were there. Obviously spokespersons for God were interpreting the disaster of 597 as God's judgment on their sins. That announcement of judgment had been the core of the preaching of the eighth- and seventh-century prophets. It derived from the old liturgical teaching that God visits "the iniquity of the fathers upon the children to the third and fourth generation of those who hate me" (Exod. 20:5; 34:7; Num. 14:18). The teaching led many of those digging canals for Nebuchadnezzar into a state of hopelessness and cynicism. Like Job, they were suffering but could not understand why. The age-old proverb circulating "in the land of Israel" was one way they could comprehend the tragedy: they were suffering for the sins of their ancestors. The proverb provided an answer, but it was not a satisfactory one: it was not just, and it left them without hope.

The problem alluded to here occurred early in the exile, but it must have continued for some years. It certainly came to a climax when news arrived that "the city has fallen!" (33:21). The destruction of the temple and the entire city was not simply the loss of some architecture. The manner in which the people's sins could be forgiven, the means by which worshipers could be declared "righteous" at the temple's gate, and the way that life could be attained — all were demolished. Is it any wonder the people were becoming despondent and even cynical over the ways of God?

3. Literary Matters

When Yahweh alludes to "this proverb" in verses 2 and 3, we must note that there were other proverbs circulating among the exiles that also needed reinterpreting. At 12:22–23 another proverb laden with pessimism, "The days grow long, and every vision comes to nought," must be replaced with, "The days are at hand, and the fulfillment of every vision." At 16:44 Yahweh cites the proverb, "Like mother, like daughter," but then instead of correcting it, applies it to Israel and her sinfulness. The citing of these proverbs helps us understand the atmosphere among the exiles and the ways in which Yahweh addressed their specific questions and their self-made answers.

The proverb quoted in verse 2, "The parents have eaten sour grapes, and the children's teeth are set on edge," is cited also at Jeremiah 31:29. In that case, however, the context is not a discussion of who suffers for whose sins but an announcement that the restoration of the people to their land and the rebuilding of the devastated ruin will make the proverb obsolete.

As for the problem over "soul" and "life" or "person" in verse 4, the Hebrew word *nepheš* used here means essentially "self" or "person." The term does not specify the Platonic soul, which is separable from the body, but rather represents the whole person, body and all. When God formed the first human out of the dirt, God enlivened the figure by breathing into its nostrils "the breath [Heb. *n^{e}šāmâ*] of life," and the figure then became "a living soul" (*nepheš chayyâ*) (Gen. 2:7). The creation story indicates that humans *are* souls rather than *have* souls, and so the translation of the various forms of *nepheš* in our pericope ought to reflect that understanding of biblical anthropology as unambiguously as possible. In any case, the understanding of the soul that "shall die" (v. 4) makes the dualistic notion impossible.

Whether we should translate the Hebrew word *ṣ^{e}dāqâ* as "righteousness," "uprightness," or "virtue" depends on what we are trying to accomplish. Certainly a contemporary audience hearing the words "uprightness" or "virtue" during a public reading is more apt to comprehend the reading than a similar audience hearing "righteousness." But our concern here is about the interpretation of the passage for preaching. Hebrew *ṣ^{e}dāqâ,* we have seen earlier, belongs in relational situations, having to do with faithful acts within a relationship. "Uprightness" and "virtue," on the other hand, do not necessarily convey the expectation of action within a personal relationship; they might be values based on a set of moral principles or one's individualistic sense of worth.

Whether one "gets" or "makes" a new heart and mind is likewise difficult to determine. The Hebrew word behind the dilemma, *'āsâ,* means primarily "do" or "make," thus the translation of the JB and NAB. However, when the preposition *l* (for) follows the verb as here, it often means "get" or "acquire." For example, at 2 Samuel 15:1 Absalom "got himself (*'āsâ l*) a chariot and horses and fifty men." And at Psalm 107:37 the hungry "sow fields, and plant vineyards, and get (*'āsâ* without the prep. *l*) a fruitful yield." Clearly, neither Absalom nor the hungry make horses, men, or fruitful harvests; they acquire them.

How to decide between the two possibilities cannot, therefore, be resolved on the basis of the word alone. What becomes crucial is the way in which the same author or his contemporaries use the same expression. In this case, Ezekiel uses the "new heart" image elsewhere only at 36:26 where he speaks the promise of God: "A new heart I will give you, and a new spirit I will put within you." Ezekiel's contemporary, Jeremiah, also speaks of Israel's need for a heart transplant: "I will give them one heart and one way, that they may fear me forever" (Jer. 32:39). Yahweh is the donor of Israel's new heart, one that will keep the people righteous before him. A "new heart" is not something the people can make for themselves, but they need to acquire one because the one they have is "hard" (2:4).

The repeated use of "O house of Israel" in verses 25–30 indicates that the Lord is not speaking to a group of individuals but to the people as a whole. Although the prophet is addressing the problem of individual responsibility before Yahweh, he nevertheless understands that the message is for the community, split and splintered though it be. The need for the emphasis on oneness during this exilic period can be seen by the oft-repeated use of this vocative in Ezekiel (20:31, 39, 44; 33:20; 36:22; 44:6) and in Jeremiah (3:20; 5:15; 10:1; 18:6), while elsewhere in the Hebrew Bible the vocative form of the expression appears only six times.

4. The Criticisms

The chapter as a whole contains several forms that combine to make a unified argument. In the material that is omitted from the lectionary, verses 5–24, we have an argument formulated in case law (if a person does this or that, then such will happen). The law type was used, among other ways, for the priests to determine who was sufficiently clean or righteous to enter through the gates of the temple, who could receive forgiveness, and who, therefore, would attain life.[47]

Within the material of our pericope we have two disputation speeches, that is, speeches that respond to and argue with a stated proposition. In verse 2 we have one such proposition, namely, the proverb about the suffering of the children for the parents' sins. The following material refutes the proverb. In verse 25 the people state the proposition that "the way of the Lord is not just," and the remainder of the paragraph refutes that statement by first throwing back on the people the accusation of being "not just" and then arguing for the possibilities for life under Yahweh's system.

The final paragraph of the chapter summarizes the whole and points to Yahweh's invitation to the "house of Israel" to repent and find life.

5. Interpretive Summary

What follows is an interpretive rendering of Ezekiel 18:1–4, 25–32:

> The word of the Lord came to Ezekiel in Tel Aviv where the exiles of Jerusalem had been gathered by Nebuchadnezzar, king of Babylon. God said, "What do you think you are doing, blaming your difficulties here on your parents by citing obsolete proverbs, especially the one that says, 'The parents have eaten sour grapes, and the children's teeth are set on edge'? From now on, this proverb, like some others you're sharing so generously with one another, is taboo. Everybody belongs to me, and I care for every person, and I hold every person responsible for him or her self."
>
> [There follows — in verses 5 to 24 — a long list of case laws regarding the guilt and innocence of individual persons and the entrance to the temple where sins can be forgiven. The Lord then continues:] "How can you people say I am unfair? What is unfair about my arrangement that when the righteous turn away from me, they shall die; and if the unrighteous turn from their evil, they shall live? You are the ones that are unfair.

"So I will judge each of you according to your own ways, not according to the ways of your parents. At the same time, I am offering you the way to life. Accept my invitation for a heart transplant. There's no reason for you to die. That's certainly not my will. My will is for life. Turn to me so that you might live!"

6. Theologies of the Passage

The nature of a disputation speech can give the impression that the entire chapter is argumentative and its results dismal. The people left in the land of Israel and those living in exile earnestly sought to understand what had happened to them as a nation and where they could turn in their despair. Obviously the answers they offered to one another were insufficient, and from Yahweh's point of view they were wrong.

Among other things, they were wrong because the people had been locked in to an understanding of forgiveness and life that was tied to their worship in the temple back in Jerusalem. Entrance through the gate to the temple was the means, they had been taught, to find God's forgiveness and to participate in the life of the Yahweh-worshiping community. Now the exiles had no access to Jerusalem, and in any case there was no longer a temple back there in the city. How could they possibly find life now?

Through Ezekiel, Yahweh came not merely to correct their old proverb but to open their eyes to a new possibility: even without the temple and even apart from Jerusalem, God held out the invitation to life. The life offered could be attained by turning from and casting away transgressions and receiving the new heart and new spirit Yahweh was prepared to give. In that new perspective Yahweh clearly promised forgiveness to those who turn from wickedness, for the concern of God is not for death but for life. That concern is most powerfully heard in Yahweh's plea, "Why will you die, O house of Israel? For I have no pleasure in the death of any one."

As a result of this proclamation in the midst of the exile, the pericope might be summarized in one of the following ways: *Against the view that the sufferings of life can be understood by age-old proverbs, God announces anew that the divine will is for life and not for death.* Or, *Having heard the complaints of the people about divine injustice, God announces that justice has always been and will continue to be administered on the basis of guilt or innocence.* In order to get at the heart of God's forgiveness, one might suggest: *While God executes justice on the basis of guilt and innocence, God delights in wiping away the past when transgressors repent of their evil ways.*

The message about giving up the old way of looking at life and concentrating on something new is picked up again in the second lesson for this day, Philippians 2:1–11. The apostle is there exhorting his readers to have a new and different mind from the rest of the world, a mind modeled on the humility of Christ.

The Gospel lesson from Matthew 21:28–32 relates to God's pleasure in one who, though earlier adamant against his parent, repented and followed the parent's will.

The pericope might serve as a vehicle to address the problem of people searching for simple solutions to difficult questions by repeating what they have heard and learned over the years. Proverbs like "You only get what you deserve" or "God doesn't give us any more than we can bear" or "God is testing you by this suffering" need to be challenged by a larger perspective from biblical theology. This passage from Ezekiel, like other ones in the book, forces us to appreciate the new perspectives that can come when we are willing to allow God's word to dispute with our preconceptions.

Part Three

SERMONS ON SELECTED PERICOPES

The Sermon as Dialogue

A sermon is an assembly of coherent words through which the word of God is proclaimed to a contemporary audience. Far from a lecture about the nature of God or a morality speech on how we should act and think and vote, a sermon is the vehicle through which God confronts people. In that sense the sermon delivered in congregations today is not essentially different from the proclamations of those witnesses of old whose preaching now comprises our canon.

Proclaiming the word of God to the listeners at hand requires focusing on the same two questions that guided us in our examination of the pericopes: (1) What is God doing? (2) What is the situation of the audience — theologically understood — in which God is doing it? Commitment to a three-year lectionary disciplines us to raise those questions over and over again, not only in light of our pet peeves and favorite issues but through the breadth of the Bible's testimony. Yet applying the biblical responses to contemporary issues requires that we understand what is tumbling around in the minds and controlling the lives of people today.

When I served as a parish pastor faced with the task of preaching every Sunday, I found the preparation of sermons both frightening and rewarding. The task was frightening because of the enormous responsibility of engaging daily in dialogue with as many people as possible and trying to interpret theologically their words and nonwords. I did not have the answers from my theological repertoire to resolve their questions about losing a job, losing a loved one through death or divorce, losing their health to sickness and disease. But I did have the responsibility to probe behind their wrestling and struggling to unveil the questions they were raising about God, about God's nature, about God's role in their predicament, and their own guilt, shame, and feelings of unworthiness.

Unveiling the questions about self and about God means participating with others in dialogue. Dialogue is the interchange between two or more persons who take one another seriously. Its goal is not to determine a precise outcome but to provide a relationship of trust in which the participants can make applications to their lives. Dialogue assumes a freedom of expression, an air of hospitality, in which each one may enter into the other's life and provide opportunity for free and authentic expression.

On one level such dialogue is itself therapeutic.[48] It allows persons to crystallize and verbalize thoughts that have been rolling around in their minds and hearts, often during sleepless nights or otherwise lonely meanderings. The freedom to extract some coherence from a jumble of intertwining ramblings and to set that selection into a communicable message provides at the very least a setting in which some self-understanding might occur. To verbalize such intimacies in relationship with another, to respond to another person's verbalization, to interact with another person's thoughts, feelings, and life — this process might present for someone in need a rare opportunity in their lives. In some cases the lack of an opportunity to interact with another in a trusting relationship might have been a major source of a person's suffering.

On another level Christians have the opportunity in dialogue to witness to God's word in a variety of ways. One of those opportunities might involve explaining to another how we have been in a situation similar to his or hers and sharing the ways in which God's word came to us to effect a new attitude, insight, or relationship. Those epiphanies, or "Aha!" experiences, as some people call them, might help the other person apply to his or her life the message and news about God's role in our life. Another way is simply to tell a story from the Bible or somewhere else — a movie, a novel, an article from a weekly news magazine — in such a way that the partner in dialogue might see possibilities for him or her self.

Whatever the manner of engaging in the dialogue, we do well to consider that dialogue can happen only when we do not insist on a certain outcome. The freedom of the dialogue and the freedom of the partners engaged in the dialogue must allow responses, applications, and decisions that are unique to the people in that situation.

What do the dynamics of dialogue have to do with the task of preaching? Three things. First, the Sunday morning sermon is not an isolated event in the preacher's relationship with the congregation, but part of an ongoing dialogue with a given audience. It is one more piece of a relationship that also occurs in daily parish ministry as well as in previous and future sermons. The sermon is part of a conversation that develops through counseling, participating in meetings, social occasions, phone calls, and the give-and-take of teaching situations. What lies behind the meaningful communication is what Reuel Howe cited as a necessary ingredient of the dialogical principle: correlative thinking. The correlation between persons, events, and things and between little meaning and ultimate meanings enables two or more persons to communicate on a significant level.[49]

Second, the sermon itself, while delivered as a monologue (that is, the preacher is the only one speaking), takes into account all that the preacher has heard and seen from her or his listeners during ministry among them. The preacher prepares the sermon with conversations and situations in mind and directs the word to the congregants' questions and strugglings. Like the biblical preaching of old, the sermon today is not generic but focused on a known audience from whom the preacher can expect nods of affirmation, frowns of disagreement, and sighs of comfort.

Third, what makes the Sunday morning presentation a sermon is its function as a set of words through which God enters into dialogue with the people. That dialogue, we have already seen, results in God's addressing the listener as law or as gospel, that is, in judgment or in grace. Like the dialogue within a human-human relationship, the outcome of this divine-human encounter cannot always be determined in advance.

How can we set the stage for such dialogue to occur in a sermon? Preachers often begin by telling a first person story. The method has the advantage of enabling the listeners to identify with the predicament the preacher went through, and that identification might assist the listeners in applying the message to themselves. One danger with this method, as I have often experienced it both from the point of view of speaker and of listener, is that the first person attention-getter goes on and on and on, leaving the listener with bewilderment about what it all means for him or her and with doubt about whether there is any reason to listen further. A sense of urgency can get lost in the opening first person narration, and once that tuning-out occurs, the preacher has difficulty getting the audience back to his or her wave length. A second danger is giving the listeners the impression that the speaker's recounting of a personal experience might not be authentic. Any suspicion that the preacher is fabricating an experience in order to make a point or simply to entertain throws an immediate barrier in the way of fruitful dialogue.

Personally, I prefer to listen to a speech — sermon or otherwise — that begins by telling me in a sentence or two why I ought to listen. I need to know at the outset that the speaker has something important to tell me, and I will lose out if I let my mind wander. After that initial sense of urgency is established, then first person narratives and retelling the biblical story have a better chance of holding my attention simply because they are now set within a context that is important to me.

Beginnings are one way to enter into the dialogue of a sermon. Another way is the use of pronouns. When we are speaking about sinfulness or the effects of sinfulness — theologically about God's judgment — the use of "you and I" as subjects and "you and me" as objects can contribute to the dialogical character of the sermon. These pronouns enable the listeners to see that we preachers are in the same predicament as the people in the pews and are publicly acknowledging that we share in humanity's sinfulness with them and everyone else. The "you and I/me" accomplishes that dialogical identification much better than a generic "we" and "us" (which sometimes sounds like an aloof editorial). Such identification of the preacher with the audience is part of the correlative principle.

When proclaiming God's grace and forgiveness, however, we do best to give it away, throw it out for public consumption: God loves *you!* We preachers know the love of God is for us, too, but in the proclamation of God's word to others, we must let the audience hear unequivocally that the gospel is for them! When we speak the good news, we are primarily God's agents acting for the sake of others, bringing the comfort of God into their lives. Taking some of that for ourselves might get in the way of the hearers' ability to receive this special gift for them.

A third method for framing a dialogue is the structuring of the sermon. How do we outline the story from the biblical pericope, the theological meaning derived from our exegesis, an analysis of the contemporary scene, and the means by which the audience can apply all that to their own lives? Admittedly, I myself have become entrenched in one particular formula for constructing the outline (my own lack of creativity will show in the following sermons). Basically, my sermons start with a one- or two-sentence introduction that tells the audience why it is important they listen. Then I talk about the problem we'll be dealing with, how its symptoms rear their ugly heads in our society and how they reflect our brokenness with God. From that point I move into the same problem — theologically understood — by describing the situation behind the biblical story (our pericope for the day). Once I am involved in the telling of the biblical story, I continue with it, telling the response of God to that situation long ago. Finally, I try to demonstrate how that same theological response provides a setting in which we might make similar applications to our own lives.

This framework can easily be outlined as follows:

Introduction: What is the sermon about?

I. What is the situation?

- A. Now
- B. Then (in biblical times)

II. What is God doing?

- B. Then (in biblical times)
- A. Now

The structure can contribute to dialogue in the sense that it starts with where the people are (on the basis of our reading of society, human nature, local concerns) and helps them identify with the people of biblical times. The sermon ends with where they are, too — forgiven, accepted, challenged — or with where God is sending them at this moment. Ending in such a way is an invitation to further dialogue because the people, having been engaged, will want to seek deeper meaning and application of the message with us and with other people, even family and friends. Between the beginning and the end (the *now*), the biblical story remains intact. Our use of the pericope to provide the message of God's word enables the audience to see that we have supplied for them not merely our own opinion about the situation at hand but a fundamental promise from the canon of faith.

The dialogical aspect of preaching combined with the integrity of the biblical message means, of course, that some sermons will tend to convey more judgment than comfort. If we take seriously that God's word confronts people as law or gospel, then we must not shirk from the responsibility of proclaiming that divine law. In our world where it seems "anything goes," we must announce the claims God lays on us both as human creatures and as baptized

Christians. Failure to do so will only allow the audience to find other gods who will surely assert different claims and lead them to further chaos. That's one side of the challenge.

And here's the other. So many people sitting in our congregations today are broken human beings. They experience so much pain we can barely fathom it, even if we have heard and seen pieces of it while providing pastoral care. Their sufferings are complicated by their involvement in a web of complex issues, each one intertangled with many others. When I look from a pulpit at the audience and see the agonies written on their faces, I recall the words from the king in Shakespeare's *Hamlet:* "When sorrows come, they come not single spies, but in battalions."

Facing people whose lives are such a web of brokenness and loss, I often consider as my task to interpret their suffering as a result of humanity's sin rather than further to accuse them of sinfulness or warn them of its consequences. They are already overwhelmed with the consequences of sinfulness. What they/we often need is a perspective that enables them/us to realize *why* we all suffer so, *why* we feel guilty, *why* we can't get specific answers to each tragedy, and then to seek the grace and forgiveness and guidance of God.

All that I have said here confirms that preaching in our contemporary world is at least as challenging and frightening as it was in the days of Jeremiah, Paul, the author of Daniel, and the author of the Book of Revelation. Where, then, is the reward for participating in this awesomely responsible task?

Perhaps the only reward lies in the opportunity to serve as God's instrument of reconciliation. The opportunity to give away the gospel of Jesus Christ makes the task of preaching rewarding. It allows the dialogue between God and the listener to continue. And continue it must! For the message itself is the power that can change lives, even our own as we dialogically prepare and deliver the word:

> By dialogue we can let God into our world because in dialogue we open ourselves to one another, and in so doing, we open ourselves to God.... Miracles have to happen. But they are forged out of everyday events, the happenings between persons: the conflicts, failures, misunderstandings and tragedies of living together, as well as out of the love and acceptance that are both the source and the environment for the working of the miracles of dialogue.[50]

The following sermons are offered not because they represent miracles of preaching but because they illustrate how for this preacher the theology and hermeneutics of part 1 and the exegeses in part 2 eventually worked their way into the pulpit. None of these sermons was prepared with the intention of submitting it for publication. Rather they were all attempts to address listening (hopefully) audiences between 1990 and 1995 with the word of God in terms of the situations in which the people lived, at least, in my analysis.

Genesis 50:15–21

Seventeenth Sunday after Pentecost (Year A)

Getting all tangled up in the struggles and agonies of life can prevent both you and me from getting a grip on what's happening. Often it's only when we look back on such times, like Monday morning quarterbacks, that we can comprehend what this or that struggle was all about.

Looking back — we call it "retrospect" — can change our view of things. We can get a clearer image when we look at things in retrospect.

When I read this or that biography of Wolfgang Amadeus Mozart, I can hardly believe that he wasn't recognized in his own time to be the unequalled genius he is considered to be today. He struggled to make a living. He desperately wanted to be admired and revered by people other than his closest friends and the citizens of Prague. But it wasn't until this century, two hundred years after he lived, that Mozart has become the favorite composer of many throughout the world. Only in this century could the famous theologian Karl Barth say, "Whether the angels play only Bach in praising God, I am not quite sure. I am sure, however, that within the family they play Mozart." Where was Barth when Mozart needed him? Not yet living, of course. But retrospect had given Barth a new appreciation of Mozart's genius.

The same is true of Vincent van Gogh, a reject from the seminary, a rejected lover, a peculiar individual remembered by some only for cutting off his ear. In retrospect his paintings have become invaluable — no one would reject them today — and a popular composer of songs sings to Vincent that "the world was never meant for one as beautiful as you." Where was Don McClean when van Gogh needed him? Not yet alive, of course. But there again is the advantage of retrospect.

Retrospect enables us to put a number of things in perspective. Things that are incomprehensible at the moment. Tragedies that confuse us and virtually paralyze us from making the next move. Loved ones die all too suddenly and unexpectedly. Marriages end abruptly, sometimes with no real understanding of what had happened. Children contract illnesses and diseases and suffer at the abusive hands of adults. Spouses and parents become incapacitated.

How can we bring perspective to some of the tragedies that overwhelm our lives? How can retrospect help?

Our lesson from the Book of Genesis brings the Joseph story to a conclusion. Thirteen chapters that eventually made it to Broadway come to a focus in our lesson. It's the retrospective view of what the whole story was about.

At the beginning of the story Joseph was a seventeen-year-old dreamer. He was extremely unpopular with his brothers because, for one thing, he was his father's favorite, and he flaunted in front of their eyes his father's gift of a beautiful robe with long sleeves. All that his brothers had to wear were Levis and short-sleeved shirts that read "My father went to Bethel, and all I got was this lousy T-shirt." And Joseph didn't endear himself to his brothers either by telling them of his dream that one day he would rule over them.

To make matters even worse, Joseph sat at home watching TV while his brothers worked out in the fields, caring for Dad's flock. No reader of the story is surprised to learn that one day, when Father asked little Joe to check up on his working brothers, "they plotted to kill him." They made their plan quickly as he sauntered over the hills, flopping his long sleeves in the breeze. And then they greeted him by stripping off his robe and throwing him in a pit to die. While they were munching on lunch a caravan came by, and the entrepreneurial spirit moved them to sell their brother as a slave.

The poor guy ended up in the service of a military man named Potiphar. The slave worked his way up to a position of some authority over the household, but Mrs. Potiphar took a fancy to her good-looking slave. Though Joseph was the perfect gentleman, he was thrown into prison for allegedly messing with the boss's wife.

You see how Joseph suffers one agony after another, and it is always the greed and jealousy and plots and suspicions of others that keep him in trouble. Where was God when Joseph needed him?

Back in prison Joseph so impressed the jailer that he was put in charge of all the other prisoners. Now we get a clue from the writer's advantage of retrospect. "The Lord was with him; and whatever he did, the Lord made it prosper" (39:23).

It turned out that the pharaoh's butler and baker ended up under Joseph's custody in that prison. They were dreamers, too. Joseph interpreted their dreams, and eventually word of his skill reached the pharaoh, who was also a dreamer. When Joseph interpreted the king's dream, he was able to avert a disaster in the land. And so he ended up in a most prestigious position, second in the land only to pharaoh himself.

As you know, the long-lost brothers came to Egypt for food. They ended up dealing with the Food Minister, who — unbeknownst to them — was their brother. There were some trips back and forth to father Jacob, and he, too, though ill, came to Egypt at Joseph's request. The old patriarch died there, and afterward the brothers came to Joseph asking for his forgiveness of the deed they had done to him years before.

Joseph responded to their request with these words of comfort and assurance: "As for you, you meant harm against me, but God made your harm turn out for good, so that many people should be kept alive, as they are today."

There it is in a nutshell. It all comes down to this sentence. Thirteen chapters make the same point as some single proverbs: "The plans of the mind belong to mortals, but the answer of the tongue is from the Lord." Or another: "Many are the plans in the human mind, but it is the purpose of the Lord that will be established."

Remember the beginning of our long story? The brothers "plotted against him to kill him," but the Lord made it work "to "keep many people alive."

Only in retrospect could Joseph see that in the midst of all the agonies of life, the ones brought about by his own ostentation and the sins of others, God was at work making good — accomplishing life instead of the intended death.

There's a lesson to be learned here. We often hear people say about a tragedy, "It was the will of God." But it is not! It is not God's will that this child get caught in a cross fire between drug dealers and police. It is not the will of God that this stalwart member of the community dies before he turns fifty, or that this marriage end, or that this person become incapacitated by a stroke. God's will is for life, "to keep alive," not death and disaster.

And yet when those tragedies come, as they surely will, God can, and often does, work good. A friend of mine, a Native American, saw four of his brothers die violently — all as a result of drugs and alcohol. He himself has never touched a drop of alcohol or tried any chemical substances. He has instead devoted his life to working at a rehab center for addicted people. He realizes that God did not cause the deaths of his brothers, but he sees that God has worked *through* their deaths to bring him into a position where he can help others find life.

The story can be told over and over again. You might have already seen it happen in your life. I have in mine. Perhaps not enough time has passed so that you are able, as Joseph was, to see that God can work good out of the evils of life.

But two things are sure. First, neither you nor I can determine in advance what God might do through this or that tragedy. It took Joseph years before he could see it clearly. We can only put our pain-filled lives in the loving care of God, and let God work.

And this is second: God is never stymied by the disasters that occur in human life. God's power is far greater than our powerlessness, and God uses that power for life.

The God who saw the sinfulness of the world crucify Jesus Christ is the one who raised him from the dead. The Gospels say about the religious authorities what the author of the Joseph story said about the brothers: "They plotted against him, to kill him." But God made their evil work out for good, the ultimate good, resurrection from the dead. The gift of life out of the relentless grasp of death. That's the God whom we worship. And that's the God in whom we put our trust.

We can't *see* God at work, but we can use retrospect. And when we do, we can eventually acknowledge in faith what God has done to work good out of the worst of things that happen to us.

2 Samuel 7:1–11, 16

Fourth Sunday in Advent (B)

It's religious to ask what we can do for God. And it's not a bad question. But more important from the Bible's point of view is to ask: What does God do for us?

Sounds like something John F. Kennedy said at his inauguration in 1960. You remember it, I'm sure. "Ask not what your country can do for you. Ask what you can do for your country." The line caught on. It called for a commitment, and it offered the invitation to people of all ages to become involved in a variety of activities, including the Peace Corps.

That was good. Unquestionably good!

A few years ago I was asked to provide some theological reflection to a group of bankers and investors who had been brought together by a nationwide church group to pool their expertise. As they publicly introduced themselves, one after another expressed delight at having been asked to do something for their church. Many lamented they had never before been invited to contribute their expertise and until now had felt left out. Now they were given their chance.

And that was good. Unquestionably good!

We all like to be doing something — something useful to someone else, something helpful to persons in need, something that's pleasing to God. "We don't like to be idle," many retired folks say to me. "We want to feel useful." And so, retired or not, we contribute our time to prepare and serve food at the Food Pantry. We exercise our bodies to keep in condition. We volunteer for this or that community or church activity. We earn our salaries to provide for our families.

And that is good. Unquestionably good!

I know that, like me, some of you feel a tinge of guilt (or an accusation of idleness) when you sit still long enough to read a book or just to think. I remember reading an article several years ago about Abraham Lincoln. It began by recounting the mystery that surrounded Lincoln during his years as a congressman in the 1840s. His peers couldn't figure him out. He didn't drink or use tobacco or bet or swear. Finally, they discovered how he was spending his time: in the library. "Bah!" said his fellow congressmen, "he is a book worm!" The implication, of course, is that it's a waste of time to be sitting around reading. He should be out there doing something.

The human desire to be doing something is unquestionably good.

But at this time of year we do well to sit back and see that it's God who is the doer.

The year was just around 1000 B.C. David was comfortably in control of his domain. He was occupying the palace of the former ruler of Jerusalem, some unknown Jebusite king. He got to this throne by his own hard work and ingenuity, by manipulating military and political forces. He must have been popping the buttons off his royal shirt as he thought about all he had done. Ever since he imbedded that stone into Goliath's Philistine forehead, he had been on a roll. But what could he do now that he had made it big?

As he jogged aimlessly through the corridors of his beautiful palace situated high on the steep slope of Jerusalem, the realization of what he could do next shot him like a thunderbolt. He could do something for the Lord! He could build God a temple. Quickly he ran to his court prophet, Nathan, and told him his plan. "It's not right," David panted, "that I'm occupying a house of cedar while God is stuck out on that windy hill in a tent. I want to build God a house!"

"Go for it!" Nathan said — exactly what you'd expect from a religious person. And the matter was settled.

But only until Nathan tried to sleep that night. God came right there into his bedroom and instructed Nathan to tell David to scratch the whole idea. "Why should he build me a house? I've been camping out in a tent for almost three hundred years now, ever since the time I brought the people out of Egypt. I like camping — the fresh air, the songs of birds, roasting marshmallows on the open fire. You tell David that he will not build a house for me. I'll build one for him. That house will be a dynasty, and it will last forever. One Davidic king after another will be born to rule the people."

You see what happened here? David felt the need to do something for God; it was only right, after all. It made him feel useful; it was even religious. But God intervened. God ruled David's plan out of order. God would build for David a family tree out of which would be born a thousand years later the Davidic king par excellence.

All that David could say to this sudden reversal of the game plan was this: "Who am I, O Lord God, and what is my house, that you have brought me so far? . . . And now, O Lord God, confirm forever the word which you have spoken concerning your servant and concerning his house, and do as you have spoken."

God took over the action, and all that the king could do was submit to God's will and work.

A thousand years later the angel named Gabriel visited a young teenager from Nazareth whose name was Mary. He said simply, "Hail, O favored one, the Lord is with you." Mary turned down the volume on her stereo box and shouted back in a mixture of horror and confusion, "What?" And Gabriel said, "Don't be afraid. You have found favor with God. And you're going to have a baby whose name will be Jesus."

"Far out!" she said. "But wait a minute! I'm only engaged; I haven't done anything yet!"

"The Holy Spirit will take care of that. You see, the child to be born is God's Son."

There it is again. Mary's immediate response was to interpret the whole thing in terms of her doing something or not doing something — just like David. But God came to announce who was in charge. God would do everything that's necessary to bring Jesus into the world — just as God established the dynasty in which Jesus was to be born.

Mary's only response when she heard Gabriel's message was this: "Let it be according to your word." Sounds like David, doesn't it? "Concerning your servant and your house, do as you have spoken."

Think about these two individuals. One a seasoned warrior, now a king, living in the splendor of his cedar palace. The other a peasant girl at the age when we confirm our young people into the faith of the church, living in who knows what — a two-room house with her parents and six siblings? Yet though worlds and a millennium apart, each of them thought they needed to do something for God.

What God was up to was doing something for you and me: bringing into the world the Christ.

Sometimes people who are overwhelmed by the commercialization of Christmas say, "We need to put Christ back into Christmas!" A clever thought, a noble sentiment, something to do for God. But impossible! It took God to put Christ there in the first place, and only God can do it year after year.

Sometimes when you and I think about all the important people God has to care about, we wonder why God should spend any time listening to your prayers and mine. But God brings Christ into your life, into the lives of kings like David and peasants like Mary, men and women, old and young.

Sometimes when you and I get down on ourselves because we haven't done enough religiously or personally, we resolve to mend our ways so we can find Christ once again. But God changes that resolve because God in Christ finds you, even when you don't think you deserve to be found.

John Newtown was a captain of a slave ship in the eighteenth century. He was involved in one of the most inhumane businesses the world has ever known. Suddenly he realized he was doing something—something awful. But instead of thinking he now had to do something for God, that he could find Christ, he realized Christ had found him. He left his profession and wrote a hymn:

> Amazing grace, how sweet the sound, that saved a wretch like me!
> I once was lost but now am found; was blind but now I see.

On this last Sunday before Christmas, sisters and brothers, ask not what you can do for your God. Ask what God is doing for you.

And then, let it be! "Let it be . . . according to your word." That is the answer of faith when God comes to do it all for us.

Isaiah 6:1–8

The Fifth Sunday after the Epiphany (C)

In church circles we talk a lot about participating in God's mission to the world. It's one thing to use that kind of talk for a congregation, but how do we fit into that role as individuals? Especially when you and I might feel we're not up to the task, and that there's really nothing we can do anyway.

When I started the first grade, we as a country were smack in the middle of World War II. That war made quite an impression on me in those early years. I remember saving my pennies and nickels to buy war bonds for tanks and planes. I remember, too, that outside the post office in my small coal-region town was a sign of Uncle Sam pointing his finger at me and saying, "Uncle Sam wants you."

I was a bit embarrassed by the whole thing. I stood about three and a half feet tall. I don't remember how much I weighed, but I do recall I was so thin that when my mother dressed me in my little soldier outfit for school, she had to pin my trousers to my shirt to keep my pants from falling down.

There I stood—all dressed in the proper attire in front of Uncle Sam—but I realized there was no way in the world he wanted me. I wasn't up to the job Uncle Sam wanted done. There was nothing I could do.

My guess is that some of you, too, have periodically felt the same way. I'm not capable of this or that. I don't have enough self-confidence to speak my mind. I'm not as articulate as other people. I'm afraid I'll sound stupid if I speak up. We tend to look around at others and compare ourselves most unfavorably. We're never quite as good as we think others are.

If we feel we're not up to the task our country expects of us, how much less we might feel up to God's call: "I want you." All our insecurities rise to the surface. There's nothing I can do!

If those feelings of unworthiness occur when we compare ourselves to other people, surely we come far short when we compare ourselves to Jesus. After all, there's nothing you and I can do.

That's precisely why we begin our worship with a confession of sins. We are about to begin an hour in the presence of God, and we all know how unworthy we are of God's presence. If there's such a thing as misery loving company, then we can all be sure we've got loads of company because all of us are in the same boat. The apostle Paul put it like this: "*All* have sinned and keep falling short of the glory of God."

And so you and I confess our sins all together because we have that sinfulness in common. And I stand apart from you only in this sense: though I am a sinner, too, I have the unbelievable privilege of announcing God's forgiveness to all of you. That done, we proceed with our worship.

Our first lesson for today and our Gospel are just for us when we harbor those feelings of being unworthy, especially when we say of God's work, "There's nothing I can do."

There was a fellow named Isaiah who went to church, the temple in Jerusalem, week after week. He wandered into the temple and wandered out. He joined in the rituals, and he sang the psalms, and he listened to the priests, and he went home again. Next Sabbath he'd go through the same routine. Something about the routine itself made him feel good, I suppose. Not much was supposed to happen in it, but there was some comfort in doing it all with a crowd of people.

All of a sudden, one day at worship when nothing unusual was supposed to happen, there was God making the divine presence known to Isaiah as God never did before. Weird looking seraphim were flying all around, singing their praises to God. Isaiah realized he was having a vision. He was peeking into eternity, where the praises to God on the throne are sung over and over.

The whole experience was too much for Isaiah to bear. He was standing in the presence of the holy God, and all he could think of was his own unworthiness — and the unworthiness of all the people in his society. Isaiah realized he was no worse than everybody else; no better either. He was just one more of a sinful people, and like himself none of them could stand upright in the face of God. There was nothing he could do.

But God sent one of the seraphim to cleanse Isaiah of his sins. The poor guy smarted from a burned lip when the strange creature touched a burning coal just above his chin. But he knew he was a new man now. No longer did he need to identify himself as a sinner; now he was a forgiven sinner! And so when God asked who would volunteer to participate in the mission to the rest of that broken and sinful society, he — the one who thought there was nothing he could do — said, "Here am I! Send me!"

And God said, "Go and say..."

How similar it all is to our Gospel story from Luke! Jesus was gathering so many crowds to hear his teaching and preaching, he decided he needed a suitable pulpit. There were two empty fishing boats near the shore; the owners had just given up for the day. Jesus asked the owner of the one boat whose name was Simon to push off from the shore a little so that the crowds could see and hear him.

After the sermon, Jesus said, "Let's go fishing." But Simon had enough of fishing for the day. He and the others had been at it all night and caught nothing. But they did as Jesus said, threw out their nets, and caught so many fish that they had to call the other boat to help them pull in the catch.

Now Peter realized that this was no ordinary teacher and preacher standing in his boat. He fell on his knees, recognizing he was in the presence of one who was holy.

He must have felt the way I did when I stood in front of Uncle Sam with my pants pinned to my shirt. Unworthy. Embarrassed. Afraid. "Go away from me, Lord," he said, "for I am a sinner."

Sounds so much like Isaiah, doesn't he? "I am a man of unclean lips, and I live among a people of unclean lips." "I am a sinner, O Lord." Both were saying under their guilty breaths, "There's nothing I can do."

Simon was right, of course. He was a sinner. But Jesus told him not to be afraid. The grace of God is stronger than the sinfulness of humanity. The presence of Jesus demonstrated that. And now Jesus invited Peter to participate with him in the mission that God had sent him to do: "From now on you will be catching people alive."

And Peter and James and John left behind the biggest catch they had ever seen. No standing on the shore to get their pictures taken. No bragging to the reporters about knowing where the big ones hide out in the early morning light. They just left it all behind — even though they felt unworthy — because Christ called them to follow.

Maybe it's necessary that, like Isaiah and Peter, you and I recognize we are not worthy of the presence of God. Maybe it's essential to know that we are sinners who can come near God only because of God's forgiveness. Maybe there's no other way than to be faced with the stark reality that God is holy and that we are sinful in order to know fully why Jesus came to die for our sins and set us free.

Maybe only then, knowing what God has done for us, can we know how badly God wants to do the same for others. And so he sends the likes of you and me to follow Jesus Christ in that mission to the rest of the people on earth—catching people alive, bringing life in the midst of death, bringing the presence of God into the lives of others who feel no more worthy than you or I.

Oh, sure, even with that call, we realize that we can't do all things well. Even knowing God's forgiveness of our sin, we realize that we might have some talent at this or that, but we dismiss those talents as trivial and insignificant. Yet when you put in your two cents and I put in my two cents, maybe together we realize that as a community of believers we can work together to continue the mission of Christ among us. None of us is worthy, but God calls each of us to contribute what we have.

Some years ago Simon and Garfunkel sang a song that went like this:

> If you cannot speak like Peter, if you cannot preach like Paul,
> You can tell the love of Jesus; you can say he died for all.

They're the words from a hymn, one that's included in our book of worship. It ends like this:

> Let none hear you idly saying, "There is nothing I can do,"
> While the multitudes are dying and the master calls for you.
> Take the task he gives you gladly; Let his work your pleasure be.
> Answer quickly when he calls you, "Here am I. Send me, send me!"[51]

Why am I getting this impression that you and I have no excuse when God says, "I want you!"? Not even if our pants are pinned to our shirts!

Isaiah 40:1–11

Second Sunday in Advent (B)

In the late 1960s and early 1970s the popular group known as the Kingston Trio sang a haunting song about the meaningless cycle of life. The song was called "Where Have All the Flowers Gone?" It was an antiwar song and fitting for its day, but it raises questions about life and death in our day, too, and about the changing nature of our lives.

It doesn't happen as often as it should, but once in a while I like to show my love for Jannine by buying her flowers. I know it cheers her up when I do. It lifts her spirits just as these flowers in the chancel Sunday after Sunday do for all of us. They're brilliant with color. To those who have a sense of smell, they add a delightful scent—so I'm told. But I have a problem with flowers. In a few days they fade away, and then they're gone.

Things that have a special appeal to us are like that. Things that mean a lot to us or to someone else cannot last forever. Things that seem to offer security in our lives can disappear. Things that people hold on to, that people can count on, can wither and fade away. "Where have all the flowers gone?"

We have seen it over the last year and a half.[52] Governments in Eastern Europe have fallen, and the powerful Soviet Union, which seemed so invincible, disintegrated. Only a few weeks ago, the prime minister of Great Britain, Margaret Thatcher, who seemed to be maintaining a strong position in world leadership, lost the support she needed to continue in office. Like flowers, governments of the world and worldly leaders wither and fade away.

And so do our traditional values. The moral standards of our day are quite different from the ones we held forty or fifty years ago. Commitments to church and community, even to our country, have dwindled. Commitments to one another in friendships and marriages do not seem to last the way they used to. The drive to get rich quick has replaced the willingness to set long-term goals and to work hard. Even values, like flowers, wither and fade away. "Where have all the flowers gone?"

It's the way life is. And sometimes it gets difficult to hope for anything better, for something more stable, for something that lasts.

The people of ancient Israel knew what that was all about. For centuries they had counted on the possession of their land as the guarantee of their claim on God. For almost as long, they looked to the glorious temple in Jerusalem as the symbol of the presence of God in their lives.

Then suddenly they were carried off to a foreign land, to Babylon. One day in that foreign place where they served as captives and worked as slaves, they heard the news that the walls of Jerusalem back home had been torn down and their beloved temple had gone up in flames. Even the things most precious to them became like the flowers that wither and fade. "Where have all the flowers gone?"

The exiles languished in Babylon for almost fifty years. The generation that remembered Jerusalem was rapidly passing away. The new generation had found other gods, other values, other flowers to watch bloom and fade. And where was the God they heard about in songs and stories from their parents? Must have faded away, too. "Where have all the flowers gone?" Or to put it in their own words from Psalm 137: "By the waters of Babylon, there we sat down and wept, when we remembered Jerusalem."

Into that rather hopeless situation comes the call of the prophet that makes up our first lesson for today. It's a strange scene really. It's a far cry from the hopeless songs of the desert. Instead it's a scene in the heavenly council in which God decides it's time to turn things around.

"Comfort, comfort my people," God said to the council. "Tell them their time of punishment is over and that they are pardoned of their sins."

One of the council members called out something about preparing for the coming of the Lord through the desert. "God's glory is about to be seen by people everywhere," the council member said. "You can believe it, because God said so."

Another voice in that heavenly council called to some innocent bystander. He was probably just hanging around in church. The voice said: "Preach."

And the human responded the way we'd expect of anyone who had seen everything change over the previous fifty years. He reacted as one who must have been singing with the Kingston Trio. He said:

"What shall I preach?
All flesh is grass, and all its beauty like the flower of the field.
The grass withers, the flower fades,
  when the breath of the Lord blows upon it;
surely the people is grass."

And the voice from the council agreed in part:

"Yes, yes. The grass does wither.
  Yes, yes, the flower does fade.
But the word of our God will stand forever."

Against all the flowers of life that fade, against all the grass that withers, God's word alone endures. That enduring word is not one of despair but of hope. Not one of disillusionment but of confidence. Not one of fear but of certainty. The word of God endures forever!

That word of God's salvation is what John the Baptist came to preach. He was the voice in the wilderness who took up the call six hundred years later to announce the coming of God. He said that God's coming salvation would come in a person who will baptize with the Holy Spirit.

That person was Jesus, and Advent points us to God's coming to us in Jesus Christ. The word that endures forever is the word in the flesh, Jesus, the Son of God.

And so, God's promise to bring salvation and to establish God's Reign over all the world is about to be accomplished in the birth, the ministry, the death, and the resurrection of Jesus Christ. God's word endures. God's word is salvation. And so, Jesus' name means, "May the Lord save!"

Margaret Thatcher's Great Britain might indeed have given up on her, and her strong position in world leadership has come to an end. Instability in Eastern Europe and in the former Soviet Union has shaken things up on God's globe. The things we stood for as a nation are often difficult to find.

But constant is the concern of God that every person ever born is made equally in the eyes of God. Constant is the nature of God to save people from the withering structures and values of the world. Enduring is the divine promise that God will one day set up a glorious Reign over all the earth. "The grass withers, the flower fades, but the word of our God will stand forever."

Commitments made between friends or spouses fail at an increasing rate in our society. The death of a spouse or of a child or a parent changes life dramatically. Holiday celebrations aren't what they used to be. But constant is the promise of Christ: "Lo, I am with you always, even to the end of the age." "Yes, yes, the grass withers, the flower fades, but the word of our God will stand forever."

That word to you and to me is to save us—to forgive us in this life and to rescue us from the judgment to come at the end of the age. That's God's word: to live with us every moment throughout all eternity.

"Where have all the flowers gone? Gone to graveyards every one." So went the song.

That is, after all, the fate of flowers. But it's not the last word. God had that. The last word: Arise!

Though the grass withers and the flowers fade, the word of God that was in the beginning and that became flesh and died, and was raised to be with us for all eternity—that word invites you to life.

Isaiah 44:6–8

Ninth Sunday after Pentecost (Year A)

The world is full of pain — all kinds of pain.[53] But the kind of pain that's most severe is the agony of abandonment. When someone you love or like or trusted walks out of your life, either with reason or no reason, the pain is excruciating. And where is the healing?

Just about four weeks ago, one Sunday afternoon, there was aired on television that classic western *High Noon.* The sheriff (Gary Cooper) was told immediately following his wedding to Grace Kelly that his old nemesis was released from jail and on his way to get revenge. He knew he had to postpone their honeymoon to take his stand, and so he set out to round up his troops. No one, not his best friends, not the sheriff he succeeded, not his deputy — no one — was willing to help. They all rejected him, and even his blushing bride headed for the train station, thus the song, "Do not forsake me, O my darlin', on this our wedding day." No wonder that when the shoot-out was over, the sheriff threw his badge on the ground in front of all the townspeople and rode away with his bride. The townspeople forsook him, and he wanted nothing more to do with their likes. Maybe you know the feeling!

The other night Jannine and I rented a movie. It wasn't exactly profound, as you can tell from the title: *A Gun in Mary Lou's Handbag.* It was the story of a young married woman who felt that her husband abandoned her for his work. He paid no attention to her, even when she prepared their anniversary dinner with candles and all the trimmings. She felt unworthy, neglected, rejected, too ordinary for anyone to notice. In her feeling of abandonment she did something crazy. She confessed to a murder she didn't commit and to an illicit affair with a man she never even knew. That got attention all right! She made new friends, especially a "woman of the night." Mary Lou dressed differently, talked differently, in short, gave up who she was to become someone more exciting. All because she felt abandoned. Maybe you know the feeling!

Recently I picked up a book that had been written fifty years ago: Richard Llewellyn's *How Green Was My Valley.* It's about a family of coal miners in South Wales, and a major player in the story was the village minister. The minister knew well the meaning of the gospel; he stood behind the workers in their strikes and debates against the mine owners; he sacrificed his pay during a long strike and along with it, his health, too. And suddenly the talking grapevine had it around town that he was seeing a young woman, and so the congregation rejected him, moving him out the next day because he was "unfit to be their minister." Maybe you know the feeling!

It's excruciatingly painful to be forsaken.

When the one who has forsaken us is God, then the pain is even more acute. Individuals feel that way these days. "I don't feel the presence of God anymore," they say. "I don't have the feeling I used to have in church."

Where is God these days?

That was the painful cry of the exiled Israelites in Babylon in the sixth century B.C.:

> "My Lord has forgotten me," they said;
> "my Lord has forsaken me."

And so they threw their mezzuzahs on the ground to ride off into the sunset with the gods who had clearly and visibly been present in the world: the idols of the Babylonians.

Here's how it happened. Years before, the people had been tried in court for their unfaithfulness to the Lord. They were guilty as can be, and so they were indicted by the Judge of the whole world. Right there in the courtroom, they heard the verdict: exile! It was bad, but they would deal with it. They'd be out on good behavior in no time. God would take them home in two years, said one prophet.

But year after year went by, and God didn't show the old Yahweh face. The Babylonian gods had their faces everywhere. It was obvious that the Lord had abandoned them after their trial and sentence. The people became like old, dry bones, withered, hopeless, cut off, hung out to dry. And so they went with the winners. Maybe you know the feeling!

Now along comes the Lord one day some sixty years later. "Everybody on the train!" God said. "We're going home!"

And the exiles said, "We don't even believe you're God anymore. You've been gone so long."

So God went on trial this time. Not the people. God!

It's no secret that in our apparently God-forsaken world there are many gods ready to fill the gap. We can easily identify some of them, the gods of greed and power and fortune and fame. But others are subtle little devils! Hardly noticeable! Especially since a god is that in which we put our trust. A god is that which we would not want to surrender without feeling some grievous loss. A god is that which gives us some sense of importance.

I'll wager you have as many gods as I, and they somehow determine how we live our lives. They might be as subtle as the attitudes we hold, the opinions we insist on, the way we spend our time, the way we always did something, our work, even the office of ministry itself. And when push comes to shove, your god and mine rise to the surface along with all the rest in our society.

Each time they do, God goes on trial. Court is in session daily. No weekends off. The issue is always the same: Who is God?

If the jury is to decide on the basis of who seems to have control over things these days, who gets all the attention from you and me and from the rest of our society, whom do you think will emerge from the courtroom as God?

After decades went by with no eyewitness evidence that their own God was still moving the world along, the Israelites went with the apparent winners. They could look up into the midnight sky to see all those Babylonian gods twinkling the night away. They could watch the Babylonian god rise on the eastern horizon every morning and set in the west every evening. They were eyewitnesses to the celestial gods.

Then the Lord came along, claiming to be the world's "one and only." That claim countered the gods of Babylon, so they all ended up in court. Our lesson from the Book of Isaiah is one of many court scenes from this prophet in which God accuses the idols of Babylon of being impostors.

> I am the first and I am the last;
> besides me there is no God.

Yahweh then challenges the idols to defend themselves:

> Who is like me? Let him proclaim it,
> Let him declare and set it forth before me.
> Who has announced from of old the things to come?
> Let them tell us what is yet to be.

And there they stand, these silent gods, positioned on their pedestals of lapis lazuli, dressed to kill. But they cannot proclaim. They cannot declare. They cannot announce. They cannot tell what is yet to be. They, in other words, are not gods. Their pleading the Fifth Amendment only accuses them.

The evidence needed to prove who is God is this: Yahweh is God because Yahweh spoke of old what would come to pass, and it did!

The point the prophet we call Second Isaiah is making is this: Yahweh has made known who is God since the beginning of the world, and it's now time to take God's word to heart. God's word now is one of comfort to the exiles after sixty years of oppression in a foreign land.

It's difficult for us today to grasp the power of the spoken word. Perhaps it's because we hear too many words, and we've learned to distrust 99 percent of them. "It's nothing but talk!" we say, when we hear one politician after another promise there'll be no increase in taxes and more food for everyone and health care for all. "It's just a commercial!" we say when one company after another persuades us that its deodorant is the one that will attract friends and influence people. We are bombarded with words, and we have learned to distrust them, along with the people who speak them, for they are, after all, mere words.

But we are not without examples of effective speech. Just a year ago Garry Wills published a book called *Lincoln at Gettysburg: The Words That Remade America*. Wills argues that far from being a casually composed address scribbled on the back of an envelope, Lincoln's address at Gettysburg was a scholarly masterpiece in which he relied on oratorical forms of ancient Greece to compose a beautifully balanced set of 272 words. But it's the power of those words that attracts Wills, words that caused an intellectual revolution: 272 words *made* history. It's nothing short of a miracle, Garry Wills writes.

The miracle of God's word is that it effects what it says. When you hear or say, "As a minister of the church of Christ and by his authority, I declare to you the entire forgiveness of all your sins . . . ," they are forgiven!

When you say or hear, "The blood of Christ is shed for you," it is shed!

When you say or hear, "The Lord bless you and keep you," people are blessed!

And that's what distinguishes God from the idols of the world. You know it. I know it. But what will convince the jury?

In that very same courtroom in ancient Babylon, God told Israel what is necessary: *you are my witnesses.*

The people of Israel, enticed as they were by the gods around them, were called to be character witnesses for God in that world. Only their witnessing to the faithfulness of God could tell the rest of the world who was God in spite of no eyewitness accounts. Their testimony was that the one who is God is *not seen* in the powers of the world *but rather heard* in the faithful and effective word, and it was present to the exiled canal diggers who felt forsaken and forgotten by God.

Some are saying these days that we live in a post-Christian world. And they mean that the church doesn't have the influence it once had in the world, that the majority consider our faith obsolete. We can lament that diagnosis. Or we can celebrate it. Perhaps the church gives its best testimony when we, like the people of Israel in exile, are not identified with the power of the world but with the power of God's word.

Think of the testimony you and I make for God when the powerful word we speak is that of a crucified Christ. Think of the impact on the jury when we live out our word of faith by committing ourselves to serving people in need. Think of the powerful character witness that is made when we stand alongside the oppressed in our world, when we work alongside the needy trying to learn what would help them most.

Now raise your right hand and swear to tell the truth, the whole truth, and nothing but the truth, so help you God!

Isaiah 61:10–62:3

The Second Sunday after Christmas (C)

On this last day of Christmas we have one last shot at trying to understand what Christmas and Christmas giving are all about.

Today, the twelfth day of Christmas, is not only the end of the season; it's also the conclusion to the song. It's the day when "my true love gave to me twelve drummers drumming." The image is clear enough, but the gifts connected with other days are somewhat strange.

It was on the tenth day of Christmas — Friday to be exact — that Jannine and I wondered about that strange gift of ten "lords a leaping." Having just read a piece on "bungee jumping" we wondered if the ten lords a leaping were bungee jumpers.

Bungee jumping is that sport in which someone jumps off a bridge or cliff into a vast empty space over a canyon or a raging river. The bungee jumper comes as close to certain death as one could ever want to come without actually dying. Of course, there's a catch to bungee jumping. Thank God for the "catch" — a piece of strong, elasticized cord wrapped around the jumper's ankles. At the last moment the cord springs into action and keeps the jumper from crashing to earth or into the river far below.

Bungee jumping is a sport that folks do just for the thrill of it. In the process they identify with people on the verge of sudden death. Other people go bungee jumping in a figurative sense, identifying with people in deathlike situations.

Some years back there was a movie about a man who went bungee jumping in that figurative way. He was a corporate executive who willingly jumped from his high-paying, three-piece-suit job to digging ditches. He wanted to know what it was like for the people who used to work for him, to know what it was to feel cold and wet, or hot and sweaty, always tired, and achy after a long day's work.

A few years back I read about another bungee jumper of sorts. This woman left a comfortable and safe job as a writer for a major newspaper. But jump she did — straight into Philadelphia's darkest streets and loneliest corners. For a while the writer became a homeless person, dependent upon the goodwill of a passerby, surviving by handouts at local shelters and soup kitchens. This jumper was subject to the elements of wind and rain and slept sometimes in a shelter, sometimes in an abandoned cardboard box. She didn't do this out of idle curiosity. Certainly not for the thrill of it. The writer wanted to experience what life was like for the poorest of the poor: to come as close as anyone would want to come to existence as a shadow of a human being and then raise her voice to society along with those with whom she identified.

Like many of you, I did a little figurative bungee jumping of my own. During my summers off from the intellectual pursuits at college and seminary I toted roofing shingles to the highest peaks, swung a hammer, hefted wallboard, put down flooring. I worked with a crew of other men, some of whom were paying off their bill to society, paying their fines for drunken brawls and infractions of the law. I worked beside those who were struggling to find a way back to life as many others know it.

Each of us — the corporate executive, the newspaper writer, myself during those summers — was a bungee jumper of a sort, hurling ourselves into a different space. But each of us had a cord wrapped about our ankles to save us when the situation turned too ugly, when the going got too rough. For each of us there was a way out — another well-paying job possibility; an editor who could blow the whistle and bring the writer home; a return to academia at the end of the summer.

Our lesson from the Book of Isaiah tells of yet another bungee jumper. These people of Israel were completely disillusioned. For years they had sat as exiles in Babylon waiting for God's promise to return them to Jerusalem. They had been promised that when that day of return would come, it would be a day of glory, of joy, of happiness. It would mean not only the restoration of Israel but the beginning of the Reign of God on earth.

The day of return to their homes did come, but none of the promised glory and joy came with it. Instead the people found only a destroyed temple, corruption, grinding poverty, and hopelessness. There stood among them a prophet we today call Third Isaiah.

Rather than speak for God, as prophets usually did, this one promised the people that he would so identify with them in their despair that he would complain on their behalf before God. He would raise his voice as the spokesperson for the people. He would never be silent before God. He would be there with the people always reminding God of the promises God had made. He would not stop until salvation came to Israel. He would continue his complaining even if it meant his death. He jumped with a bungee cord attached to his ankles.

But even that leap of complaining would not accomplish Israel's salvation. What was needed for Israel's salvation and the salvation of the whole world was one who would jump without a bungee cord.

When the time came in my summer employment to dig ditches, the complainer in me rose to the surface. I said to the boss on more than one occasion, "I thought Lincoln freed the slaves!" I was a relentless complainer. Only one thing ever stopped my griping. It was when the boss smiled lovingly at me and joined me in the ditch to help with the digging. There we were: father and son grunting and sweating and struggling together.

That's what Israel needed. That's what the world needed. To have our Father leap into the ditch with us.

John's Gospel for this twelfth day of Christmas is about our Lord doing just that. These first verses from John tell in glorious language about the word of God that has dwelt with God from the beginning. It was a safe word. A comfortable and stable scene. And then John tells us the word becomes flesh and dwells among us. The word leaps from the highest heaven and becomes one of us. The word of God, the Son of God, the one we call Jesus, completely and fully identifies with us, even to death.

The death of Jesus, in fact, is what accomplishes salvation for Israel, for you, for me, and for all humanity. This is no ordinary "leaping Lord." This is no bungee-jumping Lord. Jesus has no cord wrapped about his ankles to save him from certain death. This one truly dies and accomplishes once and for all the salvation that benefits you and me and all of creation.

This morning as we partake of the Sacrament of the Lord's Supper we experience in the most intimate way possible that benefit that comes from Jesus' death. We taste the benefit each time we hear the words: "The Body of Christ given for you." We experience again Christ's salvation each time we hear the words: "The blood of Christ shed for you."

It isn't necessary for you and me to jump without the cord. Hurling ourselves to our deaths accomplishes nothing.

But you and I can benefit humanity by being bungee jumpers of that other sort. We can bring light to the dark corners of life by identifying with those who suffer. We can raise our voices in protest like the prophet. We can speak against the people and the structures that oppress. We can stand before God and raise our voices in complaint when God seems to be silent in the face of death, despair, and destruction. And when we do, we will find God in the ditch beside us.

Oh yes, bungee jumping is quite a sport! But let us instead be bungee jumpers of another kind — "leaping lords" so to speak — and hurl ourselves into the depths of life in the service of others. When we understand Christmas in that way, the twelve drummers can conclude the season by rattling their snares to the glory of God.

Jeremiah 20:7–13

Fifth Sunday after Pentecost (A)

We have prayed today to God "our defender" to "rescue your people from despair, deliver your sons and daughters from fear, and preserve us from all unbelief." The assumption behind the prayer is that even the people of God experience despair, fear, and unbelief. The assumption is confirmed by your experiences and mine. We suffer in many ways. And our two Bible readings for today make us wonder if God is not sometimes the source of our troubles.

The other night we rented the movie *Steel Magnolias*. The story was about a group of five women whose lives constantly came together in the shop of a beautician named Truvy. There they probed into one another's business, as well into everyone else's in town. And in the process they developed for one another a powerful support group. One of that group, a young woman, Annelle, had just recently come to town. She was terribly shy and insecure at first. But as the story progressed, she became as active as all the others. She even turned to religion. Unfortunately she took her newfound religion to some extremes, and her praying over everything and her insistence on piety made her something of a joke. It turned off many of her friends, caused serious arguments with her boyfriend, and led to some sharp rebukes when her simple faith did not bring to others the comfort she intended. Her faith had got her into trouble.

I wonder if we sometimes hold back expressing what we believe for fear of alienating ourselves from other people. Might we sometimes hold back offering a prayer for a friend in distress, or a family member for that matter, because we might feel embarrassed by their reactions? Does it happen sometimes that expressing what we believe about values or injustices or morality makes us uncomfortable, to say the least? Can the fear of speaking out for God in a questionable or unfriendly atmosphere make you want to drop between the cracks?

Think of the risk in speaking out. The party has been moving along fine. Everyone is having a wonderful time. Then the conversation in one corner has become outright racist. If you put in your two cents of God-talk, everybody looks at you as though you're spaced out or just from outer space. They shrug you off, wag their heads, and for the rest of the evening you suffer from the proverbial cold-shoulder syndrome.

You're talking to a member of the family about a problem she's been having. She feels alone and unsupported, even ostracized, and so you talk about the presence of God in her life. She gives you that look of disgust, stops the conversation, tells you to get real, and leaves you sitting there.

God-talk is not the way you "win friends and influence people." Talking for God can lead to trouble, and when it does, guess who's to blame? Who sent you to do that in the first place? Who baptized you to become a priest to people in need? Who sends you out from church Sunday after Sunday to witness to the truth?

Could it be that down deep inside we hesitate to speak for God because ultimately we'll need to blame God if it doesn't work out? What if we say God will heal someone who's ill, and the person lingers in suffering? What if we promise that God will be with someone who's troubled and alone, and the person still feels forsaken by God? What if we tell someone God will give them the strength to continue, but the suffering robs the person of every ounce of strength? What if we repeat this or that promise of God or of Jesus, and there is no evidence that it's fulfilled? Might we even fall into the concern of our psalm for the day: "Let not those who seek you be disgraced because of me, O God of Israel."

There is a risk in speaking for God. Do you want to put yourselves at such risk? Do you want to put God at such risk?

Jeremiah, as young as he was when God called him to be a prophet, had enough savvy to know what would come of it. God called the young Jerry to preach the word with such force that it would pluck up and break down, as well as build and plant. Jeremiah tried his best to get out from under the weight of the burden. "I'm too young for this," he said. But God wouldn't take no for an answer. Jerry's one consolation was this: God promised to be with him and to deliver him from trouble.

The young prophet ended up in a lifetime of trouble. He went around the city of Jerusalem announcing, "Violence and destruction! God," he kept saying, "has had enough of your lackadaisical attitude, your running after other gods, and your injustices to the poor. So now, 'Here come d'judge!' "

All the handwriting was on the wall. The Babylonians were sure to destroy the city. What the people needed to know from Jeremiah was that the destruction would be God's work.

But no destruction came. The years of threat came and went. And Jeremiah felt like the proverbial fool. He became a laughingstock in town. People mocked him, as the onlookers at Golgotha would one day mock Jesus. His closest friends deserted him, as the disciples of Jesus would one day do.

Jeremiah was certain it was all God's fault. It was that call to be a witness for God that led to all the trouble. And so he complained. He accused God of seducing him. He lamented about having to speak God's word. It had become for him "a reproach and a delusion all the day long."

But even as he complained, he realized anew the promise of God years before: the promise that God would be with him to deliver him. "The Lord is with me as an awesome warrior," he reassured himself. And knowing that, believing that ultimately God would vindicate his preaching and fulfill the word, Jeremiah broke out in a song.

> Sing to the Lord! For he has delivered the life of
> the needy from the hand of evildoers!

There's a lesson in faith here. God allows us to dump everything on those divine shoulders when things go wrong—even when the things that go wrong seem to have something to do with witnessing for God. God never ignored Jeremiah's complaining. God never chided the prophet for bad taste. God never even suggested that Jeremiah should not have complained.

God can take all the complaining we have to offer. And God is especially ready for that barrage when our problems have something to do with carrying out God's work. And come they might when you talk on God's behalf, serve meals to the lonely, visit the sick, spend time with them as companions, driving them here and there. You put yourself at risk whenever you allow yourself to be God's servant.

But God promises to be with you and to deliver you, even when it seems God has left you holding the bag.

In our Gospel reading from Matthew, Jesus was in the process of sending out his disciples. He made no bones about the trouble they could get into as sheep among the wolves. After all, he said, "Disciples are not above their masters." Serving the one who was mocked and ridiculed, even deserted by close friends, means the possibility of experiencing the same trouble.

But when troubles come because of serving Christ, Jesus says, "I will acknowledge that person before my Father who is in heaven." That's the comfort Jesus promises. He will stand at our side on the day of judgment and speak on our behalf before the Creator and Judge of all the earth.

More than that, when the Risen Christ commissions the apostles again on the mountain in Galilee, he promises to be with them "'til the end of the age."

Standing at our side on the day of judgment. Present with us throughout our lives as we do God's work. That's Jesus' promise to us who are called to be members of the baptized priesthood.

With that promise we can do our witnessing without fear. And when trouble comes because of it, we can do our complaining without fear, too. At the same time we can join Jeremiah even now in singing to the Lord the song of praise: "Sing to the Lord! For he has delivered . . . !"

Ezekiel 18:1–4, 25–32

Nineteenth Sunday after Pentecost (A)

We sing to God in one of our favorite hymns, "O thou who changest not, abide with me." I wonder sometimes how a God who doesn't change fits into the world in which we live.

On that wonderful television show of bygone days, *Candid Camera,* Allen Funt performed some stunts that linger on in some of our aging memories. One time the crew of the show constructed a very realistic tree — probably of papier mâché — big enough for a man to stand inside. The tree and he were positioned alongside a sidewalk in a town, and the man was instructed to move as people walked by. As each person approached the tree, it moved one, two, or even three feet. The response from nine of the victims was the same. They stared momentarily at the tree, continued their forward movement past the tree, shrugged their shoulders, shook their heads, and moved on.

Obviously they couldn't believe what they saw. It did not fit their understanding of the world and the laws of physics. It must, therefore, have been a figment of their imagination, and so they passed by without letting the moving tree affect them in the slightest.

Only one man out of the ten stopped dead in his tracks, stared at the tree for a moment, approached it, grabbed it, and began to shake it. He wanted to know what was going on, what made this tree move. Why? How?

I wonder sometimes if you and I don't approach life like the nine who passed by. This or that experience doesn't fit our worldview, and so we close ourselves off from what's going on around us. Whether it's too frightening to admit to changes in life, or whether it's just a refusal to recognize the world is no longer the same, I don't know. I do know, though, that for some people stubbornness is a virtue, and that might indeed shut them out of the world that's developing around us.

The trees are indeed moving whether or not we are willing to acknowledge the changes. The world is no longer what it used to be, even from the time that I was a child. I grew up in a small town where the churches were the center of everything that went on. People's lives evolved around the congregations in that small coal-region town, just as they did in towns and cities where many of you grew up. The trees have moved. Church doesn't play the same role in the lives of so many people.

Think of the way information gets around today. While the telephone has been in use for many years, it is now used to send electronic mail from computer to computer or printed texts and graphics through fax machines. Radio and television waves are bounced off satellites circling the earth, and so we learn instantly what's happening in Germany or Japan or the Middle East. The world has become not only smaller but faster. The trees have moved!

If we insist the world for each of us remain the same, we might miss out on a whole new way of looking at life. Only one in ten seems willing to shake the trees that move to find out what's happening and why and how.

Some six hundred years before the birth of Jesus there lived in Babylon a man named Ezekiel. He was one of many exiles from Jerusalem the Babylonians had carried off. The tree had moved for these people. In Jerusalem they had been the upper-class folks; now they were digging canals for their new masters. In Jerusalem they had known the security of God's presence in the temple and its liturgy; now they lamented that God had forsaken them. In Jerusalem they had lived by predictable patterns, ones they could even reduce to parables and repeat over and over again.

And so this Ezekiel, a strange priest according to his own reports, was called to be an equally strange prophet. His task was to help people acknowledge that the trees had moved and to encourage them to shake the trees to find out why and how and what difference it might make in their lives.

One way he went about his task was to challenge the old familiar proverbs he heard them repeating. One day he approached a group of people with the word of God. "What is this proverb you have about the land of Israel: 'The days grow long and every vision comes to nought'? Tell them, 'God said, "I will put an end to this proverb, and they shall no more use it as a proverb in Israel." ' "

On another day Ezekiel heard them repeating another proverb — one that's in our lesson for the day. He spoke God's word again: "What do you mean by repeating this proverb concerning the land of Israel: 'The parents have eaten sour grapes, and the children's teeth are set on edge'? 'As I live,' says the Lord God, 'this proverb shall no more be used by you in Israel.' "

The people in Israel had been complaining through this proverb that they were in such a state because of the sins of their ancestors. They were sure they themselves did not deserve to suffer for someone else's sins in the past. They were convinced they were suffering unjustly. And so, the parable: "The parents have eaten sour grapes, but the children's teeth are set on edge."

The fact of the matter is, said Ezekiel, God is working a new way in which every person is responsible for his or her sins. The trees have moved! And Ezekiel is trying to get them to shake the trees rather than pass by without realizing something new has happened.

There's a whole new understanding in the relationship with God at stake. Not only is each one responsible for his or her own actions. Freedom from that old proverb frees you to turn around and to hear God's invitation to life! Don't walk by! Be open to the new! Experience it! Life has changed, and there's no going back. Shake the tree!

Jesus was saying something quite similar in his speech from our Gospel lesson (Matt. 21:28–32). He was addressing the chief priests and elders of the people within the temple precincts. He told a story and asked them to respond. The lesson, Jesus said, was that it is people who not only speak but do the will of God that will enter the Kingdom of Heaven. And on the basis of that understanding, it is the despised harlots and tax collectors who will precede the obviously religious folks into the Kingdom. "Even when you saw them flocking to John the Baptist's way of righteousness, you did not afterward repent and believe in him."

God was acting in a new way, but the religious folks were so stuck in the old that they couldn't budge. The trees had moved, but they never stopped to shake them to find out why or how or what difference it might make.

What was this new way?

The word of God had come not through ones to whom they were accustomed but through somebody new, somebody different in appearance, in message, in style. Only the outcasts of society felt free enough to shake the trees.

The world has indeed changed. The trees are moving all the time. We need to take that seriously, you and I, as we struggle with the mission of God in a new day and how to participate in it; with how to reach out in a changing world where the church is no longer the obvious center of everyone's life; with a situation in which the family structure has changed, and it becomes harder and harder to find a traditional family. What difference does it make in our involvement in God's mission that the globe has become a village where information about joys and tragedies reaches us in seconds, where in fact our lives have become intimately connected to the decisions and actions of people in the Middle East or in Eastern Europe?

And what do we do with the possibility that God can address us in new ways through the most unlikely people? How do we deal with the possibility that God can comfort and challenge us through persons of different color, different cultures, different ethnic descent, or a different gender? Isn't it even possible that the agents through whom God's word comes to us are our own children? Or friends who have never uttered a liturgical word? Or a stranger sitting beside you in the waiting room of a doctor's office?

Suppose the surprising word that comes through these surprising people is that you are not stuck in the things of the past. That you are not a helpless recipient of family patterns. That you have the opportunity to take responsibility for yourself. And that God's invitation to you is for life!

The trees keep moving, and God, the one we say "changes not," moves with them. Don't pass by the trees. Give them a good shake to find out what's going on and why and how.

You might even find in the shaking that it is God who has been inside, obviously moving to grab our attention, and to set aside the old proverbs we live by. Moving the trees just might be one of the ways God offers to us new and meaningful ways to understand our lives and the world around us. It might even be the way God calls us to participate as movers and shakers in the mission to a broken world.

Notes

1. This first chapter is the result of the author's presentation to colleagues on the faculty at the Lutheran Theological Seminary at Philadelphia in the fall of 1983. The paper, reviewed and revised, was then published in *The Mt. Airy Parish Practice Notebook* 23 (Philadelphia: Lutheran Theological Seminary, spring 1984): 1–6, 12. It is used here with the permission of the present editor, Andrew J. White.

2. Martin Luther, "Preface to the Prophets," in *Luther's Works* (Philadelphia: Fortress, 1960), 35:274.

3. Gerhard von Rad, *Studies in Deuteronomy,* trans. David Stalker, Studies in Biblical Theology, no. 9 (London: SCM, 1953), 78–81.

4. Foster R. McCurley, *Proclaiming the Promise: Christian Preaching from the Old Testament* (Philadelphia: Fortress, 1974), 36.

5. For the development of the Kingdom of God as a unifying theme throughout the Bible, see Foster R. McCurley and John Reumann, *Witness of the Word: A Biblical Theology of the Gospel* (Philadelphia: Fortress, 1986).

6. See the summary of such difficulties in Arthur M. Schlesinger Jr., *The Cycles of American History* (Boston: Houghton Mifflin, 1986), 3–22.

7. See Elizabeth Achtemeier, *Preaching from the Old Testament* (Louisville: Westminster/John Knox, 1989), 56–59.

8. Books, articles, and reports of commissions concerning methods of biblical study abound today. For a summary of this work among Roman Catholics and Protestants, as well as a concise presentation of his own outline, see John Reumann, "Methods in Studying the Biblical Text Today," *Concordia Theological Monthly* 40 (1969): 655–81. Reumann acknowledges a theological influence from Gerhard Ebeling and Heinrich Ott and a terminological one from a volume by Otto Kaiser and W. G. Kummel, *Exegetical Method: A Student's Handbook,* trans E. V. N. Goetchius (New York: Seabury, 1967).

Among the many tools available in English are Bible dictionaries, notably *The Interpreter's Dictionary of the Bible,* 4 vols. (Nashville: Abingdon, 1962); *Theological Dictionary of the New Testament,* ed. Gerhard Kittel and Gerhard Friedrich, Eng. trans. and ed. Geoffrey

W. Bromiley (Grand Rapids, Mich.: Eerdmans, 1964–74); *Theological Dictionary of the Old Testament,* ed. G. Johannes Botterweck and Helmer Ringgren, trans. John T. Willis, rev. ed. (Grand Rapids, Mich.: Eerdmans, 1974ff.); concordances such as Robert Young's *Analytical Concordance to the Bible,* rev. ed. (Grand Rapids, Mich.: Eerdmans, 1970) and *Nelson's Complete Concordance of the Revised Standard Version Bible* (New York: Nelson and Sons, 1957), as well as Bible atlases, histories of Israel, general introductions, and, of course, commentaries. Three useful one-volume commentaries on the Bible are *The Interpreter's One Volume Commentary on the Bible,* ed. Charles M. Laymon (Nashville: Abingdon, 1971); *Peake's Commentary on the Bible,* ed. Matthew Black, rev. ed. (London: Thomas Nelson and Sons, 1962); *The Jerome Biblical Commentary,* ed. Raymond E. Brown, Joseph A. Fitzmyer, and Roland E. Murphy (Englewood Cliffs, N.J.: Prentice-Hall, 1968). While each commentary should be examined on its own merit, as a series in Old Testament books the Old Testament Library volumes published by Westminster Press are particularly good as theological works, as are those in the Hermeneia series published by Fortress Press (now Augsburg Fortress).

Valuable as introductions to the various "criticisms" in biblical exegesis are the concise volumes in Fortress Press's Guide to Biblical Scholarship. The New Testament series includes Norman Perrin's *What Is Redaction Criticism?* (1969); Edgar V. McKnight's *What Is Form Criticism?* (1969); William A. Beardslee's *Literary Criticism of the New Testament* (1970); William G. Doty's *Letters in Primitive Christianity* (1973); Edgar Krentz's *The Historical-Critical Method* (1975); Daniel Patte's *What Is Structural Exegesis?* (1976). The Old Testament Series includes Norman Habel's *Literary Criticism of the Old Testament* (1971); Gene M. Tucker's *Form Criticism of the Old Testament* (1971); Walter E. Rast's *Tradition History and the Old Testament* (1972); Ralph W. Klein's *Textual Criticism of the Old Testament* (1974); J. Maxwell Miller's *The Old Testament and the Historian* (1976); David Robertson's *The Old Testament and the Literary Critic* (1977); H. Darrell Lance's *The Old Testament and the Archaeologist* (1981). These volumes are highly recommended for those who are unclear about the nature and methods of these aspects of biblical study.

9. Where such Dead Sea texts are available and where variations from the received text occur, the editors of Kittel's *Biblia Hebraica* have included a third paragraph in the apparatus at the bottom of the page on which the text appears. For those gifted in languages, the Septuagint can sometimes serve as an aid in establishing the text, for one can sometimes work backward to determine the Hebrew reading that the Greek translator had before him. Admittedly, ancient fragments, even older than the Dead Sea scroll, have been found, such as the Nash Papyrus of Exodus 20 (second century B.C.), and quite recently a sixth century B.C. inscription of the Aaronic benediction (Num. 6:24–26).

10. Especially commendable as introductions to the Old Testament

are Otto Eissfeldt, *The Old Testament: An Introduction,* trans. P. R. Ackroyd (New York: Harper and Row, 1965); Georg Fohrer, *Introduction to the Old Testament,* trans. David E. Green (Nashville: Abingdon, 1968); Arthur Weiser, *The Old Testament: Its Formation and Development,* trans. Dorothea M. Barton (New York: Association Press, 1961); Otto Kaiser, *Introduction to the Old Testament: A Presentation of Results and Problems,* trans. John Sturdy (Minneapolis: Augsburg, 1975); J. Alberto Soggin, *Introduction to the Old Testament: From Its Origins to the Closing of the Alexandrian Canon* (Philadelphia: Westminster, 1976); Brevard S. Childs, *Introduction to the Old Testament as Scripture* (Philadelphia: Fortress, 1979); Norman K. Gottwald, *The Hebrew Bible: A Socio-Literary Introduction* (Philadelphia: Fortress, 1985).

11. Theodore H. Gaster, *Myth, Legend, and Custom in the Old Testament* (New York: Harper and Row, 1969). An important contribution to biblical studies in recent years has been the production of books and articles on the sociological realities of ancient Israel. The pioneering work in this field was Norman K. Gottwald's *The Tribes of Yahweh: A Sociology of the Religion of Liberated Israel, 1250–1050 B.C.E.* (Maryknoll, N.Y.: Orbis, 1975); see also his *Hebrew Bible.*

12. See the series Guides to Biblical Scholarship cited above in note 8.

13. While forms have been described and identified for every book and for every kind of literature in the Old Testament, some basic descriptions in several areas are readily available in English. The pioneer in this discipline, Hermann Gunkel, did most of his work in the narratives of Genesis and in the Book of Psalms. His methods and concerns, while now somewhat refined and modified, are readily available in English in *The Psalms,* trans. Thomas M. Horner, Facet Books — Biblical Series, no. 19 (Philadelphia: Fortress, 1967), and *The Legends of Genesis,* trans. W. H. Caruth (New York: Schocken, 1964). On prophetic literature, especially commendable is Claus Westermann's *Basic Forms of Prophetic Speech,* trans. H. C. White (Philadelphia: Westminster, 1967). The reader will benefit from the collection of essays in *Old Testament Form Criticism,* ed. John H. Hayes (San Antonio: Trinity University Press, 1974). Finally, a thorough approach to the discipline occurs in a commentary-like series called The Forms of Old Testament Literature, ed. Rolf P. Knierim and Gene M. Tucker (Grand Rapids, Mich.: Eerdmans); of the twenty-four volumes planned about one-third are now available.

14. On the challenge to the documentary theory see especially the July 1977 issue of the *Journal for the Study of the Old Testament.* The basic article by R. Rendtorff criticizes the traditional approach, and subsequent articles by G. E. Coats, R. E. Clements, R. N. Whybray, J. van Seters, and N. E. Wagner respond to Rendtorff's argument.

15. For a comprehensive study of Deuteronomistic influence in Jeremiah, see E. W. Nicholson, *Preaching to the Exiles* (New York: Schocken, 1970).

16. Over the past several decades Brevard S. Childs has advanced the necessity for considering a pericope in the context of the entire canon. His works, particularly *Biblical Theology of the Old and New Testaments: Theological Reflection on the Christian Bible* (Minneapolis: Fortress, 1992), make significant contributions to the theological study of the Bible.

17. See Theodor H. Gaster, "Sacrifices and Offerings, OT," in *The Interpreter's Dictionary of the Bible,* (Nashville: Abingdon, 1962), 4:153–54.

18. See my essay "The Quality of the Sacred Mountain," in *Ancient Myths and Biblical Faith: Scriptural Transformations* (Philadelphia: Fortress, 1983), 125–82.

19. See von Rad, *Studies in Deuteronomy,* 74–91.

20. For the arguments that the Deuteronomists are responsible for the prose section of Deuteronomy, see Nicholson, *Preaching to the Exiles.*

21. For a summary of views concerning the passage and an excellent study of the whole story, see Tucker, *Form Criticism,* 41–54.

22. On a passage as complicated as this one, the reader will do well to consult a detailed commentary on the pericope. Especially recommended are the following: Gerhard von Rad's *Genesis,* rev ed. (Philadelphia: Westminster, 1972), 319–26; Claus Westermann, *Genesis 12–36,* trans. John J. Scullion, S.J. (Minneapolis: Augsburg, 1985), 512–21.

23. See Gaster, *Myth, Legend, and Custom,* 201–10.

24. See the commentary on this passage by James Luther Mays, *Hosea,* The Old Testament Library (Philadelphia: Westminster, 1969), 161–65, and that of Hans Walter Wolff, *Hosea,* trans. Gary Stansell, Hermeneia (Philadelphia: Fortress, 1974), 206–14.

25. See James B. Pritchard, ed., *Ancient Near Eastern Texts Relating to the Old Testament,* 2d ed. (Princeton, N.J.: Princeton University Press, 1955), 31–32.

26. Ibid., 259.

27. The essay is in Vetus Testamentum Supplement, no. 1 (1953), 120–27; reprinted in Gerhard von Rad, *The Problem of the Hexateuch and Other Essays* (New York: McGraw-Hill, 1966), 292–300.

28. Von Rad, *Problem of the Hexateuch,* 300.

29. Arndt Meinhold, "Die Gattung der Josephgeschichte und der Estherbuches: Diasporanovella I," *Zeitschrift fur alttestament-liche Wissenschaft* 87 (1975): 306–24; D. B. Redford, *A Study of the Biblical Story of Joseph (Genesis 37–50),* Vetus Testamentum Supplement, no. 20 (1970); George W. Coats, "The Joseph Story and Ancient Wisdom: A Reappraisal," *Catholic Biblical Quarterly* 35 (1973): 285–97; Claus Westermann, *Genesis 37–50,* trans. John J. Scullion, S.J. (Minneapolis: Augsburg, 1986).

30. See my discussion of the Joseph story in *Genesis, Exodus, Leviticus, Numbers,* Proclamation Commentaries: The Old Testament Witnesses for Preaching (Philadelphia: Fortress, 1979), 59–63.

31. This generally held assumption has been recently challenged, how-

ever, by George W. Coats, *Rebellion in the Wilderness* (Nashville: Abingdon, 1968).

32. *I and II Kings,* trans. John Gray, The Old Testament Library (Philadelphia: Westminster, 1963), 362.

33. Above all, see *Theological Dictionary of the Old Testament,* 2:253–79. To use Kittel's *Theological Dictionary of the New Testament,* look up *diatheke* in vol. 4. An excellent article on "covenant" by George Mendenhall is available in *The Interpreter's Dictionary of the Bible, A–D.*

34. For a discussion on the meaning of Jesus "walking on the sea," see my *Ancient Myths and Biblical Faith* (Philadelphia: Fortress, 1983), 58–61.

35. See Otto Kaiser's commentary *Isaiah 1–12,* trans. R. A. Wilson, The Old Testament Library (Philadelphia: Westminster, 1972).

36. See Gerhard von Rad, *Old Testament Theology,* trans. D. M. G. Stalker (New York: Harper and Row, 1965), 2:151–55.

37. See Kaiser's *Isaiah 1–12,* 96.

38. For further reading on the Syro-Ephraimite crisis, see Martin Noth, *The History of Israel,* 2d rev. ed. (New York: Harper and Row, 1960), 257ff.; or John Bright, *A History of Israel,* 3d ed. (Philadelphia: Westminster, 1981), 273–75.

39. It is the position of Kaiser, *Isaiah 1–12,* 96–106, that "the young woman" refers generally to many pregnant girls in the land who, upon the birth of sons, will rejoice by naming their children Immanuel.

40. For further theological implications of the passage, see ibid., 105–6.

41. For a discussion on Second Isaiah and the exodus, see Rast, *Tradition History,* 61–68.

42. For a description of "salvation" forms, see Claus Westermann, "The Way of the Promise through the Old Testament," in *The Old Testament and Christian Faith,* ed. Bernhard W. Anderson (New York: Harper and Row, 1963), 200–224, esp. 202–9.

43. Claus Westermann, *Isaiah 40–66,* trans. David M. G. Stalker, The Old Testament Library (Philadelphia: Westminster, 1969), 138–40. Westermann admits he is following Duhm in the suggestion of adding vv. 21–22 to vv. 6–8.

44. Gerhard von Rad, *Old Testament Theology,* trans. D. M. G. Stalker (New York: Harper, 1962), 1:370ff.

45. Klaus Koch, *The Prophets,* trans. Margaret Kohl (Philadelphia: Fortress, 1982), 1:56–62.

46. Interpretations of the confessions of Jeremiah have ranged from the traditional one in which they reflect the prophet's personality and faith crises to the current approach that considers them later insertions into the book without any connection to the life and times of Jeremiah. Two recent studies have challenged the current position. A. R. Diamond suggests the confessions are authentic to Jeremiah but have been redacted by the Deuteronomistic editors to serve purposes of their own (*The Confessions*

of Jeremiah in Context: Scenes of Prophetic Drama, Journal for the Study of the Old Testament, Supplement Series, no. 45 [Sheffield: JSOT, 1987]). Kathleen M. O'Connor argues that the confessions legitimate Jeremiah as a prophet and provide a setting within the prophet's life for their original proclamation (*The Confessions of Jeremiah: Their Interpretation and Role in Chapters 1–25,* Society of Biblical Literature Dissertation Series, no. 94 [Atlanta: Scholars Press, 1988]).

47. See the discussion by Walther Zimmerli, *Ezekiel 1,* trans. Ronald E. Clements, Hermeneia (Philadelphia: Fortress, 1979), 376–77. For a different approach within a comprehensive study of the chapter, see Gordon H. Matthies, *Ezekiel 18 and the Rhetoric of Moral Discourse,* Society of Biblical Literature Dissertation Series, no. 126 (Atlanta: Scholars Press, 1990). Matthies argues that the purpose of the chapter is "to motivate the transformation toward a new and cohesive social order" (219).

48. I am indebted to psychiatrist Ralph M. Reeves, M.D., who, through his unpublished paper "Optimal and Suboptimal Modes of Dialog" and through numerous private discussions, has enabled me to appreciate the therapeutic nature of dialogue.

49. Reuel L. Howe, *The Miracle of Dialogue* (New York: Seabury, 1963), 42.

50. Ibid., 152.

51. *Lutheran Book of Worship* (Minneapolis: Augsburg; Philadelphia: Board of Publication, Lutheran Church in America, 1978), hymn no. 381.

52. This sermon was preached in a congregation on December 9, 1990.

53. Unlike the other sermons in this collection, this one was addressed to an assembly of clergy who were gathered at the Lutheran Theological Seminary in Philadelphia for a week-long session (1993) devoted to preaching from the Old Testament.

Scripture Index

OLD TESTAMENT

NEW TESTAMENT